WILDERNESS
U.S.A.

WILDERNESS U.S.A.

NATIONAL GEOGRAPHIC SOCIETY

WILDERNESS U.S.A.

PUBLISHED BY THE NATIONAL GEOGRAPHIC SOCIETY
MELVIN M. PAYNE, *President*
MELVILLE BELL GROSVENOR, *Editor-in-Chief*
GILBERT M. GROSVENOR, *Editor*
FRANC SHOR, *Executive Editor for this series*

Introduction by
SIGURD F. OLSON
Author of The Singing Wilderness, The Lonely Land, Listening Point, Runes of the North, The Hidden Forest, Open Horizons, Wilderness Days; *wilderness consultant to the Secretary of the Interior, the Director of the National Park Service, and the Izaak Walton League of America; former President, The Wilderness Society; former President, National Parks Association*

Essays by
EDWARD ABBEY
Author of Desert Solitaire, Slickrock, Appalachian Wilderness

FRANK CRAIGHEAD, JR.
Senior Research Associate, Atmospheric Sciences Research Center, State University of New York; President, Environmental Research Institute; co-author of A Field Guide to Rocky Mountain Wildflowers

MICHAEL FROME
Author of Strangers in High Places: The Story of the Great Smoky Mountains, Whose Woods These Are, The Varmints: Our Unwanted Wildlife

HARVEY MANNING
Author of The Wild Cascades, The North Cascades National Park, Backpacking: One Step At a Time; *editor of* Mountaineering: The Freedom of the Hills

JOHN P. MILTON
Author of Nameless Valleys, Shining Mountains; *co-editor of* Future Environments of North America; *a director of Friends of the Earth; President, THRESHOLD: An International Center for Environmental Renewal*

ROBERT O. PETTY
Associate Professor of Biology, Wabash College; President, Resource Chapter, Indiana Division, Izaak Walton League of America

Chapters by
DAVID HISER, ROBERT LAXALT, STEVEN C. WILSON, DAWNETTA WINTERS and TOM ALLEN, SEYMOUR L. FISHBEIN, NOEL GROVE, DAVID F. ROBINSON, and VERLA LEE SMITH *of the National Geographic Staff*

Drawings by
DILL COLE, GEORGE FOUNDS

Photographs by
ENTHEOS, LOWELL GEORGIA, FARRELL GREHAN, RONALD A. HELSTROM, DAVID HISER, ROBERT W. MADDEN, MARTIN ROGERS, *and others*

First printing 325,000 copies
Library of Congress CIP data page 343

A VOLUME IN THE
WORLD IN COLOR LIBRARY
PREPARED BY
NATIONAL GEOGRAPHIC BOOK SERVICE

Staff for this Book

SEYMOUR L. FISHBEIN
Editor

MIKE W. EDWARDS
Associate Editor

CHARLES O. HYMAN
Art Director

ANNE DIRKES KOBOR
Illustrations Editor

ROSS BENNETT
JULES B. BILLARD
EDWARD LANOUETTE
DAVID F. ROBINSON
VERLA LEE SMITH
Editor-Writers

MARY SWAIN HOOVER
DIANE S. MARTON
SHIRLEY L. SCOTT
HARRIET H. WATKINS
ANNABELLE WITHERS
Editorial Research

WILHELM R. SAAKE
Production Manager

CONNIE BROWN, *Design*

KAREN F. EDWARDS, *Production*

BARBARA G. STEWART, *Illustrations*

PAMELA MUCCI, *Assistant*

JOHN R. METCALFE
JAMES R. WHITNEY
Engraving and Printing

JOHN D. GARST, JR.
VIRGINIA L. BAZA
BETTY CLONINGER
NANCY SCHWEICKART
SNEJINKA STEFANOFF
MILDA STONE
Map Design and Production

WERNER JANNEY, *Style*

TONI WARNER, VIRGINIA THOMPSON
Index

363 illustrations, 302 in full color

Foxtail barley sprays its gold over the green of the Great Swamp Wilderness, New Jersey; Rudi Schonbeck. Page 1: Alone with his shadow, a backpacker tramps the wild; Sam Abell. Pages 2-3: Lakes like giant footprints keep company with peaks more than two miles high in Maroon Bells-Snowmass Wilderness, Colorado; David Hiser. Page 7: Spray Falls drapes a gorge in Mount Rainier National Park; Steve Marts.

CONTENTS

A LONGING FOR WILDERNESS

Sigurd F. Olson

I began guiding canoe parties through the waterways of the Quetico-Superior country along Minnesota's border with Canada shortly after World War I. All roads ended near the little town of Ely, my home, with only an immensity of space and grandeur beyond: shimmering, island-dotted lakes reverberating to the calling of loons; rapids full of song; cliffs, forests, bogs. To me this could never change. It would always be wilderness.

But suddenly people were talking of "a road to every lake," and chambers of commerce were trumpeting the hope of developing "The Playground of a Nation." I imagined the silence of such waters as Lac la Croix and Saganaga shattered by the din of cars and motorboats, their shores lined with resorts. That threat was followed by another: the prospect of seven hydroelectric dams with impoundments as deep as 80 feet, submerging rapids, campsites, whole river systems.

During this time I took a canoe trip along the border to see the country again before anything happened to it, a sort of voyageur's farewell to the wilderness. At Lac la Croix I climbed Warrior's Hill to get the sweep of the great historic waterway, its fleets of rugged islands with their pines leaning away from the winds, the smooth glaciated campsites, the brooding stands of timber on the mainland.

The next day I portaged around the thunder of Curtain Falls, threaded the maze of Crooked Lake and camped on a barren isle in the very center of the swirling cauldron where the Basswood River comes plunging in. The moon was full and as always it was a place of magic until I remembered the threat. In my mind's eye I saw an apron of concrete and steel holding back the flood, the rocky gorge empty, the surging moon-drenched brilliance gone, its music stilled forever.

The following night I camped on another island above the brawling rapids of the river I had ascended, sat there in the dusk listening to the loons and the distant roar, watching the black silhouette of jagged spruce against the western sky, and I knew that man needed such beauty and solitude far more than electric power and stockholder's dividends, and that somehow the land must be saved.

The same realization had come to others. I made a canoe trip with Will Dilg, organizer of the Izaak Walton League of America, who vowed to make protection of the region a prime league objective. A Quetico-Superior Council was formed to draft a wise plan of zoning and management for the area. Men we'd guided contacted congressmen, officials, editors. Thousands who never portaged or paddled saw the effort to save the Superior National Forest and Canada's Quetico Provincial Park

The promise of spring freshets clings to shadowed wilds of the North Cascades, where man and snow are but visitors
ENTHEOS

as a struggle to save a part of primitive North America. The tide had begun to turn when the U.S. Forest Service established the Superior Primitive Area in 1926. Known today as the Boundary Waters Canoe Area, it is the only national forest unit dedicated to canoe travel in our National Wilderness Preservation System.

In most of the nation untamed land had all but vanished before any action was taken to save some. The awesome fastness that greeted the colonists of Jamestown has been whittled and hacked, roaded, mined, suburbed, dammed. By generous reckoning some 6 percent of the old 48 states—less than 180,000 square miles out of more than three million—can today be considered wild. The picture brightens when the emptiness of Alaska is counted in, but there too the wilderness is shrinking. An area estimated to equal two Rhode Islands succumbs to the bulldozer and the cement mixer in the United States every year. Ecologists studying the complex life chains of natural areas often use the word "resource" when speaking of our remaining wilderness, perhaps mindful of Aldo Leopold's observation that "our tendency is not to call things resources until the supply runs short." Leopold was writing of this dwindling treasure in 1925, a year after he had persuaded his Forest Service superiors to establish a national wilderness—the first one—in New Mexico.

At that time and for four decades afterward it was simply by the stroke of an administrator's pen, always subject to a bureaucratic change of heart, that wild land was rescued in the national forests. But events were in motion which would yield lasting results. They reached a climax in 1964 when Congress passed the Wilderness Act, securing by law "the benefits of an enduring resource of wilderness" not only in the forests but also in national parks and wildlife refuges. The late Howard Zahniser, executive director of The Wilderness Society, provided for the act a wilderness definition that soars with the spirit of tumbling streams and virgin forests: ". . . an area where the earth and its community of life are untrammeled by man, where man himself is a visitor who does not remain."

Roadless and resortless, these protected lands are in most instances beyond the grind of motors. You enter on foot—yours or a horse's—or perhaps by canoe or on skis. Wildlife refuges may restrict visitors to daylight hours or ban them entirely so that fauna will not be disturbed. But for the most part the wilderness is open and beckoning. You can hike, scale peaks, fish the creeks for trout, hunt in the national forests and many refuges. Or just stretch out in a meadow and watch a hawk soar. You follow trails that may have felt the tread of moccasins. Sometimes you come on a campsite lavishly appointed—by wilderness standards—with fireplace and grill, or even a lean-to. But usually you make your own site with your tent and perhaps, if downed wood is plentiful, a small blaze to cheer the night.

Many wilderness users are family groups, sometimes trekking with a youngster riding papoose-like in a back sling. Clubs and outfitters sponsor group outings, usually subscribed months in advance. Colleges utilize wilderness as a classroom, with on-the-spot studies in ecology; sometimes these courses, borrowing from Outward Bound programs, include solo hikes and rock climbs to heighten self-awareness. The challenge of living among woods and cascading streams has even been used in experiments designed to help hospitalized mental patients shake off defeatism and gain confidence for returning to the everyday world.

For the tenderfoot a bit of orientation may be necessary before wilderness yields its good tidings. Feet unaccustomed to hiking boots and seats unacquainted with saddles may rebel at the introduction, and the absence of a convenient hot-dog stand may at first seem cause for alarm. But soon even first-timers are back in the grooves

From a onetime factory worker came an early voice crying out for "the great fresh, unblighted, unredeemed wilderness." John Muir moved men from conservation to preservation; his spirited writings helped create a system of national parks.

When a factory mishap in 1867 injured an eye, Muir at 29 lay in a darkened room for a month, recalling old treks in the wild and dreaming of new adventures. Healed, he turned from promise as an inventor "to the study of the inventions of God."

The camera caught him in 1908 on a trip with the Sierra Club. Fired with his zeal from its earliest days, the club works to save a nation's wild heritage.

of ancestral experience. Leopold once described two young canoeists who were rapidly making the adjustment when he met them on a river bank in Wisconsin.

What time is it? they asked. "For two days," he wrote, "they had lived by 'suntime', and were getting a thrill out of it. No servant brought them meals; they got their meat out of the river, or went without. No traffic cop whistled them off the hidden rock in the next rapids. No friendly roof kept them dry when they mis-guessed whether or not to pitch the tent. No guide showed them which camping spots offered a nightlong breeze, and which a nightlong misery of mosquitoes; which firewood made clean coals, and which only smoke." The wilderness, Leopold added, gave them "their first taste of those rewards and penalties for wise and foolish acts which every woodsman faces daily, but against which civilization has built a thousand buffers." Perhaps, he said, every youth needs an occasional outdoor adventure to learn the meaning of the freedom to make mistakes.

That freedom can be experienced in some 11 million acres of designated wilderness. The total will more than double with inclusion of areas that are well along in the designation process. Still more millions of acres will be surveyed and added to the national system in the future, and state governments are saving roadless and natural areas too. Wilderness — statutory wilderness — leaps from sea to shining sea: from the beach of Monomoy National Wildlife Refuge near Cape Cod to the islets of the Three Arch Rocks refuge off Oregon's coast. Pelican Island Wilderness in Florida musters a mere six acres of tangled mangroves; the Selway-Bitterroot encompasses 1,240,618 acres of Rocky Mountain high.

Increasing millions of Americans each year seek out these unspoiled lands. It may be a hidden corner where, miraculously, a mere breath of the primeval has been saved, perhaps the Great Swamp in New Jersey. A dab of sedge and slough, some stands of beech and oak, only 3,660 acres in sum, the Great Swamp Wilderness

Cathedral Rocks, arrayed behind Bridalveil Fall and mirrored in the Merced River — such images eased Muir's convalescence and honed his urge to see Yosemite. Few had trod this wondrous gorge, though many, perhaps Muir among them, had admired it in Albert Bierstadt's painting of 1863.
In 1868 Muir reached California by ship, then Yosemite on foot. For six years he haunted the vale and wrote of its splendors, living by odd jobs as he scaled cliffs, tracked down glaciers, and read its biography in the rocks.
His moving pleas helped make it a national park in 1890. In such places "the galling harness of civilization drops off, and the wounds heal ere we are aware."

survives 25 miles from Manhattan's towers. Such places are hints of the beauty there was. People go to them for glimpses of the old America and come away refreshed.

Others crave action and horizons far beyond civilization. No tiny pockets tucked in suburbia for them! They must know the vastness and adventure of the old frontiers. They seek the remote reaches of such little-known rivers as Alaska's Noatak, draining the barren lands of the Arctic. They must bend against the bite of tumplines on the portages of the Quetico-Superior, glory in the roaring rapids of the Salmon in Idaho. They must battle wind and storm, know hunger and hazard—and the bond of comradeship forged on the out trails of the world.

Once in Alaska I followed a creek near the Valley of Ten Thousand Smokes. The salmon were running, their vivid red bodies crowding the shallows. Everywhere were signs of the great brown bear: half-devoured fish floating downstream and enormous bear tracks in the mud. I broke out of a tangle of alder and saw at the end of a pool, not a hundred feet away, a brownie with its eyes on me. We were frozen into a primeval scene: I and this hunter at bay, face to face with the eternal challenge, life or death. For what seemed to be two or three hours—in truth, no more than two or three minutes—we stared at one another. Then we went our separate ways.

From the West beckon the realms of mighty ranges: North Cascades National Park in Washington, the John Muir Wilderness in California, the Teton Wilderness in Wyoming. Each of these encompasses more than half a million acres of noble spires corrugated with rill-veined valleys. One does not forget the glory of soaring domains. I remember a morning in Alaska's Wrangells when parting clouds revealed the grandest spectacle of snow-capped peaks on our continent, and an autumn day in the Never Summer country of the Colorado Rockies, with the aspens solid gold and elk bugling in the thickets. When men and women come down from such mountains—*their* mountains for a day, a weekend, a fortnight—they come as people always have from lonely heights, spiritually regenerated.

There are those who feel that only in the great swamps and flowages of the South, in the cypress stands of Georgia's Okefenokee or the mangroves of the Florida Everglades, can they understand the true meaning of wilderness. And in a sense they are right, for it was from such watery places that terrestrial life evolved. Development has eaten out great chunks of Florida's subtropics, and thirsty cities and farms have drained much of the sustenance. Yet wild beauty remains, and flashes of it sear my mind: a rosy drift of flamingos against blue sky; three deer leaping through a silver spray of billowing saw grass; a cougar's fresh track on a muddy bank.

On the plains and prairies, remnants of grassland and the raw grandeur of the badlands lure wanderers to such places as the Wichita Mountains Wildlife Refuge in Oklahoma and Theodore Roosevelt National Memorial Park in North Dakota. Desert trails are harsh, yet men brave them willingly to roam the richly colored canyonlands of Utah or the cactus-studded fastness of Arizona. Who can deny the magic of night on that stretch of Sonoran Desert along the Mexican border known as Cabeza Prieta, under stars so bright they all but blaze? I remember the smell of greasewood and sage, and a dark valley alive with the tremulous music of coyotes. To me this unchanged land was one that night with all the great deserts of the world—and I understood why men through the ages have gone to them to gain perspective on their lives.

Mountains, deserts, swamps, forests, lakes and rivers and shores: Whatever the type, be it large or small, wilderness is balm for the tensions of the world, a place to meditate and commune with our past. In the mists of morning, ghosts speak to us of waterways flowing full and clean to the sea. When we cross the prairies it is hard to realize that until the last century they had never felt the plow, or that vast herds of buffalo roamed at will. We still have untamed space, nearly overwhelming in its magnitude, though its herds are not buffalo but caribou. Amid the glacial lakes and stunted, twisted spruce in the Alaskan taiga—the land of "little sticks"—you can hear them moving up a slope. The sound is a faint but distinctive clicking as ligaments rub against foot bones, a whisper from a virgin continent.

The pioneers who journeyed west across the plains and mountains knew the wilderness as a place of hardship. Broken wagons, spavined oxen, and lonely graves were the waymarks of their trails. Snowbound in the Sierra Nevada, the Donner party resorted to eating dogs and hides—and human flesh when the hides gave out. Struggling across Death Valley, a party of forty-niners cursed the harsh country until, as one remembered, "it seemed as if there were not bad words enough in the language to express properly their contempt and bad opinion. . . ."

But the wilderness could be tamed, and taming it meant that a man could possess land. So the pioneers chopped and burned and plowed their way into the heart, elbowing aside and often slaughtering the Indians, not stopping until they reached the Pacific. Wild land was an inexhaustible commodity in 19th-century America. Homestead laws enabled more than a million families to acquire more than 248 million acres in the prairies, plains, and western mountains. Railroads were granted 150 million acres, war veterans 61 million, the states more than 300 million for such purposes as supporting schools and building wagon roads and canals.

Out of their desperate years the settlers knew a fierce pride of accomplishment. The wilderness discarded Old World notions of aristocracy; on the frontier a man proved himself in the crucible of survival. In time the pioneers developed a sense of continental belonging to the land, a loyalty welded of hope and struggle. The wilderness molded them—and us—as a people. "American democracy . . . was not carried in the *Sarah Constant* to Virginia, nor in the *Mayflower* to Plymouth," wrote historian Frederick Jackson Turner. "It came out of the American forest, and it gained new strength each time it touched a new frontier." But in the very process of conquering the wilds, the pioneers were chopping their spiritual roots.

"Land is an organism," wrote Aldo Leopold, a forester who saw the southwest's wilderness not as a grab bag of resources but as an interweaving of life with man himself part of the fabric. In 1924 this pioneering ecologist convinced the Forest Service to designate the Gila Wilderness Area, first of scores of tracts set aside long before passage of the Wilderness Act.

"When we see land as a community to which we belong," he wrote in the still-popular Sand County Almanac, "we may begin to use it with love and respect. There is no other way for land to survive the impact of mechanized man. . . ."

The world we face now is a strange one, the great silences replaced with clamor, the hearts of our cities garish with blinking neon and foul with the stench of pollution. We look at the slums, at the never-ending traffic, the shrinking space and growing ugliness, and are appalled. Is this, we ask, what our forebears struggled for? Is this the great American dream?

We enjoy comforts never known before, but they are not enough; somehow, someway, we must make contact with naturalness, the source of all life. The frontiers are still too close to forget and the memory of wilderness goes far back into the eons when man lived close to the earth and was in tune with the ancient rhythms. We still listen to the song of the wilderness and long for a land we have lost. Civilization has not changed emotional needs which were ours long before it arose. This is the reason for the hunger, this the true meaning of wilderness and the search of moderns for places where they can know it again. The battle to save the last remnants is not only a struggle for freedom and beauty, but for the spirit of man in a world that seems to have lost its balance and perspective.

"Something will have gone out of us as a people if we ever let the remaining wilderness be destroyed," the author Wallace Stegner warned some years ago, "if we permit the last virgin forests to be turned into comic books and plastic cigarette cases; if we drive the few remaining members of the wild species into zoos or to extinction;

A living legend in his brief 38 years, Bob Marshall fought for wilderness— and tested himself against its challenges—with boundless energy. Author Olson recalls hikes with "this physically and spiritually powerful man" that might begin at 3 a.m. and end some 19 hours and 50 miles later.

Born a wealthy Easterner, Marshall scorned the use of "machinery to get the jump on Nature." His persuasive voice among Forest Service colleagues helped swell a still-growing system of wild lands, and won stricter controls on their use. Bob Marshall Wilderness honors his memory; the Wilderness Society he organized in 1935 draws thousands to his cause.

if we pollute the last clear air and dirty the last clean streams and push our paved roads through the last of the silence. . . . The reassurance that it is still there is good for our spiritual health even if we never once in 10 years set foot in it."

Though the yearning spirit in us often obscures them, there also are practical reasons for saving what's left of wilderness. Man is a manipulator of nature—more so now than ever as he seeks by pesticides, defoliants, fertilizers, irrigation schemes, and cloud-seeding chemicals to grow food and fiber with heightened efficiency. But he is far from a complete understanding of the processes he manipulates. In the complex ecosystems of natural domains he has a laboratory in which to study the interaction of species, environmental trends, evolution. And in undisturbed flora and fauna he has a storehouse of genetic diversity the future may prize.

As early as the 1830's the frontier artist George Catlin suggested that the government create a preserve where the world in ages to come could view the wild freshness of nature. At midcentury the rustic philosopher of Walden, Henry David Thoreau, was advocating much the same thing. "In Wildness is the preservation of the World," he declared; why should not some be saved for "our own true recreation"?

S uch men were setting the stage for John Muir. How best to type this bearded wilderness fanatic? Incorrigible wanderer, inventor, naturalist—he was all three. But with a pen in his hand he was something more: a poet on a crusade. Writing, he once grumbled, is "like the life of a glacier, one eternal grind." But grind he did: nine books, hundreds of newspaper and magazine articles, letters. As no man had before, Muir infected Americans with the joy of nature and alerted them to the dangers of mindless exploitation.

"Climb the mountains and get their good tidings," he exhorted. "Nature's peace will flow into you as sunshine flows into trees." He campaigned to save Yosemite, the mountains of all the West, the glaciers, fiords, and forests of Alaska. Domestic sheep grazing the fragile high country he condemned as "hoofed locusts." He fought for trees, especially the sequoias. "It took more than 3,000 years to make some of the trees in these western woods . . ." he once wrote. "Through all the wonderful, eventful centuries since Christ's time—and long before that—God has cared for these trees . . . but he cannot save them from fools. Only Uncle Sam can do that."

Muir and the handful of men who thought as he did arrived on the scene at a desperate time. "The Age of Extermination," naturalists have called the last half of the 19th century, an era of rampant and ghastly abuse of both wildlife and landscape. Eastern forests were largely devastated and lumbermen were sawing away at the public lands of the West. In the Deep South spoonbills, flamingos, ibises, egrets, and other plume birds were being blunderbussed to provide trimmings for milady's hats. Hunters were blasting to oblivion the passenger pigeon, once the most numerous American bird. Buffalo were gunned down by the millions.

But the country had been alerted. Responsible public servants began to act. Presidents Benjamin Harrison and Grover Cleveland created the first forest reserves from public lands in the 1890's. "Lockout!" shouted loggers and stockmen. But the reserves remained. Gifford Pinchot, America's first native-born professional forester— he had studied silviculture in Europe—argued that forests should be "managed" for the national good. "Managed" meant trees could be harvested, but the principal manager would be the government. Reforestation would be an important element. It was thus that he advised his friend, President Theodore Roosevelt.

Pinchot's utilitarian approach disappointed Muir, who saw a canopy of conifers as a temple. But as T. R.'s counsel the forester achieved much for which Muir's modern disciples are grateful; Roosevelt built the forest reserves to 172 million acres, including many of the most magnificent tracts which afford us pleasure today. That was not the only signal achievement of this conservation-minded president. Naturalist and hunter, he "gave the vanishing birds and animals the benefit of every doubt," as a zoologist noted, creating the first national wildlife refuge on Florida's Pelican Island in 1903 and later 50 others. He also set aside 18 areas of historic or natural interest, including Grand Canyon, the Petrified Forest, and Muir Woods.

A wilderness, Aldo Leopold wrote in 1921, when he was an assistant district forester in the Southwest, should be "big enough to absorb a two weeks' pack trip." It should be devoid of "roads, artificial trails, cottages, or other works of man." In 1919 Leopold had met a fellow Iowan, Arthur Carhart, a landscape architect employed as the Forest Service's first fulltime recreation engineer. Carhart described his own efforts to rescue 313-acre Trappers Lake in the White River National Forest in Colorado. Ordered to execute a design for siting summer cabins, Carhart argued—successfully, as it turned out—that houses and a road would destroy the beauty. He had seen the Quetico-Superior and thought it also should be saved, and a few years later was involved there in the fight to keep out roads.

Leopold had his eye on a fine wilderness in the Gila National Forest in New Mexico—a region of piñon and ponderosa pines, box canyons, and peaks soaring beyond 10,000 feet. Deer and turkey were abundant. "Report on Proposed Wilderness Area" is the title of a memorandum he submitted in 1922. It declared:

"Object. To preserve at least one place in the Southwest where pack trips shall be the 'dominant play.' . . .

"Function. A 'National Hunting Ground' is the one form of recreation which has not been provided for or recognized by the federal government. . . ."

Leopold had spent his boyhood hunting and fishing along the Mississippi River, and well into manhood the hunter's instinct pulsed in his veins. He once applauded

Four men pulling, two poling, made a rapid transit a century ago on liquid highways near what is now the Boundary Waters Canoe Area. Voyageurs before and adventurers since have dared this labyrinth; Robert Marshall and author Olson—to whom this realm is home—together paddled its pure lakes and streams.

Artist Frances Anne Hopkins portrayed herself and husband about a century ago as unruffled riders in the big canoe. Trader Hopkins met the wild's rigors when he had to: A friend called the transplanted Englishman "a regular voyageur" who had learned to eat "horse flesh, dog and every thing . . . like one who has been travelling all his life."

the "splendid progress" of a campaign to rid New Mexico of such predators as wolves and mountain lions. The evidence, however, is that Leopold did not view designated wilderness in the single dimension of sport. Save only the tilling of the soil, no outdoor activity "bends and molds the human character like wilderness travel," he wrote in the American Forestry Association's magazine in the 1920's. "Would we rather have the few paltry dollars that could be extracted from our remaining wild places than the human values they can render in their wild condition?" He urged support for preservation of tracts in both forests and national parks.

On June 3, 1924, a Gila Wilderness Area of 750,000 acres was created in a memorandum signed by the Southwest district forester. Two years later the chief of the Forest Service urged other administrators to designate wild lands, and in 1929 wilderness preservation was adopted as official Forest Service policy. In later years the Gila's boundaries would contract as foresters bowed to local pressures for mining, logging, and highway rights-of-way. But something very profound in the history of preservation had happened there among the box canyons and pines.

Eventually Leopold traded the rifle for the bow and arrow, and then those for the notebook, acquiring stature as a conservationist and ecologist. Thousands were influenced toward the rescue of the land and its resources by the compact but powerful essays in his slim classic, A Sand County Almanac. Once when we were discussing my own studies of wolves in Minnesota I chided him for having been an advocate of extermination. "We've come a long way since then," he answered. Just how far Leopold showed in his magnificent essay, "Thinking Like a Mountain," about the shooting of a she-wolf on a Southwestern peak. I quoted to him that day a paragraph from the essay, as he closed his eyes and remembered:

"We reached the old wolf in time to watch a fierce green fire dying in her eyes. I realized then, and have known ever since, that there was something new to me in those eyes—something known only to her and to the mountain. I was young then, and full of trigger-itch; I thought that because fewer wolves meant more deer, that no wolves would mean hunters' paradise. But after seeing the green fire die, I sensed that neither the wolf nor the mountain agreed with such a view."

A fellow conservationist of the 1930's dubbed Robert Marshall "the most efficient weapon of preservation in existence." He approached everything with vigor—most of all, wild land. Marshall thought nothing of backpacking 40 or 50 miles a day, usually wearing tennis shoes, and several times paced off an incredible 70. At the end of one of those days he declared: "A man must work for his wilderness enjoyment. Only when he's hungry, thirsty, and dog-tired can he really know what it means." With Bob Marshall involved, there was no chance the fledgling wilderness movement would be neglected.

We made a trip together in the Boundary Waters Canoe Area when he was the Forest Service's chief of recreation. "We'll go in paddling and come out the same way, no launches, no airplanes, no mechanized transportation of any kind," he had written me. "I want to see the country as the voyageurs saw it, and travel it as they." The trip was all adventure and delight—or nearly so. Once we came on a portage route which had been straightened by the Civilian Conservation Corps. "A cellophane trail," Marshall called it in disgust. "Portages are sacred. We must leave them alone. There are plenty of straight trails in America." He felt that campsites used by Indians and frontiersmen were best; they had "atmosphere and feeling."

In 1931 Marshall returned from a 13-month adventure in the Alaskan Arctic overflowing with zeal. He rained pleas for safeguarding wild land (Continued on page 25)

A hiker tramps a trailless meadow in Desolation Wilderness, California

Where Man Is a Visitor

If he sidesteps the flower, he crushes the grass instead.
If he stays on the trail, he spares them both—but with every footfall
a puff of dust blooms and blows away, a bud on a trailside bush
snags his sleeve and is snapped off. Another bud will sprout, another flower,
another blade of grass. But another hiker may come to the meadow, and another;
too many, and it becomes a patchwork of green grass and brown earth.
Wilderness is a fragile treasure, an exquisite gearing
of soils and seasons and species with only limited ability to accommodate
the intrusions of man. "... to cherish we must see and fondle," warned Aldo Leopold,
"and when enough have seen and fondled, there is no wilderness left to cherish."

A packtrain winds into Bob Marshall Wilderness, a broad chunk of Montana well suited to such use

Young backpackers round a switchback in Desolation Wilderness

"**D**on't fall down. You'll get trampled to death." A strange thing
to hear in the wilderness—but the lament of a hiker on the popular
John Muir Trail echoes more and more on footpaths slowly turning into
backcountry freeways. As fragile as the wilderness itself
is the wilderness experience, a subtle elixir that each compounds for himself
out of beauty, peace, challenge, silence, solitude. How to preserve
that experience even as the numbers of those who seek it increase?
Permit systems, time limits, restrictions on party size help to keep groups small
and scattered. Where packtrains are permitted, they often must
pack in food for beast as well as man. "Carry out what you carry in,"
say signs at trailheads—and yet litter still mars the face of the wild
and moves hiking clubs to organize clean-up hikes. But those who love wilderness
enter it humbly, taking from it only memories, leaving behind only footprints.

A register at Glacier Peak Wilderness, Washington, yields data on usage

19

Maroon Bells-Snowmass Wilderness has been protected by the Forest Service since 1933.
But herdsmen had been grazing their sheep here long before that.
And so the sheep remain, munching the shoots, churning the roots in high meadows

Pyramid Peak juts at middle left, North and South Maroon Peaks vie for top honors at right

of several wild areas under a clause in the Wilderness Act that recognizes such prior use.
Planners weigh the impact if the animals stay and the loss
to stockmen if they go—and while the debate unfolds, the sheep nibble on.

Like battle lines in a war the forest lost, logging roads
scar a clear-cut ridge. Protected wilderness spares the trees
for man's delight, but the lingering blight of a big
clear-cut can upset the ecology of adjacent wild land.
Too much protection can change a forest as well, and not always
to man's liking. Constant fire suppression allows a buildup
of natural litter that might one day flare up beyond
fire fighters' control and kindle an entire woodland. Yet small,
lightning-caused fires—one of nature's ancient tools—
can prune an understory, clear away debris, and burn
themselves out, often without hazard to the forest.

Students learn of forest needs in Montana's Bitterroot National Forest, where extensive clear-cutting has stirred dispute

Wilds of Montana's Lolo National Forest may be affected if nearby clear-cuts muddy streams, disturb wildlife, alter water tables

Drought mires an Everglades alligator, turning its once-green realm into gray ooze and whitened stalks

Sun cracks a mosaic of marl, a layer
deposited in shallows by tiny
aquatic organisms called periphyton

Too little water, and the gator wallows in mud where once he fished;
pools dry up in the Florida sun, and the Everglade kite that fed in them
dwindles to near extinction. Too much water, and the rookeries
of nesting birds flood out. Everglades National Park depends for its life
not only on nature's rains but also on man's wisdom far beyond its boundaries,
where blossoming developments drink ever deeper from the "River of Grass"
flowing in from Lake Okeechobee. As with the 'Glades, so with wild lands anywhere:
civilization can make a poor neighbor. Arctic oil crews spook the caribou.
Colorado ski resorts draw throngs to the edge of wilderness;
many venture in on side trips that can overcrowd the wild. Polluted air
drifting in from distant cities sometimes kills trees in healthy forests.
Each tree that withers warns anew that wilderness is not yet safe.

upon officials in Washington. Several of our greatest forest wildernesses—the Pasayten and the Three Sisters in the Cascades, the Selway-Bitterroot in the Rockies, to name but three—were established while his powerful voice sounded in the Capital. As a Forest Service official he won stricter regulations for the protection of wilderness tracts; outside the government he helped found The Wilderness Society, today one of the strongest voices for preservation.

"We can never have enough of Nature," Thoreau wrote. "We must be refreshed by the sight of inexhaustible vigor, vast and Titanic features. . . ." Thoreau spoke for Marshall and for all the unheralded citizens who continued the fight to save parts of the earth inviolate. All endured heartbreak and frustration while seeking to arouse a bureaucracy or a public dominated by the frontier view of land and the belief that the local economy mattered more than a gift of ages.

I was drawn inevitably to other areas where wilderness and beauty were threatened. One day I stood with friends on the beach of Indiana Dunes watching the whitecaps of Lake Michigan march in from the north. For thousands of years the winds had howled down that 300-mile stretch of water, building the beach and hurling its sands onto the giant living dunes behind it. Again the old question: Must open space and the natural legacy of millenniums always be sacrificed? As we looked across at the twinkling lights of Chicago and the blood-red sky above the blast furnaces of Gary, the answer was the same as it had been in the Quetico-Superior long before: "People need glimpses of the primeval for the good of their souls. They need it far more than another industrial complex."

At Point Reyes, a short ride north of San Francisco's Golden Gate, I walked with other friends one day when the Pacific was blue and the air rich with the scent of laurel, lilac, and lupine. We climbed a promontory and looked down on the roaring surf, alive with glistening sea lions. This was the Point Reyes that Drake and Spanish explorers had sighted long before the gold rush. It was hard to believe that in a few years suburbia would engulf it. I already knew the battle slogans: People or Scenery; Ghettos or Homes; Taxes or Poverty. In time most of Point Reyes, like the Indiana dunes, became a national shoreline, but opponents still skirmish over how much of the park land should be preserved in the wilderness system.

I stood among the redwoods as chain saws felled the giant trees; in Dinosaur National Monument in Utah and Colorado when a dam threatened not only the canyons but the sanctity of the entire national park system; in the forests of the Olympics; on Cape Cod National Seashore. Always the thin rank of wilderness proponents manned the ramparts. And emerging everywhere was a dream of giving wild places, long embattled, surcease and solid protection—not through an order from a government department, too easily rescinded, but by the force of law.

So, the wilderness champions banded together—thousands of individuals and members of such organizations as The Wilderness Society, the Izaak Walton League, and the Sierra Club—and asked Congress for help. Their battle was not won easily; it meant redirecting a nation's way of thinking. Mining companies opposed the wilderness concept, one spokesman even charging that it played into the hands of the Soviet Union. Sheepmen condemned wilderness as a breeding ground for predators. Cattlemen argued that "ever-increasing pleasure areas" would result in carelessly set fires. The parent bodies of the three federal agencies whose lands would be involved —the Department of Agriculture for the Forest Service, the Department of the Interior for the National Park Service and the Fish and Wildlife Service—declared that the proposed legislation would interfere with their management activities. Eight years passed from the introduction of the first bill until the Wilderness Act cleared Congress and was signed by President Lyndon B. Johnson on September 3, 1964.

"A compromise among human beings with conflicting desires," a Wilderness Society worker characterized the act. Bowing to mining interests, it permitted prospecting to continue in national forest wildernesses until the end of 1983. Cattlemen and shepherds would still be able to graze their herds in wilderness meadows (though officials have reduced the number of grazing permits). The ban against motorized equipment was skewed to permit a few "established" practices: Planes could continue to land hunters and hikers deep within the Selway-Bitterroot, for instance, and motorboats still could ply parts of the Boundary Waters Canoe Area.

But there was, at last, a National Wilderness Preservation System, composed of lands that retained their "primeval character and influence, without permanent improvements or human habitation . . . with the imprint of man's work substantially unnoticeable." A wilderness was further defined as having "outstanding opportunities for solitude or a primitive and unconfined type of recreation"; it must be at least 5,000 acres or, if smaller (as are a number of wildlife refuges), capable of being preserved in "an unimpaired condition." Areas that won the designation would continue to be managed by their respective agency landlords, but the rules of the act would apply: no roads, power lines, dams, resorts, logging.

President Johnson's signature put into the system that day in 1964 more than nine million acres which the Forest Service had been administratively protecting, beginning with Leopold's Gila. These 54 tracts included the Boundary Waters Canoe Area and lands the administrators had classified before 1964 as "wilderness" (areas of 100,000 acres or more) or "wild" (between 5,000 and 100,000 acres). Also in the national forests in 1964 were 34 parcels, 5.4 million acres in sum, called "primitive." These consisted of lands that were candidates for upgrading to "wilderness" or "wild" status, though some also were marked by fire roads and other works of man. For the most part they were being protected from further encroachment so that some day the parts predominantly valuable for wilderness could be elevated on the scale. The act required that the national forest Primitive Areas now be reviewed for inclusion in the wilderness system, subject, as all new wildernesses would be, to congressional approval.

In the national parks all roadless areas of 5,000 acres or more were to be reviewed, and in the wildlife refuges all roadless areas of that size as well as roadless islands. The backcountry parts of parks and monuments in particular had been held in a natural state; logging had been banned in all of them, mining in all but four units. The refuges, though less rigidly protected (they are open to mineral leasing), also contained undeveloped lands. Within these two systems more than 175 parks and refuges have been identified for wilderness consideration.

Beyond its definition and guidelines, the Wilderness Act's most important feature is a provision for citizen involvement. In preparing recommendations to the President on each candidate area, officials must publicize the proposals and invite public expression. Of course this procedure also allows opponents of wilderness to be heard. But the advocates nearly always outnumber the other side by lopsided margins. For example, the Forest Service's wilderness plan for the Gore Range-Eagles Nest Primitive Area in Colorado generated nearly 19,000 written responses—letters, postcards, and petition signatures—and elicited statements at hearings from 213 persons. These last represented groups as diverse as the American Legion, the Denver Audubon Society, and a high school biology club. By far the largest response was registered in favor not of the Forest Service's plan for a 72,000-acre wilderness but of one larger by more than two-thirds—a resounding plea for preservation.

Years, perhaps decades, will pass before the task of protecting wilderness is complete. Ten years were allowed for the agencies to review potential areas; other years will go by as Congress ponders their recommendations, perhaps expanding some boundaries and shrinking others as local pressures come into play. The Alaskan backcountry may someday provide enormous new areas; the Alaska Native Claims Settlement Act authorizes the allocation of some 80 million acres for national parks, refuges, forests, and wild and scenic rivers.

Meanwhile, the Wilderness Act's silence on other land of great potential—especially the 56 million acres of roadless but undesignated lands in the national forests—has triggered numerous disputes. Only a fifth of these so-called "de facto" areas have so far been proposed for wilderness study; conservationists hope to see all the roadless lands reviewed under the Wilderness Act procedures. Other disputes simmer over the drawing of wilderness boundaries in some of the national parks and refuges, and still others over the future of public lands held by the Bureau of Land Management in the West. Though not subject to the act, the Bureau has selected several areas, mainly in the canyonlands, to be administratively kept as wild land; some 60 others are under review.

And what should be done with forests that once, perhaps half a century ago, heard the ring of axes and breathed the smoke of frontier cabins? The question has raged east of the Mississippi, where most of the national forests were once logged.

There's a special charm for me in places that have reverted from farm to forest, as in much of the Appalachians. Of course the enormous chestnuts are gone, victims of blight, and along with them virgin pines and hemlocks that towered in the silence. But the generous rain of the eastern mountains is a potent restorative. And so one now finds in cut-over forests thriving stands of hardwoods, spruce, fir, and white pine, conjuring a sense of wildness as the predecessor forest must have to settlers.

"Alaskan Poppies"—discarded 55-gallon oil drums—bloom on the permafrost as civilization's arctic outposts bring in fuel and oil for thirsty engines. Drums by the scores of thousands bestrew the North Slope, relics accumulated since the 1940's in a vast deepfreeze where litter may last for centuries. Modern oil crews take pains to clean up trash, reseed scarred tundra— and sway ecologists who fear the impact a planned pipeline may have on the arctic wilds.

ENTHEOS

Then, without warning, you come on an old stone wall, a chimney of fieldstone, a lilac bush growing wild. Relics of our heritage, they are a poignant dowry bestowed upon the land, giving a deeper meaning to wilderness. But as the Forest Service has interpreted the Wilderness Act, such places are trammeled.

To officials besieged with mail from conservationists, or listening to hundreds testifying at hearings, it must often seem that wilderness lovers want the whole continent restored. What they really want is *enough* wilderness—whatever the sum may be, and no one can know it yet—to satisfy the millions who seek its pleasures.

Were John Muir to return today to his beloved High Sierra in peak season, one writer has noted, he would meet a ranger who might instruct him thus: "Bullfrog and Timberline Lakes are closed to camping and grazing. In the Evolution Basin and at Kearsarge Lakes wood fires are prohibited. You can stay only one night at Paradise Valley, Woods Creek, Rae Lakes, Kearsarge Lakes, Charlotte Lakes, Sixty Lakes Basin, Junction Meadow, and Bubbs Creek. Oh, and please remember to camp at least 100 feet away from lakes and streams. Thank you and have a good trip." Such a thicket of restrictions has become necessary in many areas to protect vegetation from trampling, streams from pollution, and solitude from crowds. In an ever-growing list of park and forest wildernesses, campers must obtain a permit to spend the night. Demand has simply outstripped supply.

Many national forest wildernesses were created in areas of little value for timber—too remote for profitable logging, too high or too dry to yield more than scrub. As the yearning for wilderness grows, the Forest Service responds that it must provide other goods and services also. A quarter of the nation's lumber and plywood is cut on its lands; car and trailer campers must be considered; there is more pressure for ski areas and resorts. No national policies sort out the priorities. So our wilderness system continues in yeasty ferment, and the ideal is far away.

A few years ago I looked out over an expanse of wild country from Sherman Pass, high over the Kern River in Sequoia National Forest. The trail had led upward from sagebrush and rabbit brush, up through piñons and scrub oak, with patches of Indian paintbrush flaming along the way. At the top the trees were wind-tortured, scraggly, frayed—seemingly as old as the rocks. I caught the blue flash of a Steller's jay, heard the faint nasal tones of nuthatches. A buzzard wheeled overhead, coasting the currents. Far to the north rose the mass of Mount Whitney, brooding over the ancestral home of the famous golden trout.

It saddened me to learn later that loggers had set upon this great realm and that a road was inching across the mountains, even through Sherman Pass. An opportunity was lost here for relieving some of the pressure on other Sierra wildernesses, and as the saws and tractors ripped across the Kern Plateau, a bit more of the heart and soul of America, of the wilderness that shaped us, was destroyed.

The millions who quest after the peace and glory of wild places must, like their compatriots in decades past, live with such disappointments—and fight on. The Wilderness Act is a foundation, a great victory for the land, a lode of law which will reward future struggles with victories that are not fleeting. There is hope, too, in the deepening awareness that man cannot forever exploit resources with the abandon of a pioneer in a boundless domain. Man is slowly learning to live in harmony with the earth, using his vast technology to right past wrongs, to clean despoiled rivers and poisoned air. "It has never been man's gift to make wildernesses," Wallace Stegner observed. "But he can make deserts, and has." The choice is ours. I have faith that the wild places will win out.

Foundation pilings crumble near Shenandoah National Park, Virginia

Men labor, build, and move on. But the power of wilderness remains,
refreshing the human spirit during hours of leisure, healing her own wounds
when men have gone. Sometimes the lesions mend—and quickly, as nature
measures time. Around the stumps of an old mill, where a wilderness used to be,
the green promise of another wilderness to come entwines afresh.
But some wounds cannot heal. To build a dam and flood Alaska's Yukon Flats
(overleaf) might destroy one of North America's prime waterfowl nurseries,
whence more than two million ducks and geese take wing southward in an annual
gift of life. There is wildness now to save, and more if left to heal.
"Men's failures are often as beautiful as men's triumphs," wrote Robinson Jeffers,
and the wild's "returnings are even more precious than [its] first presence."

Pacific waves batter a rocky headland at Cape Johnson, on a 50-mile strand of wild shore within Olympic National Park.

FROM OLYMPIC SHORES TO THE HIGH SIERRA

Harvey Manning

Whenever I look from Seattle westward over Puget Sound to the Olympic Mountains, the ragged summit line reaching nearly 8,000 feet above tidewater, my eye comes to rest at a rather low and obscure point on the horizon. Exactly there, on a July evening of 1938, I first went wild.

After supper the Boy Scout leaders let the fire go out to save wood. To keep warm at our mile-high camp, pooped kids crawled into sleeping bags. Others of my fellow Scouts ran whooping and hollering around the ridges. I compromised, wandering alone up the trail beside a step-across creek, all that remained of the Quilcene River which at lunchtime down in the big trees had been so wide and loud. Abruptly the creek ended, or rather began, in a spring gushing from under a rock. On my first high mountain hike I had found the source of the Quilcene!

Farther on, the way entered a meadow decorated with small evergreens and splashes of yellow, red, and blue. To earn the money for Scout camp I'd mowed lawns and weeded flowerbeds until I hated lawns and flowers. But these lawns would never have to be mowed, and even the weeds were flowers. The trail led up to Marmot Pass and I assumed that meant a highway. But when I reached the 5,900-foot pass I realized the nearest road was the rough track we'd left that morning, nine miles and a gallon and a half of sweat ago. Scree and trees fell steeply into darkness and the faint roar of the Dungeness River; the peak-jumble beyond was silhouetted against a sky banded crimson, pink, orange, gold. No highways were out there, no soda fountains or candy stores. Only the wild, wild mountains of Olympic National Park and the first sunset of my life I ever really looked at.

Until that evening at Marmot Pass, I thought no wilderness was left except in polar wastes and tropic jungles. Many more lessons to the contrary followed in my third of a century of walking from Pacific beaches to glaciers nearly three miles above the sea; from jungle to desert; from flower garden to lichen-black crag.

Three great lumps of wilderness dominate the Far West map. They lie in the Sierra Nevada, the Olympics, and the North Cascades. Two chains of smaller preserves extend north and south: one running the 500-mile length of the volcanic Cascades from Washington through Oregon into California; the other, 900 miles along coastal ranges from Oregon to Mexico. Not to be forgotten are quiet corners of mountain and canyon farther inland, and islands and reefs in the Pacific.

THE FAR WEST

Numbered sites are established Wilderness Areas; most lie in national forests. Unnumbered entries are units officially considered for wilderness. A figure after the name is wilderness acreage, not total acreage of the primitive area, national park, or wildlife refuge. Pages cited offer fuller description; page 337 lists contacts for obtaining further details on particular areas.

WASHINGTON

1 Pasayten W. 505,524. See page 37.

Turnbull NWR. Marshes, lakes. 200 species of birds.

North Cascades NP. 515,880. See page 37.

San Juan NWR. 361. Rocky islets harbor birds. Restricted use.

2 Glacier Peak W. 464,741. See pages 37 and 82.

Olympic NP. See page 33.

Mt. Rainier NP. See page 50.

3 Washington Islands W. 179. Three wildlife refuges. Petrels, puffins, auklets. No public use.

Little Pend Oreille NWR. Forested mountains. Deer.

4 Goat Rocks W. 82,680. Snowfields embrace meadows. 95 miles of trails. Mountain goats.

5 Mt. Adams W. 32,356. Excellent climbing, hiking. Lava ridges.

OREGON

6 Three Arch Rocks NWR W. 17. Nine small rocks in Pacific. Sea lions, seabirds. No public use.

7 Mt. Hood W. 14,160. Sand and pumice dunes on upper slopes.

8 Eagle Cap W. 293,775. Bighorn sheep on 9,845-ft. white limestone Matterhorn. More than 60 lakes.

9 Strawberry Mountain W. 33,653. Fairly easy hike up 9,044-ft. peak.

10 Mt. Jefferson W. 99,600. Glaciers, "parks." Craggy summit.

16 Oregon Islands NWR W. 21. Bird haven. No public use. New proposal would include #6, #16, and 56 more islands.

17 Kalmiopsis W. 76,900. Rocky, low-elevation canyons. Many rare plants. Rough trails.

CALIFORNIA

18 Lava Beds NM W. 28,460. Lava caves. Rugged; no trails.

19 Marble Mountain W. 214,543. Spectacular mountain of crystallized marine organisms.

20 South Warner W. 69,547. 27-mile Summit Trail. Glacial lakes, grassy meadows.

Salmon Trinity Alps PA. 223,340. Wild Coast Range crest. Ghost towns, abandoned mines.

21 Thousand Lakes W. 16,335. Trail to 8,676-ft. Magee Peak, an extinct volcano. Lakes formed in lava potholes; cinder cones. Suited only to short trips.

22 Lassen Volcanic NP W. 78,982. Dozing volcano. Hot springs.

23 Caribou W. 19,080. Gentle plateau. Many lakes. Good trail system from Silver Lake.

24 Yolla Bolly-Middle Eel W. 111,091. From some spots on trails hikers can see Sacramento Valley and Pacific Ocean at the same time.

25 Desolation W. 63,469. Trail runs 20 miles from Echo Lake to Emerald Bay. Fisherman's paradise; 130 lakes.

26 Mokelumne W. 50,400. Hand-hewn log cabin of hermit, who mysteriously disappeared after 20 years, still stands.

Point Reyes National Seashore. 5,150. Trails lace forested Inverness Ridge, coastal bluffs.

Emigrant Basin PA. 106,899. Granite outcroppings. Deep canyons, alpine meadows.

Farallon NWR. 140. Rocky islands in the Pacific Ocean. Birds and sea lions. Limited use.

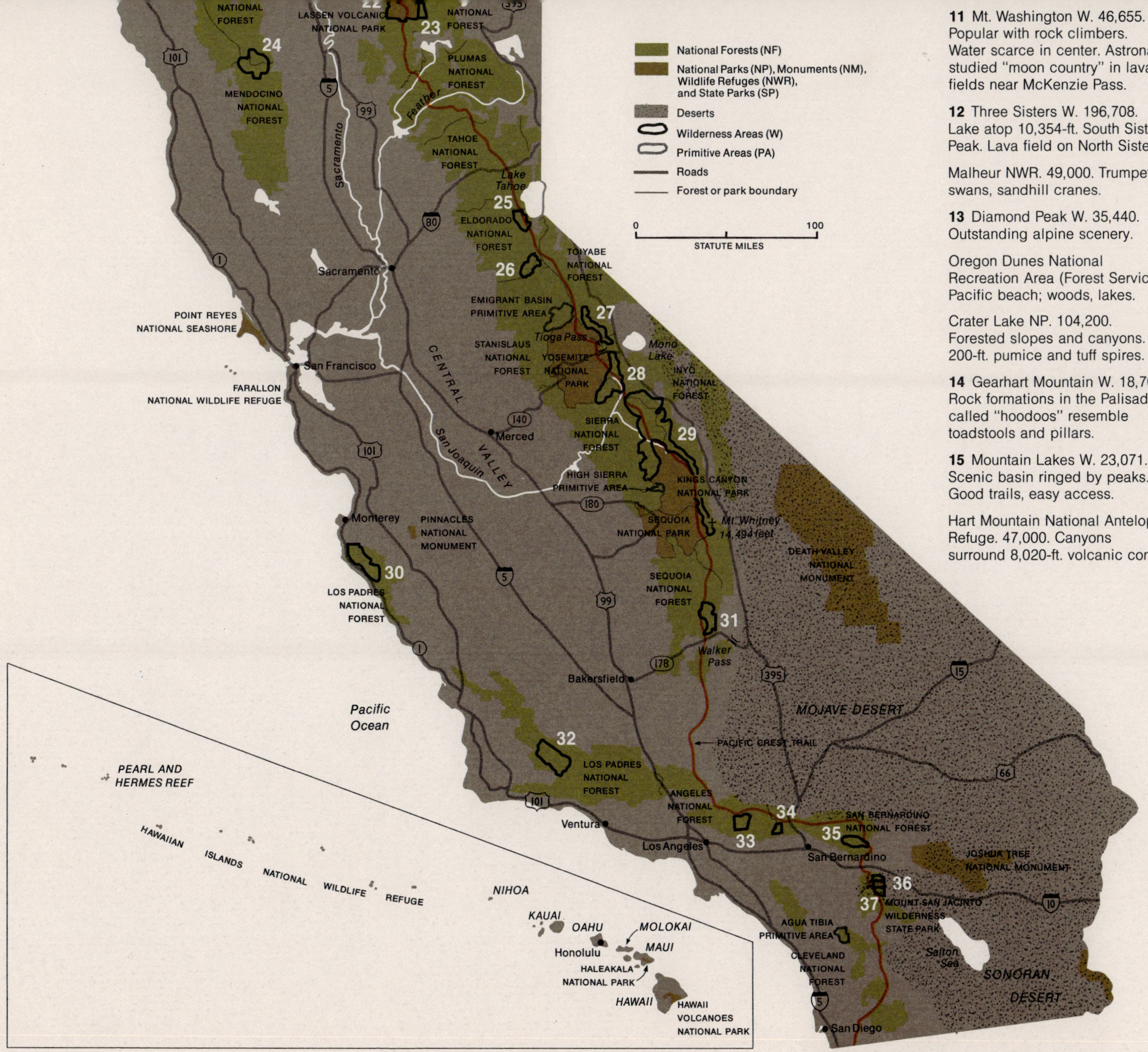

11 Mt. Washington W. 46,655. Popular with rock climbers. Water scarce in center. Astronauts studied "moon country" in lava fields near McKenzie Pass.

12 Three Sisters W. 196,708. Lake atop 10,354-ft. South Sister Peak. Lava field on North Sister.

Malheur NWR. 49,000. Trumpeter swans, sandhill cranes.

13 Diamond Peak W. 35,440. Outstanding alpine scenery.

Oregon Dunes National Recreation Area (Forest Service). Pacific beach; woods, lakes.

Crater Lake NP. 104,200. Forested slopes and canyons. 200-ft. pumice and tuff spires.

14 Gearhart Mountain W. 18,709. Rock formations in the Palisades called "hoodoos" resemble toadstools and pillars.

15 Mountain Lakes W. 23,071. Scenic basin ringed by peaks. Good trails, easy access.

Hart Mountain National Antelope Refuge. 47,000. Canyons surround 8,020-ft. volcanic cone.

27 Hoover W. 42,800. Rugged. Glacial canyons; snowfields. Sudden extremes of weather.

Yosemite NP. 646,700. Study area north and south of Tioga Road (closed in winter). Alpine flora and fauna.

28 Minarets W. 109,559. See page 63.

29 John Muir W. 504,263. See page 36.

Sequoia-Kings Canyon NPs. 721,970. See page 36.

Death Valley NM. See Southwest section, page 104.

High Sierra PA. Proposed as Monarch W., 36,021. See page 36.

Pinnacles NM. 7,313. Volcanic spires. Canyons. Good trails. Semi-arid.

30 Ventana W. 95,152. Popular area, excellent hiking.

31 Dome Land W. 62,211. Granite domes. Semi-arid region.

32 San Rafael W. 142,918. Includes condor refuge.

33 San Gabriel W. 36,137. Rugged; trying trails.

34 Cucamonga W. 9,022. Sharp peaks, steep slopes.

35 San Gorgonio W. 34,718. Alpine flora, fauna. Water scarce; rough going off trails.

36 San Jacinto W. 21,955. Wild, pristine mountain crest. Risky for novice hikers.

37 Mt. San Jacinto Wilderness SP. 13,521. Granite peaks, subalpine forests. Bighorn sheep.

Joshua Tree NM. See Southwest section, page 102.

Agua Tibia PA. 11,920. Desert mountains. Climax chaparral belt.

HAWAII

Haleakala NP. 19,270. Colorful lava flows of dormant volcano.

Hawaii Volcanoes NP. Slopes of active volcanoes.

Hawaiian Islands NWR. 303,936. Hawaiian monk seal. Seabirds. Permit required; landings hazardous.

National Forests (NF)

National Parks (NP), Monuments (NM), Wildlife Refuges (NWR), and State Parks (SP)

Deserts

Wilderness Areas (W)

Primitive Areas (PA)

Roads

Forest or park boundary

0 ——— 100
STATUTE MILES

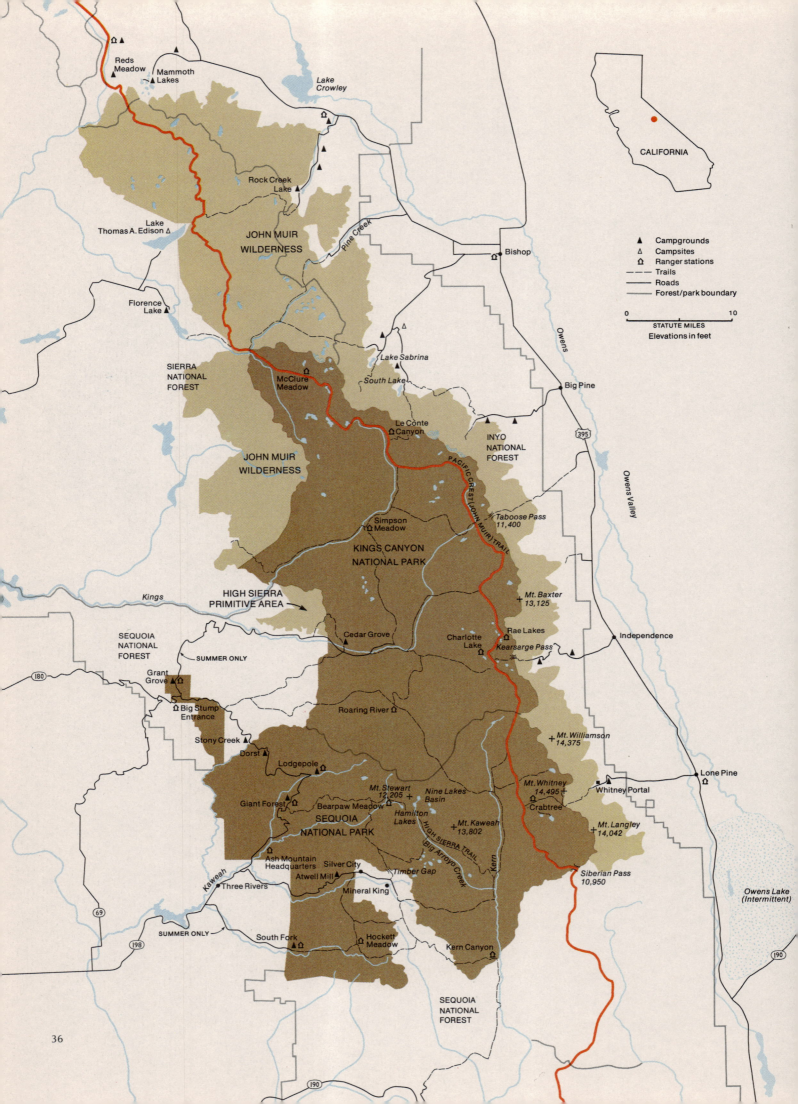

Reds Meadow

Mammoth Lakes

Lake Crowley

Rock Creek Lake

Lake Thomas A. Edison

JOHN MUIR WILDERNESS

Pine Creek

Bishop

Florence Lake

SIERRA NATIONAL FOREST

McClure Meadow

Lake Sabrina

South Lake

Big Pine

Le Conte Canyon

INYO NATIONAL FOREST

JOHN MUIR WILDERNESS

PACIFIC CREST (JOHN MUIR) TRAIL

395

Owens

Owens Valley

Simpson Meadow

KINGS CANYON NATIONAL PARK

Taboose Pass 11,400

Kings

HIGH SIERRA PRIMITIVE AREA

+ Mt. Baxter 13,125

Cedar Grove

Charlotte Lake

Rae Lakes

Kearsarge Pass

Independence

SEQUOIA NATIONAL FOREST

180

SUMMER ONLY

Grant Grove

Big Stump Entrance

Roaring River

+ Mt. Williamson 14,375

Stony Creek

Dorst

Lodgepole

Mt. Stewart 12,205 +

Nine Lakes Basin

Mt. Whitney 14,495 +

Whitney Portal

Lone Pine

Giant Forest

Bearpaw Meadow

SEQUOIA NATIONAL PARK

Hamilton Lakes

HIGH SIERRA TRAIL

Big Arroyo Creek

Mt. Kaweah 13,802

Crabtree

Mt. Langley 14,042

Ash Mountain Headquarters

Silver City

Timber Gap

Kern

69

Kaweah

Atwell Mill

Three Rivers

Mineral King

Siberian Pass 10,950

Owens Lake (Intermittent)

198

SUMMER ONLY

South Fork

Hockett Meadow

Kern Canyon

SEQUOIA NATIONAL FOREST

190

190

CALIFORNIA

▲ Campgrounds
△ Campsites
⌂ Ranger stations
--- Trails
— Roads
— Forest/park boundary

0   STATUTE MILES   10

Elevations in feet

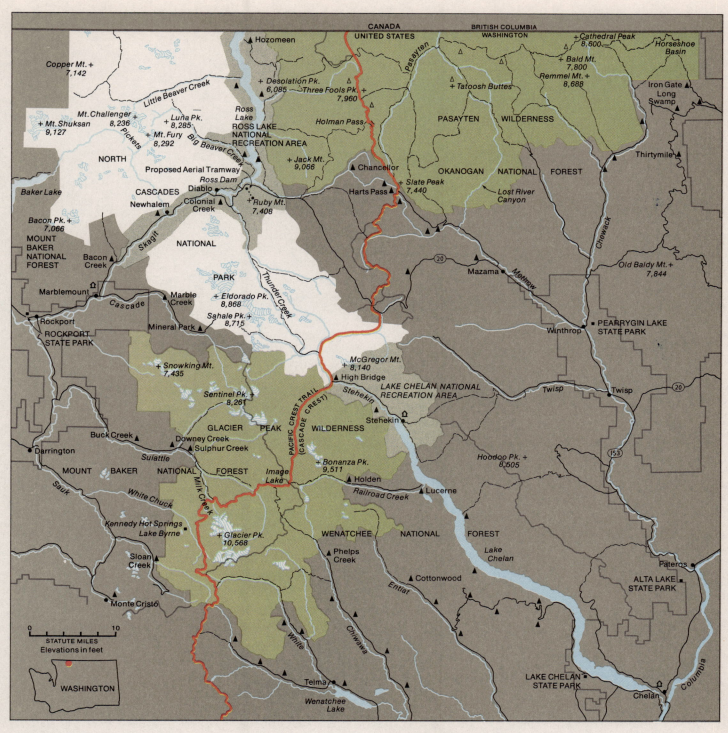

HIGH SIERRA

Plunging canyons, alpine meadows, lakes, and peaks that rise "like the wall of some celestial city"—the grandeur of the High Sierra fills this popular complex of park and forest land. Through it winds much of the John Muir Trail, a 212-mile route that largely coincides with the Pacific Crest Trail and passes near scores of peaks rising above 13,000 feet.

Kings Canyon and Sequoia National Parks, with their magnificent sequoia groves, total 847,000 acres, of which 85 percent is slated for wilderness protection. Most of the backcountry is accessible only on foot or horseback; no road crosses the Sierra crest within the parks. Thousands cross from Giant Forest to Mount Whitney on the High Sierra and John Muir trails. From Cedar Grove in Kings Canyon a trail leads to the rugged High Sierra Primitive Area—the proposed Monarch Wilderness which is less crowded than the park lands.

Straddling Kings Canyon like a giant wishbone, half-million-acre John Muir Wilderness is carved from two national forests. On the west visitors find access from roadheads at reservoirs such as Florence and Edison lakes. From Owens Valley, where campgrounds and pack stations fringe the wilderness, visitors head for Whitney or trout-stocked lakes, some in glacial cirques above timberline. Special preserves on Mount Baxter and Mount Williamson shelter the rare California bighorn sheep.

NORTH CASCADES

Bristling spires of "America's Alps" crown a primitive realm of rain-drenched forests, glaciers, cascading streams, and—in the east—sunny groves of pine and dry shrub lands. Deer and mountain goat, cougar and bear range the majestic fastness.

Of the 674,000 acres that comprise the national park system units, more than three-fourths are recommended for wilderness preservation—even chunks of the more heavily developed Ross Lake and Lake Chelan National Recreation Areas. In the national park, climbers find challenge in the Eldorado Peak area or in the remote Picket Range. Rangers urge careful outfitting and a minimum of two to a party. For the less hardy a proposed tramway at Ruby Mountain would provide a bird's-eye view of the peaks.

A year-round ferry on Lake Chelan brings visitors to Stehekin near the Pacific Crest Trail. Backpackers funnel south along the trail to Glacier Peak Wilderness and its breathtaking white volcano, or north toward the park.

The new North Cascades Highway (Route 20) makes Pasayten Wilderness more accessible in the summer. Campgrounds and outfitters dot the southern edge; interior campsites are little more than clearings. From Horseshoe Basin, where riding is popular, a trail leads west past Cathedral Peak to wilder lands beyond. Lost River Canyon offers rugged hiking; meadows at Tatoosh Buttes glow with wild flowers in season.

Has anyone ever intimately known all three brave chunks and two noble necklaces and the marvelous miscellany? Conceivably. As for me, I wander even my home hills as a stranger still, as full of awe as in that long-ago sunset at Marmot Pass.

In my second Olympics summer, I walked my first glacier, the Anderson, one of more than 60 in these mountains, and was wonderfully terrified by the jump-off-and-pray glissade from Flypaper Pass. Sliding on my rump a mile a minute down a precipice of snow, I howled in fear and glee, slowing finally to a stop far out in the glacier flat, amazed to be alive and unbroken. Later that summer, I beat brush up from the Dosewallips River to the narrow slot between walls of Mount Deception and Mount Mystery, entered Deception Basin, and from the top of a raw moraine looked down to a stream bursting from Mystery Glacier.

Where but in my mountains lived so many free animals? Deer grazed in evening shadows. Marmots whistled from boulder-top lookouts. Goats casually ambled over frightening cliffs. One summer day in parkland headwaters of the Lost River, I felt almost crowded, simultaneously seeing two black bears, two coyotes, and a band of several dozen elk. Another time a nervous gray bird, perched on a river boulder—dipping, dipping, dipping—startled me by suddenly diving into the rapids and striding along the stream bed totally submerged. Ever after, meeting a water ouzel, I found myself empathetically dipping, dipping at the knees. Once on the crest of a ridge I turned a blind corner and nearly stepped on a golden eagle. The enormous creature nonchalantly spread its wings and sailed over the valley.

So my passion grew. Though ultimately other wild lands competed, always I remembered my first home and have yet to experience elsewhere that special glory of Olympic National Park, a unity of surf, forest, meadow, glacier.

It starts on the strip of sand, shingle, and driftwood where wilderness of ocean ceaselessly attacks wilderness of continent. Except at midpoint, the 50-mile beach is roadless. When alpine gardens are deep in snow I go to the beach to explore tidal-pool gardens of seaweed, green anemones, red and purple starfish, white barnacles, and blue-shelled mussels. Snail shells scurry mysteriously, having been appropriated by tiny hermit crabs. Sandpipers run along the spindrift; crows and gulls scavenge; bald eagles circle. A dog-like face pops out of foam-flecked water near the shore. Soft eyes stare; I bark in greeting. Then a breaker curls over the seal's head and it ducks beneath the explosion. Groups of whales come in spring to cavort in the depths. From the beach I see monstrous backs breaking the surface, black fins cleaving green rollers, plumes of spray exhaled high in the wind.

At dawn I have looked out from the rim of the continent, hearing in surf the pulse of eternity, and at noon a few miles inland, walked into cathedral gloom of the Hoh River rain forest, fed by up to 150 inches of annual precipitation. Sea fogs in every season seep through the valley, bathing giant Sitka spruce, western hemlock, and big-leaf maples so swollen with moss and ferns they seem not true trees at all but weird survivals from earth's distant past. Olympic peaks were born 12 to 20 million years ago of sediments and lavas uplifted from ancient seas. During the Pleistocene the shales and sandstones, spiced by basalts, were shaped by ice into horns, arêtes, and cirques. Abruptly above Hoh Valley rises the culminating peak, 7,965-foot Mount Olympus, gleaming white.

Water is its element, the thrust and swirl of cold mountain torrents seemingly the theme of its cheery song. The water ouzel, or dipper—"plump and compact as a pebble . . . whirled in a pot-hole," Muir wrote— bobs up and down 40 to 60 times a minute, then dives. The slate-gray "teeter bird," a familiar sight to Western wilderness travelers, can swim underwater or walk the stream bed seeking insects. On a rock in midstream, on a ledge, or behind a waterfall, the female weaves a hollow globe of moss and grass—with side entry— to shelter her new brood.

DRAWING BY GEORGE FOUNDS

One January three of us snowshoed 18 miles through rain forest to Glacier Meadows, aiming to climb Olympus. Arriving simultaneously with a blizzard, we tunneled down into a buried lean-to and for days, as the storm raged and hopes of the summit faded, strove to warm the cave with dead branches plucked from sub-alpine trees. The ice-encrusted wood stubbornly resisted combustion, giving little heat but vast quantities of smoke which filled our burrow, our noses, our eyes. One afternoon, to clear our lungs we bundled up and wandered the Blue Glacier aimlessly, naught visible but snow under boots, snow driving furiously into eyes, and the frosted rope connecting to dimly seen companions. For all we could tell, we might have been on the Greenland icecap. After miles and hours someone shouted over the gale, "Why the hell are we here?" Yelled another, "Damned if I know!"

That wasn't really true. We knew.

The 700-mile Cascade Range is really two ranges under a single name. Southward from Snoqualmie Pass — a 50-mile drive from Seattle — extend the volcanic Cascades, a relatively simple arch uplift accentuated through the ages by myriad spewings and spittings of hot rock. Northward lie the more complex North Cascades, where the arching and volcanism are superimposed on sediments, granites, gneisses, schists, and whatnot, so fractured and jumbled that geologists only recently have puzzled out the structures.

My acquaintance with the Cascades began at Snoqualmie Pass in the close-to-city Alpine Lakes region, where some 600 lakes large and small, low and high, fill cirques and troughs of vanished glaciers. Along the Cascade Crest Trail a day's walk may pass as many as a dozen lakes, set amid tall trees, in flower gardens, or in barren rock bowls beneath cliffs. Families picnic on fringes of the wild land. Fishermen roam the interior. Generations of Boy Scouts have been introduced to high adventure here and generations of climbers — me among them — have learned their craft on the numerous sharp little peaks. The Alpine Lakes country is surely one of the nation's finest wild areas so near the homes of so many people.

The Cascades drama builds steadily northward.

From dim dawn to dark noon of a September day in 1949 half a dozen members of the Mountaineers, a climbing and conservation club based in Seattle, plugged across endless fog-bleary snowfields. We climbed col after col and descended couloir after couloir, and finally navigated a sea-like glacier whose edges were lost in mist. We knew vaguely we were on our objective, an 8,868-foot peak named Eldorado. Miners had picked at its base before the turn of the century, but the summit had first been attained in 1933 and only seven or eight times since.

Immersed in a cloud, we cautiously kicked steps along the knife-edged snow crest, keeping ropes taut, jamming axes deep. Faraway rivers echoed in the unseen emptiness below. At last the crest dipped. Nothing was left to climb. We gathered for lunch on a mass of boulders, feeling eerily disconnected from earth.

Suddenly a hole opened in the clouds — and as suddenly closed. Convulsive yells blew sandwiches out of our mouths. What *was* that huge peak we had glimpsed? More holes, more monster mountains, more enormous glaciers. The map was sketchy, giving few names. Nineteen years later, in 1968, our obscure Eldorado was famous as a climax peak of the south unit of the new North Cascades National Park.

In the intervening years I discovered wildness beyond any I'd known. Soon after Eldorado our group of nine Mountaineers nearly doubled the number of people who had penetrated the heart of the hostile Northern Pickets: We were the fifth party to ascend Mount Challenger, the fourth on Luna Peak. The morning we were to attempt

Mount Fury a July blizzard obliterated the sharp crags. In driving sleet we hoisted packs and commenced a daylong retreat over glaciers back to Whatcom Pass and the miracle of green grass and trees, the security of trail. Again, not until 1968 did the Pickets gain fame as the "pole of remoteness" of the range and as the core of the north unit of North Cascades National Park.

Remembering the living wall of Mount Fury, blocks of ice breaking loose from hanging glaciers and thundering in slow-motion billows of white dust—down, down, down to the dark moraines and loud torrents of Luna Cirque—I do not automatically concede the superiority of higher mountains elsewhere.

To be sure, the highest nonvolcanic summit in the Cascades is 9,511-foot Bonanza. But mountains are less impressive for height above the sea than for their height above adjacent valleys, their *tallness*. Even omitting the two volcanoes, Baker and Glacier Peak, North Cascades peaks are extraordinarily tall, many standing 5,000 to 7,000 feet above their bases. With winter snows piling to 20 feet or more, timberline dips as low as 4,000 feet, making a very large and snowy alpine zone. The Cascades north of Snoqualmie Pass contain 756 identified glaciers, more than 100 square miles of ice. Though not impressive to an Alaskan, the glacier area is approximately half the total in the Lower 48 states.

My early approaches were from the west, from Puget Sound lowlands, along rivers whose names are incantations (Sauk, White Chuck, and Suiattle; Cascade, Skagit, and Nooksack). I trekked through lush forests of fir, hemlock, and cedar; upward in parkland and moraine; finally to glaciers and rough-cut walls and spires.

The classic trips were the mean ones: when the trail quit in a thicket of slide alder and vine maple and we were bruised and abraded and humiliated before breaking free from the greenery; or when a snowmelt-raging creek washed over a slippery footlog and I strove to convince my wife that true happiness lay on the far side of the flood. No vacation was satisfying without its proper ration of rain and fog, no summer complete without at least one screaming three-day blow. Never apologizing for the weather, west-side loyalists extol the intimacy of red, white, and yellow heather gardens in the gray, drifting mist and explain that sunshine is the brighter for its rarity.

There is, of course, an east side. Eventually there came a (Continued on page 49)

Portfolio Notes

OPPOSITE: *Olympic Mountains, fit home for the gods, also please mountain goats. The bearded steeplejacks, ranging from the Yukon to the northern Rockies, were imported to the Olympic Peninsula, now thrive on its cloud-castled crags.*
KEITH GUNNAR

PAGES 42-43: *From the flank of 8,715-foot Sahale Peak, climbers survey an icy solitude of North Cascades summits. View is southwest from the national park into Glacier Peak Wilderness. To gain this vantage, experienced mountaineers toil half a day upward from Cascade Pass, in left foreground. To look over their shoulders, photographer and pilot hovered precariously close in a helicopter.*
JAMES P. BLAIR, NATIONAL GEOGRAPHIC PHOTOGRAPHER

PAGES 44-45: *Winged explosion—teal, mallards, widgeons, and other wild ducks roil a pond in Malheur National Wildlife Refuge, Oregon. Here, on* marshes, lakes, and semi-arid uplands more than 230 bird species of the Pacific flyway nest or tarry during migration.
ENTHEOS

PAGES 46-47: *Thousands annually pay homage to the king of Oregon mountains, 11,235-foot Mount Hood. On a clear day His Majesty can view Portland, 50 miles away, and vice versa. Peak eroded and volcanic fires banked, Hood still fumes, yet probably is more often climbed than any other snow-mantled summit in North America.*
DAVID FALCONER

PAGE 48: *Headlong down a stony stairway a stream purls from a mile-high meadow near the eastern edge of Three Sisters Wilderness. Though more than half of Oregon is federal land—mostly grazing lands and national forests—areas now in or officially proposed for wilderness total less than 1.7 percent of the state.*
RAY ATKESON

vacation week when I wasn't in the mood for bulling through wet brush under a sodden pack. Over the crest I went to blue skies of the rain shadow. From sunny ridges above Lake Chelan I looked westward to black Pacific storms pummeling unseen peaks and drenching my old haunts. There was something to be said for dry boots.

Glaciers and precipices are smaller and fewer here than in the west. But views are less misted, the hiking summer longer. And I quickly fell in love with the trees of the rain shadow. In valleys grow gaudy-barked ponderosa pine and ghostly white aspen; on ridges the multitrunked whitebark pine which endures after death as a masterpiece of intricate silver sculpture; on alpine slopes the dense-limbed Engelmann spruce, and especially the Lyall larch—its feathery needles turn orange-gold in autumn and drop off, then new needles sprout in an ethereal springtime green.

The east also supports a more varied assemblage of large animals: bighorn sheep, elk, and an occasional moose strayed from Canada. Most domestic sheep and cattle are gone from the highlands and with them the herdsmen who for half a century gunned down every wild creature suspected of a hankering for mutton or beef.

That menace abated, certain wild species are drifting over the international boundary to reoccupy primeval homes. The grizzly bear and the wolf, never entirely absent from the range, are occasionally being sighted in gun-free North Cascades National Park and in Pasayten Wilderness to the east. My own ears tell me another target species is thriving: I particularly remember a night on Bald Mountain in the eastern part of the Pasayten Wilderness listening to coyotes bark and howl under red and green shafts of sky-dancing northern lights.

At 8:30 a.m. the *Lady of the Lake* departs from the town of Chelan, amid apple orchards and brown semi-desert hills, and begins the 55-mile voyage up narrow, fiord-like Lake Chelan, which fills the channel of a Pleistocene glacier. Sagebrush gives way to pine forests, rounded ridges to cliffs thrusting 7,000 feet above the shores. At 12:30 or so the boat docks at lakehead, half a day and most of a century from breakfast. Hikers board a little shuttle bus. After a slow and jouncing ride up the dead-end Stehekin River road, they walk trails into Glacier Peak Wilderness or North Cascades National Park.

Nine miles up the Stehekin lives the Ray Courtney family, their cabin located (very carefully) between two avalanche chutes which in winter and spring rumble with snows sliding down 8,140-foot McGregor Mountain. Ray's family homesteaded on the lake some 80 years ago. The Courtneys constitute a fifth of the valley's year-round population of 40 or so; their closest neighbors and the one-room log schoolhouse attended by Ray—and now his children—are five miles away.

The Courtneys are not confused or uncertain about why they live where they do, on the flat between river and cliff which the original settler called the Garden of Eden. Some years ago, when a movement began to "improve" the valley by petitioning the Public Utility District to supply power, Ray stood up in town meeting and risked ostracism by saying of electric lights, television, and refrigerators, "You folks who need these things can get them a whole lot easier than by bringing in the P.U.D. All you have to do is buy a boat ticket to the other end of the lake." Electricity came to Stehekin—but not to the Garden of Eden. Most of the people who sought to civilize the valley have moved away. The Courtneys remain, and on every visit I wonder if I'll have the fortitude to return downlake to the 20th century.

McGregor (or "Courtney Peak" as their friends know it) is nearly in the center of the North Cascades. At the base, when winter snows pile to the cabin eaves, wilderness waits just beyond the windowpane. In 1892, about the time Ray's grandfather staked his homestead, the townspeople of Chelan, dismayed by the prospect of wealthy Easterners and European noblemen coming in bunches to slaughter the mountain goat and grizzly bear, raised the call for a national park in the North Cascades. A sawmill owner objected and that was the end of that—a sequence to be repeated through the years as other park proposals were put forth.

At length the U. S. Forest Service took the preservation initiative, and in the early 1930's designated the North Cascades Primitive Area along the international boundary. Several years later the legendary Bob Marshall drew up a grand plan for a wild land centered on Glacier Peak. But after his tragically premature death, the wilderness philosophy seemed to lose ground in the Forest Service.

Citizens revived his dreams, in 1957 organizing the North Cascades Conservation Council to spearhead a coalition of the Mountaineers, the Sierra Club, and other concerned groups. Under relentless prodding, the Forest Service in 1960 established the Glacier Peak Wilderness. A victory? No. The voice of the timber industry had been so loud that the designated area held more ice and rock than trees; it was a mere fragment of Marshall's vision. Sadly, the Council and its allies turned from the Forest Service to other channels of action. An epic struggle followed and in 1968 President Johnson signed the North Cascades Act, creating a two-unit North Cascades National Park and the Ross Lake and Lake Chelan National Recreation Areas, for a total 674,000 acres under Park Service administration. In addition, the Act slightly enlarged Glacier Peak Wilderness and established Pasayten Wilderness from the Primitive Area, a total 988,505 acres of national forest wild land.

A victory? Yes, a splendid one—but measured against the opportunity, a defeat too. Less than half the climax country was accorded protection. With a few notable exceptions, to us in the conservation movement the rule seemed to be cliffs and glaciers and flowers for wilderness, everything else for industry. Thus, 1968 was not the end of preservation efforts, but rather a way point.

Logging continues in high-elevation forests, cutting trees that were centuries in growing. We still face proposals for dam-building that would gain a dribble of new kilowatts but drown miles of virgin forests and free-flowing streams. What I regard as a grievous flaw in the Wilderness Act would permit a copper company to dig a vast open-pit mine in the heart of the Glacier Peak Wilderness.

Similar threats hang over wild land throughout the West. Not in the Cascades of Washington and Oregon, the Sierra of California, or anywhere in the Pacific states has the National Wilderness Preservation System approached the minimum limits I believe the future will require. As for the Olympics, a sad irony for me personally: Marmot Pass, my first high home, is outside the 896,599-acre national park, outside dedicated wilderness. How that can be I never will understand. Nor accept.

To grow up in Puget Sound country is to be dominated by a stupefying mountain of snow. With the Climbing Course of the Mountaineers so close by, it was perhaps inevitable that one bleak predawn I would be roped into one of those teams in parkas and cramponed boots heading into Rainier's cap of swirling clouds. I knew I'd never make it. But my only honorable route back to the good green world led upward with my companions. Higher and higher we climbed on that sterile glacier, chopping a ladder up the icefall, weaving between fathomless blue pits, fear submerged in a patient rhythm: *step,* inhale, exhale, *step.* Suddenly no more snow. We entered the sky. Alive and 14,416 feet tall!

Single-leaf piñon

Whitebark pine

Knobcone pine

Sugar pine

I surveyed my domain north to Canada, east into desert haze, west to the ocean, and south halfway down Oregon. Infatuated with Rainier, with all volcanoes, I dreamed of a giant's walk, stepping from Rainier to St. Helens to Adams. Over the Columbia River to Oregon's Mount Hood, Jefferson, Three Sisters, and on across the California border to Shasta and Lassen.

The isolated grandeur of the fire peaks and the rawness of an unfinished earth still being created attract climbers and hikers alike. The Cascade arch, mainly rounded and forested from Snoqualmie Pass southward, seems designed as a subdued setting for the violence of volcanoes—hundreds of them, big and small. Some are relatively new, some so old only the cores of once-huge masses remain. The farther south the greater the abundance and variety of cinder cones, lava domes, and flows. Many appear to have been liquid rock just yesterday. And as geologists measure time, they were.

Glacier Peak blew clouds of pumice to Alberta 12,000 years ago; Baker erupted five times in the 19th century and continues to smoke occasionally; hot springs bubble from both. St. Helens scared the local Indians early in the 19th century. Live steam leaks from Rainier's crater and sides. Sulphur fumes of Hood and Adams can make climbers sick. Mount Mazama, formerly about 12,000 feet high, exploded catastrophically 6,600 years ago. Pumice showered throughout the Northwest and part of Canada. The peak collapsed into the emptied lava chamber, leaving a caldera which filled with snowmelt and became Crater Lake. Lassen earned national park status after erupting some 150 times beginning in 1914. Though calm since 1921, the hot and churning pools of Bumpass Hell testify to fires unbanked.

The largest of the fire mountains are also ice mountains. Every Washington volcano, the five highest in Oregon, and Shasta in California all carry glaciers; where none are left, moraines reinforce the impression of a new-made land.

They are mountains of color: the white of ice and snow; the exuberant red and brown and yellow and black and gray of lava; the blue of lakes; the rainbow blossoms of lush meadows, the vivid green of forests. They are wild mountains too, in part—too small part. Mount Rainier National Park does not contain the entire mountain. The Goat Rocks and Mount Adams Wilderness Areas are almost entirely lava, snow, and flowers, with virtually every sawmill-worthy tree carefully omitted. Mount St. Helens has been logged to timberline on all sides but one.

The Oregon volcanoes have been treated very shabbily. The Wilderness Areas of Hood, Jefferson, Washington, Three Sisters, and Diamond are hardly spacious enough for hikers to escape the racket of chain saws and logging trucks working upward to the meadows. Of the various campaigns seeking preservation for wild lands, perhaps the most interesting is that involving French Pete Creek, one of only two sizeable forested valleys in western Oregon that are still pristine. When the appropriate United States Senate committee was unable to conduct field hearings on the proposal, citizens held their own in Eugene. Formal testimony was presented by public officials, scientists, representatives of industry, and outdoor clubs. The state's Senators subsequently entered the entire transcript in the Congressional Record. Such initiative may help achieve, someday, an Oregon Volcanoes National Park.

If mountain-building eruptions in the Cascades are a speculative threat, mountain-building earthquakes are a recurring fact in southern California. Whether or not the smog-and-freeway-menaced citizens want this added excitement, many enjoy the results. Hundreds of thousands declare with their boots the importance of the

Foxtail pine

Patterned to outlast hard times, cone-bearing trees tenant some of the driest, coldest, windiest spots where trees grow. Taproots probe deep to find sustaining soil; boughs bend to the wind. Tough, waxy needles exhale a minimum of moisture, waiting green and unwilted through drought, unfrozen by winter cold. Cones cradle seeds that may stay vital for decades. Pines, the most varied genus, number 17 species in the West. From cones of the single-leaf piñon on eastern Sierra slopes Indians gather edible seed kernels. Cones are life insurance for the knobcone, usually freeing their seeds only when the tree dies. The regal sugar pine, largest of pines and with cones up to two feet long, grows at middle elevations. Around timberline are found the whitebark and the foxtail, named for the brushy masses of needles at the branch tips.

DRAWINGS BY GEORGE FOUNDS

wilderness in unsteady fault-block ranges of their home horizons. Indeed, the nation's freeway capital may justly lay claim to being the hiking capital as well.

The Coast Ranges hold the area's two largest wilderness preserves, Ventana and San Rafael. At elevations to 7,000 feet their creeks, forests, and broad-view ridges are especially popular in winter and spring when higher mountains are deep in snow.

The heights which ring Greater Los Angeles contain pocket preserves so heavily traveled they are less old-style wilderness than city-parks-on-the-outskirts—and what's wrong with that? We need both. In fact, recreation planners and sociologists increasingly stress the importance of spacious natural areas near population centers. Undeveloped except for trail systems, they provide opportunities year-round for quick and easy surcease from urban crush, opportunities considered a godsend by a good many city people. A short drive from home they walk in chaparral, that mixture of manzanita and a dozen other shrubs "too low to give shade, too high to see over, too thick to go through." When in bloom, the "elfin forest" is delightful to the eye and nose. On higher paths hikers enter stands of ponderosa pine, incense cedar, sugar pine, white fir, and lodgepole pine. They may leave the city after breakfast with the thermometer reading 95° F. and by lunchtime be punching steps in snow on 11,502-foot San Gorgonio Mountain, the "rooftop of southern California." On San Jacinto Peak, which in five miles thrusts 10,700 vertical feet from desert, six life zones tier one continuous slope, Sonoran and alpine floras growing as close neighbors.

These are, in terms of use, among the most valuable wild lands in America. As more and more Angelenos take to their feet, how much trail country will be enough? Certainly not the few hundred thousand acres their close-to-home wilderness preserves now contain. Four times that amount of wild living room would scarcely meet projected future needs. Obviously the time has come in southern California to think carefully before building new roads, in fact to consider unbuilding.

The full moon and the evening star rose together out of Nevada to the east, glinting in breeze-rippled waters of Lake Aloha, shining day-bright, night-soft on snows and granites of the Crystal Range. I gazed over Desolation Valley, feeling dimensions of the long-vanished glacier. Aloha's waves lapped rock. Frogs sang all around. I watched a mouse cleaning up camp crumbs. Though far from my northern home, in the Sierra Nevada of California I *was* home.

It was partly the people who had drawn me here. Perhaps no other wild area of the West has known so fascinating a company of wanderers: the Paiutes who called the mountains *Inyo,* or the dwelling place of a great spirit; the Spanish who from a distant view described *una gran sierra nevada*—a great snowy range; Jedediah Smith and his mountain men; the forty-niners in search of shining gold. And the young Scot who came to Yosemite backcountry in 1869 as supervisory (Continued on page 57)

Portfolio Notes

caretaker to 2,000 sheep and in the following 46 years enriched the Sierra—and wilderness everywhere—with his shouts of glee. Unlike land-taming frontiersmen of his era and ours, John Muir reveled in the unruliness of nature. He rode an avalanche rejoicing; walked to the hot edge of a forest fire the better to see trees become instant torches; climbed a tall pine in a gale to feel the sway; dodged boulders shaken from Yosemite cliffs and exulted in "A noble earthquake!"

And in my own time came men like Dave Brower, who led the Sierra Club to national prominence and more recently, as founder and president of Friends of the Earth, has extended his definition of "home" to encompass the entire planet.

A quest for historical roots also leads to the Sierra, for something important to our nation and world began here. In 1864 a memorable seed was planted: Federal lands in Yosemite Valley and the Mariposa Grove of sequoias were given to the State of California "for public use, resort and recreation." And then there was that incredible time in September of 1890 when Congress in the space of seven days established three new national parks. The trio—Sequoia, Yosemite, and General Grant National Parks—gave momentum to the idea first clearly stated 18 years earlier with the creation of Yellowstone National Park. Among the finest subsequent accomplishments of the conservation movement were the doubling in size of Sequoia in 1926, extending its boundaries from big trees to big mountains, and creation of the hard-won Kings Canyon National Park in 1940 (including the old General Grant Park). Further, in that poignantly recalled era of the 1920's and 1930's when the Forest Service was chief exponent of the wilderness concept, Primitive Areas set aside in the Sierra were noble expressions of its farsighted idealism.

The Sierra Nevada is the largest unbroken chunk of mountain in the Pacific states. Some 400 miles long, the range overlaps the volcanic Cascades at one end and abuts southern California fault blocks on the other. It spreads as much as 80 miles wide from foothills bordering the great Central Valley to the eastern scarp. The High Sierra, defined as the country above 9,000 feet, is about 240 miles long and 15 to 25 miles wide. Summits approach 10,000 feet near Lake Tahoe and in a north-south progression rise to 13,000 feet at mid-range and to 14,000 in the Palisades and Whitney groups. More than 500 stand above 12,000 feet.

The High is wild. National forests contain six Wilderness Areas and two Primitive Areas, totaling 976,622 acres. In addition, some 1.3 million acres of the three national parks are proposed for the National Wilderness Preservation System. The Sierra thus holds the most extensive protected wild lands in the Far West.

Such things the map told me. I chose Desolation Wilderness, close to the northern limits of the High Sierra, for my introduction to things the maps can't say. With all the misgivings of an alien, I hoisted pack and set forth on the trail. There I met the Sierra juniper, pushing its stubby-thick trunk and wiry limbs from cracks in granite knolls. Gashed by falling rocks, torn by avalanches, split by lightning, it embodies half a thousand years of stubborn vitality. The pilgrimage was already a success. I'd found a magnificent new tree to love.

Before again shouldering pack, I wanted to see if the famous eastern scarp measured up to the advertising. The Sierra structure is majestically simple compared to the North Cascades. To tell its story in barest outline, the crust bowed upward in a north-south line; stresses cracked the arch lengthwise; and the keystone of the arch collapsed and sank. The Sierra block was left high above the easterly blocks that dropped to form Tahoe, Owens, and other valleys. The range is still a-building. Blocks are on the move, as evidenced by some twenty earthquakes a year.

Driving south from Lake Tahoe, I watched the scarp grow steadily sharper, taller. In the Owens Valley I let out a Muir-like whoop, looking up from a level of less than 4,000 feet to the 14,495-foot summit of Mount Whitney 12 miles away. The tallness was impressive—but it was the length of the wall that staggered me. For 150 miles the most classic clean section of the scarp extends north and south, beyond sight—the most humbling mountain front, I think, in North America. Route 395 at the base of the range on the east provides a year-round approach, leaving the crest unbroken by roads for 170 miles, from Walker Pass to Tioga Pass.

Returning north, I took Tioga Pass Road westward through the scarp, in a matter of minutes ascending a steep-walled chasm from desert heat to cool green meadows of 9,900-foot Tioga Pass. Then began the long, gradual descent of the west slope. I found the drama of the eastern scarp fully matched by the glacier-gouged western canyons—Yosemite, Tuolumne, Kings, and Kern.

The highway dropped from blue Sierra breezes to brown lowland heat. Mountains were lost in smog of the Central Valley, yet their invisible presence was felt. With rainfall as little as five inches yearly, the valley should have been parched; instead it was green with orchards, vineyards, and fields of vegetables. How could this be? The answer: The Sierra receives 70-80 inches of annual precipitation in the north and 35-40 in the south and every drop is used and reused with a thoroughness that makes a Northerner feel profligate. West-slope rivers flow from reservoir to reservoir, turning turbines as many as eight times, and when the last kilowatt has been squeezed out, they irrigate the Central Valley's agribusiness. Virtually all the east-slope creeks which once watered the Owens Valley were pre-empted by Los Angeles in the early decades of this century. Torrents tumbling from Whitney are, several days later, flowing from faucets in the megalopolis.

Having seen the outside of the range, east and west, I was ready to venture inside again. At 6,800-foot Crescent Meadow in the Giant Forest of Sequoia National Park, I lifted a ten-day burden onto my back and took to the High Sierra Trail leading across the range toward Mount Whitney. I began amid the massive reddish trunks of the world's largest trees. Not long ago the sight of blackened duff and charred firs beneath the patriarchs would have caused alarm. But after a century of overprotecting trees from fire, the Park Service now uses controlled burns to return forests to their natural balance. As Park Superintendent John McLaughlin remarked, "We're always doing what we think is wise—but as we learn more, our wisdom changes. What was 'right' 10 or 20 years ago may be wrong now."

Past the sequoias were forests of sugar pine and yellow pine, incense cedar and fir. Chaparral openings gave views of the Middle Fork Kaweah River, thousands of feet below. Ahead, dimmed by haze, loomed peaks of the Great Western Divide, which in this double-crested section of the Sierra parallels the Whitney line of summits.

Never was I more than several steps from the sight and smell of flowers. I recognized scores of old friends from the north. Spectacular strangers, though, forced the exclamations—dozens of anonymous little blossoms, blue, and white, and yellow, and violet, and pink, and orange.

Sierra granite, I discovered, is a many-splendored rock: large-crystaled or fine-grained, glowing with pink feldspar or dark-spotted with hornblende. Cliffs are black-streaked where snowmelt nourishes moss and algae; bowls are bright white where avalanches scour. Monotony in Sierra granite? Never.

After 16 miles I was at 8,200 feet, technically not yet High but feeling definitely so in the cirque called Valhalla. Here near the shining white precipice of Angel Wings lie the lovely Hamilton Lakes. Several dozen hikers were camped atop buttresses or under pines. Few had pitched tents. Having by this time come to trust the benign Sierra sky, I left my tarp in the pack and simply unrolled sleeping pad and bag on granite sand. Certain of my neighbors, obviously old hands, were traveling without shelter, virtually without clothing. Sierra packs seem to average considerably lighter than those typical of the Cascades, and that's a mercy.

One afternoon Dana Abell, the backcountry ranger for this section of trail, arrived at the lake with garbage bag and shovel. I followed as he picked up litter, scattered fire-ring rocks, and greeted hikers. Dana exemplifies a new breed, called backcountry rangers in the Park Service, wilderness rangers in the Forest Service. These men and women, often teachers or students, patrol the trails, check travelers for wilderness permits, and observe the impact of human use on fragile areas. But more than that they act as hosts, always ready to supply information and advice. I've come to look forward to encountering them and mining their lodes of lore about areas they know so much more intimately than we passers-through.

My last evening at the Hamilton Lakes I wandered to the shore and sat on a slab sloping gently into glassy water. Most other hikers had left. The only sounds in the still air were from the waterfall sliding down the cirque wall, the splash of fish leaping for insects. As sunset colors faded on peaks above, dark shapes fluttered at the edges of my vision—bats pursuing flying bugs. A single star sparkled in the sky— and in the dark mirror of the lake—then scores, then hundreds, then thousands of stars. Sitting unmoving, entranced, I suddenly realized the lake had vanished and my granite slab dipped not into water but into the star-filled sky. In a rush of vertigo I felt myself falling, falling into infinity. Time to go to bed.

Next morning I switchbacked up walls of the cirque, topping the Great Western Divide at 10,700-foot Kaweah Gap. Nine Lake Basin sprawled below. Across the stark valley rose the gaudy-hued Kaweah peaks—culminating in 13,802-foot Mount Kaweah. No mistake, I was High at last. I picked a way down to a creek through sharp-edged blocks of granite. Dropping my pack, I stripped and jumped into a pool. Later, I followed the creek upward along a series of waterfalls toward the lakes. I reached the first, rounded the green shore, and walked the waterfall avenue to the second and biggest lake. Seven more lay in loftier bowls but I was content with these two of the nine—High Sierra landscapes are larger than they look.

Aerial photos of the upper range give the impression of a barren moonscape. Far from it. The naked, treeless rocks actually hold myriad little green spots—ferns pushing from cracks, deltas of grass and knolls of heather, dwarf willows along creeks—and everywhere blossoms, blossoms, blossoms.

Descending from the basin through Big Arroyo, I met yet another new tree, the aptly named foxtail pine, then followed a mile-long corridor of smooth slabs that made me wish for roller skates. Farther along, beyond Kern River, the High Sierra Trail meets the John Muir Trail, threading 212 high-country miles from the summit of Mount Whitney to Yosemite Valley. I was tempted, but my food was running low. On the last of my ten trail days

Waiting for the next glacier to come by, stranded stones tell of an episode in earth's past when thousand-pound boulders were flotsam on rivers of ice. As the mountain-molding glaciers melted, migrant rocks became standout features of Sierra landscapes. Large or small, embedded in soil or perched like a ball on a wall, they are called "erratics" when of different composition from the rock below.
DRAWING BY GEORGE FOUNDS

I paused at Timber Gap for a farewell gaze across the wide Kaweah valley to the beginnings of my 42-mile journey. Then I descended to Mineral King, a quiet little valley in Sequoia National Forest whose serenity has been threatened by a monster ski development. If there is one thing Sierra wilderness does not need, it is easier access, such as a cog railway and trams would provide. The number of backcountry visitors in the national parks here more than tripled in a recent four-year period. And as many as 1,200 hikers have reached the top of Whitney in a single day!

During my auto tour of the Sierra periphery I saw so many hitchhikers with packs on their backs it seemed half of California was "on the loose." Those I gave rides were not out to roam highways; they were between trails. True, solitude can still be found. Even on the popular High Sierra Trail I met only three or four people a day beyond Kaweah Gap, and old hands tell me of secret valleys where they can walk a whole week and not see a soul. But there were moments in Desolation and Valhalla when I felt I was not exploring wilderness but strolling a city park.

The Park Service and Forest Service are experimenting with techniques to preserve the quality of the backcountry experience—and to protect the land from the crush of too much love. Wilderness rangers already have proved indispensable. Wilderness entry permits became a requirement in California national forests in 1971, and in Oregon and Washington in 1972. Initially the permits were used mainly to gather data about usage and to teach outdoor manners to newcomers; ultimately they will be employed to control the number of visitors to delicate ecosystems.

In many places camping within 100 feet of lakes and streams has been banned, since a major threat is water pollution. Some basins have been closed to wood fires, others to camping altogether. Ranger Dana Abell told me that many campers who originally objected to the campfire ban now are enthusiastic, saying, "Until I stopped building fires I never saw the stars!" Party size is being limited, use of pack and riding animals restricted. Both agencies are moving slowly and carefully into the era of regulation to avoid premature and officious overcontrol.

Having come to know and trust the concern and humility of such men as John McLaughlin, I personally am confident the people of the National Park Service and Forest Service eventually will find the course of wisdom in wilderness management. But only citizen-activists can give the managers sufficient raw material: Less than half the presently wild Sierra is guaranteed to remain so for the future; all (not a compromising some, but *all*) should be.

I hate to nag, but must. My first term of Sierra school has not made me an expert, yet has made me a patriot. The Sierra wilderness is part of my home now.

∽ ∽

July—Night deepened in Nine Lake Basin, under sunset-flushed Sierra peaks. A hummingbird darted through shadows at red bells of heather and violet trumpets of penstemon, then rested on a rock beside me as if gazing down Big Arroyo to the multitude of flowers awaiting it come dawn.

August—A cloud crept over our camp on the shore of still-frozen Ice Lake, swallowing moon and stars and North Cascades crags, leaving only larches growing from yellow pumice thrown out by Glacier Peak 12,000 years ago. A companion threw wood on the coals, saying, "Let's have a John Muir fire!" High-leaping flames cast our spectral shadows on the fog, like ancient wild-land gods come to join the circle.

Several weeks and nearly a thousand miles separated the two evenings, but for me they were one. Foxtail pine and Lyall larch, Sierra sun and North Cascades mist, roof-of-the-world granite basins and valley jungles do, after all, add up. Each wilderness walker, though, must find his own sum.

Hawaiian Cinderella, the rare and lovely silversword plant graces bleak cinder slopes high on the west side of Haleakala Crater on the island of Maui. Called ahinahina (silver-hair), it matures in 7 to 20 years, blooms but once, then dies. Another world, lush and verdant as the silversword's is arid, inhabits the east side, watered by trade winds. The green sanctum of Kipahulu Valley (opposite) has been called the last true Hawaiian wilderness. Among moss-hung ohia lehua trees, ferns, lobelias, and other native vegetation dwell several rare and endangered species of birds. One, the Maui nukupuu, found in 1967, was thought extinct.
DRAWING BY GEORGE FOUNDS
OPPOSITE: ROBERT WENKAM

PACKTRAIN IN THE MINARETS

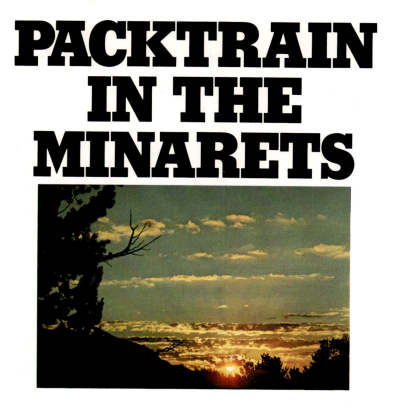

Verla Lee Smith

We are two miles high and climbing, under a searing August sun, plodding into the cobalt sky of California's High Sierra. Koip Peak Pass—the next X penciled on our trail map—keeps company with giants: spires of glistening granite, aloof, treeless, studded with gemlike lakes. The "Crown of the Sierra" John Muir called these nobles—Dana, Gibbs, Conness, Lyell, Maclure, Ritter, and "nameless compeers." Koip, the 12,979-foot compeer in our sights, bears the Paiute Indian name for mountain sheep. I do not wonder why.

We had stared speechless when the trail vanished up this wall of unruly rock, reddish and barren as the devil's back acre, rising 3,000 feet to the horizontal mile. I remembered Muir's definition of a Sierra pass: "any notch or cañon through which one may, by the exercise of unlimited patience . . . lead a mule or a sure-footed mustang; animals that can slide or jump as well as walk."

"Are you sure there's a trail up there?" a small girl asked finally.

"Positive," Pete Nelson, the trip leader, assured her, "288 switchbacks."

The number was fictional—Pete admitted it later. But while the zillion zigzags of the dusty path inched under our bootsoles, I believed it.

We were not koips but 32 city folk, including children 6 to 14, Sierra Club families on a trek into Minarets Wilderness, one of about 200 outings the club sponsors annually. We bivouacked at a campground in Tuolumne Meadows near the eastern portal of Yosemite National Park. A dozen burros would carry tents, food, stoves, fuel, and weighty camp gear, sparing the hikers for the rigors of high-altitude trails. Beginning at 9,700 feet, the planned 36-mile route winds up and down the rock-ribbed spine of the Sierra Nevada, often above timberline. Easing the trek with a lay-over day at each primitive campsite, we loop back via the John Muir Trail. Detailed planning by leaders Judy and Pete Nelson allows others without much wilderness

Young master of cloud ships mounts his conning tower, a time-gnarled pine overlooking Alger Lakes on the Sierra east flank. One of the most aspiring high-country conifers, the whitebark grows on rock ridges to 11,000 feet. Maturing at about 250 years, some survive centuries longer, their supple trunks buffeted by wintry gales. A grove of living whitebarks borders the distant shore.

Trails to wander, peaks to climb, lakes to fish or loll beside, and sunsets like wildfire lure throngs of visitors to the Minarets each summer.

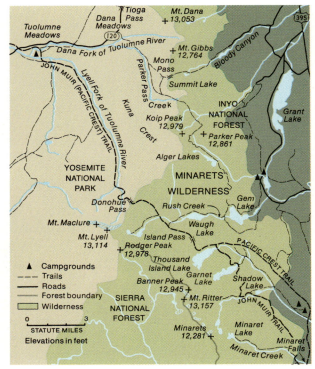

The map shows the region including Tuolumne Meadows, Tioga Pass, Dana Meadows, Mt. Dana +13,053, Mt. Gibbs +12,764, Mono Pass, Summit Lake, Bloody Canyon, Dana Fork of Tuolumne River, JOHN MUIR (PACIFIC CREST TRAIL), Lyell Fork of Tuolumne River, Parker Pass, Kuna Crest, Parker Creek, INYO NATIONAL FOREST, Grant Lake, Koip Peak 12,979, Parker Peak +12,861, Alger Lakes, YOSEMITE NATIONAL PARK, MINARETS WILDERNESS, Donohue Pass, Rush Creek, Gem Lake, Mt. Maclure +, Mt. Lyell 13,114, Waugh Lake, Island Pass, Rodger Peak +12,978, PACIFIC CREST TRAIL, Thousand Island Lake, Garnet Lake, Shadow Lake, Banner Peak 12,945 +, Mt. Ritter +13,157, JOHN MUIR TRAIL, SIERRA NATIONAL FOREST, Minarets 12,281 +, Minaret Lake, Minaret Falls, Minaret Creek.

▲ Campgrounds
‑ ‑ ‑ Trails
——— Roads
——— Forest boundary
☐ Wilderness
0 ——— 3
STATUTE MILES
Elevations in feet

A grubstake, a map, a means of transport . . .

The makings of a nine-day Sierra Club family burro trip assemble at roadhead. Reminiscent of the retinues that once transported supplies to prospectors in isolated ore fields, pack-trains now tote camp gear for city people seeking the treasure of recreation in sublime mountain settings.

Nelson family teamwork — Judy pitching, Karen catching — separates pre-measured foods by day of intended use. Judy, who majored in home economics, planned the menus.

Nature lavishes water on these mountain wilds; such dehydrated foods as this cereal with freeze-dried berries shaved pounds, as did cache-and-carry system of food supply. Hired packers put a cache along the route at midweek, reducing the initial load and the number of burros needed. Where pasture is scarce, stock feed must be carried. Sturdy and usually affable, burros make good trail companions as well as sparing hikers' backs. Dunnage was limited to 20 pounds per person. David Lorey (top) hoists a man-size load.

Minarets Wilderness, established in 1931, includes 109,559 acres of Inyo and Sierra National Forests, ranging from nearly 8,000 to 13,157 feet in altitude. The Sierra crest forms a common boundary with Yosemite National Park.

Best known of the Minarets' network of trails — some steep and rugged, some easy — honors John Muir, who knew the region intimately and fought to preserve it as wilderness. Muir's footsteps were the first atop Mount Ritter; a century ago he measured the advance of Mount Maclure's mini-glacier.

Then as now, Tuolumne Meadows served as jump-off for high-country treks. The Sierra Club Muir helped found began its outings in 1901 in the belief "wilderness will be preserved only in proportion to the number . . . who know its values firsthand." Today numbers must be limited.

experience to participate. One family, the Schaffers, are novices. But, unlike trips catered by hired packers, ours is cooperative. Everyone shares in the chores: cooking, cleanup, making and breaking camp, and loading and leading the burros from one site to the next. Even the youngest have duties.

After an al fresco steak dinner at Tuolumne, Pete lined up the junior troops. "Your jobs are to get firewood, to help look after the burros, and keep their equipment together. Say we lose a lead rope, the party can't move until we find it."

"Did you ever lose a burro?" six-year-old Chris Boyd asked.

"No. I haven't lost a kid yet either," Pete deadpanned, "but I'm allowed ten percent. What is it you do if you're lost?"

"STAY WHERE YOU ARE AND BLOW YOUR WHISTLE."

"Good. Every night we'll have whistle-blowing practice. Remember, you don't blow any other time unless you get lost. Now when I count three everybody blow."

Shuttling animals, packs, and people to trailhead at Dana Meadows next morning, we loaded the burros—each with a 75-pound burden—and set out on the historic Mono Lake Trail. First tramped by Paiute and Miwok Indians trading across the range, it became a supply path for prospectors in the late 1850's when gold fever spread from western foothills over the Sierra crest. Men with bonanzas in their eyes must have drunk from the same sparkling stream bordered with yellow monkey flowers where we paused for rest and a midmorning snack of bread and cheese.

Sky-dyed Summit Lake inlays a glacial basin at tree line near 10,604-foot Mono Pass. Here the group camped for a day of unplanned recreation: frog-chasing and Frisbee for youngsters, nature study and exploring for parents.

Brimming in spring from rain and snowmelt, lakes shrink by midsummer. Seeds sprout on indented shores, sedges stipple the shallows—portents of a dry future. Many older glacier-carved lakes at lower elevations, filled with sediment from centuries of runoff, have changed to meadows enameled with grass and flowers. Most

of some 1,500 lakes remaining in the range lie in the High Sierra, the subalpine and alpine life zones above 9,000 feet.

Beyond the pass, Mono Trail heads down Bloody Canyon, a bouldery defile threaded first by Indian traders, then by prospectors—"men who would build a trail down the throat of darkest Erebus on the way to gold," Muir wrote. Gold fever struck at Mono Pass in the 1870's. Cabins remain from the Golden Crown and Ella Bloss Mines—big promise, little payoff—now under consideration for the National Register of Historic Places.

The burros, idly nibbling grass, came to life at the faintest rustle of a knapsack. Inveterate beggars, they expected a handout of at least a piece of candy.

White clouds flocked overhead. The Sierra is kindest to campers in July and August. There is little rain; meadows are dry, streams low and fordable. Burros, we discovered, dislike wet feet. The lead animal often had to be muscled across, but the rest of the packstring usually followed willingly. Streams challenge people, too. One youngster, new to footlogs, sat down and inched across, feet first.

When the trail branched and we started the ascent to Mono Pass, Judy Nelson's daughter Karen asked, "Mom, can I walk ahead of you uphill?"

"*Anybody* can walk ahead of me uphill," Judy answered. We both moved aside.

Of a journey in 1869 Muir wrote: "I entered the [Mono] pass, the huge rocks began to close around in all their wild, mysterious impressiveness, when suddenly . . . a drove of gray hairy beings came in sight, lumbering toward me with a kind of boneless, wallowing motion. . . ." They proved to be Mono Indians clothed in skins of sage rabbits, carrying salt to trade for Yosemite Valley acorns. The hairy beings we met wallowing out of Minarets Wilderness were backpackers—we traded greetings.

At the pass a whoop went up. The boys broke into a run and, in less time than it takes to say "Sierra yellow-legged frog," were busy chasing them in Summit Lake.

A storm greeted us. Thunder muttered. Lightning stroked Kuna Crest as we unloaded the burros and turned them to pasture. Racing hail and rain, we pitched camp.

LOWELL GEORGIA

The first day's trek was the shortest—five miles—but at 10,000 feet the air pressure is about a third less than at sea level, and a lowlander's heart and lungs work harder to get enough oxygen into the bloodstream, especially during strenuous exercise. A few people had altitude sickness, marked by headaches, dizziness, or nausea. Others, feeling hearty enough, welcomed a layover day simply to relax. Six of us joined Pete on a hike up a peak to the site of an old plane crash; he wanted to see that the wreckage had been cleared away, a service Sierra Clubbers often perform.

We headed south over dry hills dotted with clumps of whitebark pine, abloom now with orange and yellow tents, for the pines make fine windbreaks. Raised veins of dirt patterned the bare ground. The work of "wee beasties," pocket gophers, Pete said. Diggers of intricate burrows, in winter they make tubes in the snow where they pack dirt from their diggings. When the snow melts, long mounds of earth appear. One land-happy gopher can plow up a hundred pounds of subsoil a week.

Midway up the ridge we explored a man-made tunnel, remnant of the Golden Crown Mine of the late 1870's. Of 350 gold and silver claims once on file in Tioga District, few traces remain. Beyond the ridge we picked up a grassy trail meandering along a stream, snowbanks on the one hand, scarlet paintbrush on the other.

The easy footwork over, we began to climb cross-country, treading glacial pavement, shiny rock ramps where a sliding glacier scratched its signature. Climbing civilized stairs does *not* condition the legs for climbing uncivilized rocks, I learned. As we clambered over jumbled boulders of a moraine and strained up near-vertical planes of bedrock—none of them divided into neat seven-inch segments—rubbery muscles and bankrupt lungs kept screaming Stop. Each time, with rest, some miracle put back breath and energy to go a few feet higher.

The view, too, was breathtaking. East past the brow of the mountain we could see beyond the Sierra scarp to a different land below. Perhaps ten miles from where we dipped cups into an ice-slivered pool newborn from a snowfield, Mono Lake shimmered lifeless and unreal, a blue-yolked egg fried on the desert sand. Mark Twain wrote in *Roughing It* that a stray dog once dived into Mono's briny water and, yelping, took off at 250 miles an hour.

As we resumed climbing, our exertions paid off. We came upon a ghost from a bygone era, the ruined hut of some son of a forty-niner and what could have been all his earthly goods. A pit dug into the hillside had been walled with loose boulders. Its walls and plank roof had collapsed but within were tools of a hardrock miner's trade—drift pick, bellows, auger, ore bucket, windlass, and sticks of No. 1-XX Hercules Powder, still dangerous though crumbled to dust. Here, too, were rusty pots, a three-tined fork, a pair of boots. It looked as if the owner had one day piled all his gear into the hut and left for the winter, perhaps with his dream still intact.

We moved onto the snowfield, slippery in the August sun. We walked sideways, digging in at each step. But lacking lug soles, I did more sliding than climbing.

Pete was standing over me. "Lee, here's where you get Nelson's crash course in

LOWELL GEORGIA

Glacial skeleton fleshed out by lingering winter snow beckons a cross-country climbing party led by Pete Nelson. Ancient ice rivers contoured parts of the Sierra uplift, scalping soil from slopes, gouging U-shaped valleys. But glaciers that now patch peaks are of recent origin; tree-ring studies on bristlecone pines indicate these were formed about 400 years ago.

David Lorey tugs at a relic found high on the slope: a prospector's ore bucket. Mine tailings revealed no overlooked trove; far more colorful were lichens clinging to rocks crossed en route. Nature's velvet chisel tames rock by growing upon it, breaking it down. Humans try another way, shown by Janet Schaffer, apt pupil of Pete's rock-climbing school on layover day.

Alchemy of sunset brews potable gold by the lakeful. Luminous in the slanted rays, this lupine at lakeside and the multitude of hardy species at high altitudes must double-time into bloom. As in the Far North, growing season is short; frost may occur any month of the year. A denizen of cold lakes, the Sierra yellow-legged frog adapts to the climate by lengthening its life cycle. Overwintering as a tadpole in ice-topped waters as high as 11,500 feet, it matures the second summer. The species exudes an odor like garlic.

snow work." He handed me his ice ax with instructions: left hand on the shaft, right grasping the steel head with the point down. "When you start to slide, plunge the point into the snow and fall forward over the handle. It can keep you from a fast sleigh ride onto the rocks below."

He went to lead the queue on up the steepening incline while I had ice-ax falling practice in the rear. Each pause had cost us climbing time. Two of us were on evening cook crew, due back at camp before long. We turned back short of the summit.

Quantities of food had been figured for man-size appetites. Meals usually ended with a dab of each course left over for the burros. No dish was a disaster unless the burros refused it. Such tempting delicacies as tomato bisque, freeze-dried chicken casserole with sherry, and chocolate crushed-peppermint pudding must be a high spot in the lives of pack stock that work the Sierra. At night when the stars glittered and our long-eared canaries out in the pasture set up a serenade like rusty pump handles, we assumed it was the music of contentment, not indigestion.

Next day, near Koip Pass, the youngsters—well ahead of the burros—vied with each other for first position. Among them was Chris Boyd. The six-year-old dynamo

71

Laden burros balk and blow, then with some urging from the wranglers have another go at scaling the Sierra spine, here shingled in metamorphic slate. Switchbacks furrowing flanks of Parker and Koip Peaks make a pass of an impasse, but should travelers meet, so narrow is the trail that one must back up and wait.

Burros, smaller and slower than mules, are self-confident and excel on rough terrain. "But," says Pete Nelson, "I've had to take them over ground where their confidence failed. One time I had to make them glissade down a snowfield. They did just fine." Passes normally are free of snow by mid-July— though summer temperatures in the Minarets can vary from 85° F. to below freezing.

had started out that morning lagging behind the others, limping badly from a fall. But as we topped the first ridge, he had caught up. "You just keep on walking," he told me. "And when you ouch five times, it gets better." Now, maneuvered out of the lead, he announced, "I could care less if I'm last."

Far below, the dinky donkeys started the ascent. As we neared the saddle, the trail ahead leveled. At last, alone in a primordial world of burnished rock, sky, sun, and not much else, we collapsed beside a sign: Koip Peak Pass, 12,350 feet.

The illusion vanished in a roar from the sky. *Boom! Boom! Boom!* Three military jets, their contrails like triple chalk lines on a clean blue board. The lines diffused into artificial cirrus clouds, then winds smeared them into cryptic scrawls.

Winds skimming over the pass brought out jackets and cut our lunch break short. With the vista of Alger Lakes before us, it was hard not to ignore switchbacks and go scree-sliding. Though urged by Judy Nelson to keep the brakes on, several eager beavers barreled down the zigs and zags. Out of earshot when the trail forked, some went left, some right. Later at campsite when we counted noses, Chris was missing.

An anxious search followed. While others retraced the two trails, I looked along the outlet of Alger Lakes, a ravine where water coursed in an almost-human hurry, where a dry, sunny bank—incredibly—harbored a ledge of snow. Flowers—pink, yellow, white, lavender—splashed the far bank. Straining for sound, I thought once I

LOWELL GEORGIA

Panorama from 12,979-foot Koip Peak dwarfs people and pack animals in the foreground. Rest and reward for the long, dusty haul wait at idyllic Alger Lakes—a wilderness campsite equipped only with clear water and a view.

heard a whistle, but it must have been a bird somewhere down the canyon. It was fairly open terrain, and we had hours of daylight left. Even so, it was a great relief to all when Chris was found—napping—back along the trail.

After a long delay the burros appeared high on the ridge, bringing on a burst of song, "The burros come marching one by one. Hurrah, hurrah." The reason for the delay: Peter the mountain-eater and a few "volunteers," with Koip Pass already under their belts, had taken on Koip Peak for dessert.

Nobody ventured far from Alger Lakes next day. A sign-out book on a rock collected notes such as: "Nelsons—exploring Rock Island. Boyds—fishing." Wanting a closer look at an alpine garden, I went back along the lake outlet. At a spot just below that ledge of misplaced snow I lazed on a log listening to the song spilling down from those hard, wild peaks. Jays clamored nearby. Dragonflies whirred, hovering like helicopters and alighting on pads of bloom. Intrigued by the variety in the flowers, I counted 39 kinds in this one small area: purple fireweed, lupine, cow parsnip, swamp whiteheads, yarrow, Bigelow sneezeweed—and dozens of strangers. One delicate star-shaped bloom was so tiny I found it only by falling on the soggy turf. The sod, spreading out from the bank, had no solid footing. Underneath I could hear the stream rushing.

Back at camp, a rash act was in progress. Using a spoon as mirror, Doug Boyd was shaving. Anti-razorites booed. Roberta Schaffer eyed her husband's stubble. "The second night out I woke up suddenly to hear this scratching sound," she said. "I thought 'Oh, no—a bear,' and punched Ron. When he sat up the noise

LOWELL GEORGIA (ALSO OVERLEAF)

Commissary, sky-high and
horizon-wide, is where
it's at: coffee; camaraderie;
a skillet to fry Alan's "most
beautiful trout," a golden;
hands to help with Katie's
pigtails. Everything from
soup to pie goes into the
Sierra Club cup; youngest
spoonhandler Chris Boyd
readies his for the next
course. Presiding at the pot,
chef-for-a-day Doug Boyd
signals satisfaction with
his concoction, a stew
given character with a dash
of this and a jigger of that,
and dubbed "Doug soup."

Overleaf: Cold glances from
peaks like 12,978-foot
Rodger keep most visitors
out of frigid Rush Creek;
risk of water pollution now
rules out swimming in
Minarets lakes and streams.

stopped. So he said if it was anything it must have gone away, and he lay back down. Then I heard it again. The 'bear' was his whiskers scratching the nylon tent."

Our baptismal shower had been the only rain. Some of us stowed our tents to sleep under the open sky. A sleeping bag needs less level ground, giving a wider choice of bedsites. A needle-padded spot between two lodgepole pines near streamside got my vote. I slept poorly, however; the ground turned lumpy and hard. In the darkness I twisted and turned and plumped up the down bag. Finally, I could see. The two trees and my pine needle mattress had slid upslope—Rush Creek rushed at my feet. It could have been a far more dramatic awakening.

The late show in the sky made sleep seem a waste of time. The night was moonless. Here in the heights with no gaseous man-made curtain to interfere, each still point of light seemed an entity, starbright. I felt I could vouch for every one of the 7,000 said to be visible with the naked eye. Then out of the northern swirl of the Milky Way they started throwing stars away. For a while a meteor a minute streaked downstage. We had missed the peak of the annual Perseid meteor shower by days, but all sky reviewers at breakfast next morning agreed the spectacle was still a smash.

Friday was our last layover day. Pete Nelson, Ronald Bentley, and three teenagers had heard a mountain calling. At sunup they shouldered ropes and ice axes to tackle Mount Lyell. For the rest of us, it was a morning of leisure posing no weightier problems than how to drape a six-inch flapjack over a four-inch cup without losing all the syrup. The pump-handle chorus started singing out in the pasture and some of the kids ran out to feed and pet them.

An impromptu excursion shaped up: an unhurried walk back along the John Muir Trail to Island Pass. Later that day, from the high ledge overlooking Thousand Island Lake we savored a spectacular southward view of the Ritter Range and the mosquetop spires for which Minarets Wilderness is named. These dramatic pinnacles challenge mountaineering experts, though most have been climbed.

Across the lake the sun slanted down from a windswept saddle between two snow-flanked peaks, the light shattering in a million fiery points on the rippled surface. Roberta Schaffer and I huddled against the bank out of the wind, close to the boulder where her husband, Ron, stood plying his new trout rod.

There seemed a timeless quality, an enchantment, about this tranquil place as if nothing ever had been or could be improved upon. Even erratics—rounded rocks incongruously placed by long-gone glaciers—looked at home exactly where they were.

Under the boulder where Ron stood, on a small rock shelf in a shaded cranny at waterline, I spotted a tiny frog—or thought I did. It sat motionless so long that I began to doubt my eyes. I flipped a pebble, thinking to make it jump. Still it sat, unmoving, unfroglike. Nearly an hour later when the fishermen gave up and we were heading back to camp, the frog was still on base. Young Steve Georgia poked at it with the end of his fishing rod, and finally the frog moved. But instead of giving ground or diving as the tip came near, the frog attacked. Repeatedly it lunged, stretching its yellow legs, trying to bite the rod. Once it latched on and clung until Steve shook the pole hard enough to dump the tiny pugilist into the water. Back up it came like a man climbing onto a raft, back to the same precise spot as if it meant to hold that one rock forever. That's how we left it.

Kindness and candy are all it takes to get along on the trail with a burro, or so I thought resting snug and smug beside a shaded creek after the bruising haul over Donohue Pass. Muir Trail up and down the 11,050-foot pass is mostly big granite boulders filled in with little granite boulders—murderous walking for us, worse

Trail partners round a barren bend approaching Gem Pass. Younger children, preferring a hurry-up-and-wait pace to the animals' steady plodding, usually clustered in a group ahead of the packtrain. Most, like Danny Schaffer, occasionally took a turn at the lead rope on an easy grade.

Unshod burros pick their own footing—they know the trails. But if the load becomes loose or unbalanced, they may —mulishly—refuse to move.

LOWELL GEORGIA

for the animals. After placing their front feet, they must use savvy instead of sight as they jump their back feet forward. My admiration was boundless, and Licorice, my trail partner, was welcome to all the candy in my pack. I gave him a double treat as we started on. He had a surprise for me, too. Now that the hard going was over, he declared his independence, butting me down. So much for my asinine formula.

We made our last camp near the head of the timbered canyon where Lyell Fork gathers trickles into a tumult and roars off to the Tuolumne. A water ouzel—fabulous Muir-bird—bobbed in the rapids. Had there been no such Pilgrim-hued bird "not afraid to go wherever a stream may go, and to sing wherever a stream sings," Muir surely would have invented it. The ouzels did not sing for us, but that afternoon from a granite penthouse I watched them dip and dive.

My bed-rock, a great, gray boulder sheared vertically on the streamside—perhaps by the glacier that gouged Lyell Canyon—might have served as an archetype Sierra Nevada: east face sheer, west side gently sloped. Not so Spartan a perch as it appeared, the rock boasted a bedsize top shelf perfectly leveled by wind and weather. As a finishing touch, a resolute pine—head-high—was making its niche in the solid stone. A touch of green, a hint of shade. Beautiful landscaping.

Stars. Pine-whispers. The afterglow of a campfire crackling with song and good talk, redolent of woodsmoke and wool socks steaming. Nightlong, the lullaby of the Lyell. Frost next morning, wall-to-canyon-wall.

One of Muir's least appreciated gifts to humankind was a clock-controlled contraption he made for dumping people out of bed in the morning. We could have used it. Frost or no, promptly at five-thirty, when cooks were due in commissary, Pete's voice rang out, "Cooks are due in commissary." While the echoes still rang, our leader leaped the stream and strode the meadow toward the burros to the shattering strains of "Oh, What a Beautiful Mornin'." I hated to leave the world's best solid granite mattress but the song was appropriate.

Down the crystalline meadow of the canyon, long before the sun tops the mountain rim, we fall in behind a burro called Rainbow, and if there is any better way to spend a brisk summer morning, I do not know it. Leg muscles hardened on up-and-down terrain now revel in luxury. At our approach white-crowned sparrows dart into the shrubbery. Juncos hop in switchbacks under the young conifers, picking up seed. A Belding ground squirrel strolls out of the way, casually, as if passing packtrains are an everyday nuisance. Only a few feet back he stands straight as a bowling pin, guarding his burrow. Melting frost hangs for a few final minutes as glistening droplets. Then dust replaces dew on the arching blades.

As sun pours into the canyon we meet hikers and more hikers. We need no calendar to say it's Sunday nor map to tell us we are getting close to roadhead. In places, too many feet have trampled too-famous John Muir Trail into four separate, parallel troughs of dust. We start to wonder: Is the Lyell still safe to drink? Danny Schaffer has caught cold and the dust irritates his eyes. Urged to stay ahead of the animals, he whispers, "But Dad, I don't *want* to set the pace."

"Will we get low-altitude sickness when we go home?" someone wondered.

"That's the kind I have all year," Ron Schaffer offered. "Mountains cure it."

Though our thoughts are already taking separate directions, Tioga Pass Road and the menacing noise of automobiles comes too soon and too suddenly. Weathered, grimy—and proud—we cluster like koips waiting for the traffic to break.

Take your time, I thought, far from anxious to leave this austere and shining land with its walls of evergreen and granite and its ceiling of stars.

The Spell of Solitude at Glacier Peak

Dawnetta Winters

*"I had to find a place to be
alone with my thoughts,
away from the city's throb
and teeming crowds.
So I put some food in
a pack . . . a sudden decision."*
Thus the author (opposite),
recalling the pressures
that led to her first wilderness
retreat, voices a need felt
by so many of her generation.
Burgeoning on trails
like the new green of
springtime, carrying home
and sustenance on their backs
and in their minds,
young people head for
unpeopled places—
*"to grow in the open air
and to eat and sleep with
the earth,"* in the words
of Walt Whitman.

What do they find in
places like Glacier Peak
Wilderness? The counterpoint
of sunlight on somber
trunks of Douglas fir;
the benediction of soft,
misty rain on a forest path;
flowery meadows, freshets
spilling from snowfields;
the icy hulk of a recluse
mountain. Savoring each
aspect, sensing relevance
in all, the wanderer
glories in solitude that
is not loneliness.

ENTHEOS. OPPOSITE: DOUG WILSON

Colors of morning rise behind Glacier Peak like a flower blooming, each petal unfolding a glow of light. Pink wisps of cloud race past the white volcano looming so close across a valley that I can count wrinkles and gashes in its cape of ice. My breath makes its own small cloud in the crisp air as I slip from my sleeping bag and find a place amid shimmering lupines to greet the sun.

I am pleased that I climbed the steep trail to camp beside Lake Byrne these last two days of my lone hike in the North Cascades. It is a high lake, at 5,500 feet, on a ridge where daylight comes early and lingers after timbered river valleys are swallowed by shadow. Last night a thin sheet of ice grew across its blue waters.

Carrying my largest cooking pot, I walk toward the stream that pours from the outlet. The sound of rushing water rises above the rhythmic breath of the winds, the drip-drip on mossy banks, the morning songs of birds. I start to sing, too, because I am happy, because I want to hear my sound, to join the harmony.

My kitchen is a pit walled by stones supporting a grill. I set about building a fire, laying the tinder, carefully stacking small twigs along a larger stick, blowing gently until flames begin to leap and dance and fragrant smoke curls like incense. While water heats for my tea and cereal, I find a spot in the sun, lean back against a rock, and draw in warmth like a sponge. Later, perhaps I will explore the far side of Lake Byrne or hike to Camp Lake a mile away—the choice is all mine. The sun is in no hurry. I may lie here, this last day in the wilderness, and be a smaller sun.

Nine days ago, I entered Glacier Peak Wilderness from the west, taking a Forest Service trail up the Suiattle River Valley. Carrying a 47-pound pack, I strained to match the quick steps of Ben Englebright, wilderness ranger from Image Lake, who pointed out plants and birds along the river terraces and areas where avalanches had crashed down Miners Ridge, felling trees and piling up debris. It had been a heavy winter. Now in August there was plenty of snow around, but before I parted with Ben at the Image Lake junction, I met enough people to call that trail well-traveled. I planned to pick up the Pacific Crest Trail and explore the Glacier Peak area at close range, not confined to a schedule, leaving the trail when I felt like it.

The Suiattle, milky with glacial silt, foamed below the log suspension bridge I crossed the second morning. The air was heavy and damp and clouds concealed the sun. Canopied by giant firs and hemlocks, the moist dark ground ahead was rich with decaying plants that nourished tiny foam flowers and plump mushrooms. Ferns and prickly devil's club with platter-size leaves draped the narrow path. Cool fingers

of fog had touched all the foliage with glittering jewels. It was a mysterious, quiet place with only an occasional bird calling from some high branch. I wondered what alert eyes might be following along the path as I moved deeper into the evergreen temple, a magnificent sample of the forests for which the wet Pacific side of the Casades is famous.

It was not long before I was introduced to the Cascades rain, equally famous. I hiked on until afternoon, then pitched my tent and holed up to enjoy this phase of nature from inside my sleeping bag. Warming myself by sipping hot tea, made quickly with a small pack stove, I watched the rain, wondering how long ago these drops were dancing with the sea. I followed in imagination as they slid gently from leaves into the soil, finding a stream, then a river, and at last the sea again. Soon rain songs gave me the soundest of wilderness sleep.

Under clear skies next morning, I watched a beautiful young doe slip quietly through the brush beyond a nearby stream. Gracefully she took her morning drink and vanished into the forest. A few minutes later I spotted a coyote pup. But he

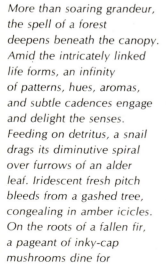

More than soaring grandeur, the spell of a forest deepens beneath the canopy. Amid the intricately linked life forms, an infinity of patterns, hues, aromas, and subtle cadences engage and delight the senses. Feeding on detritus, a snail drags its diminutive spiral over furrows of an alder leaf. Iridescent fresh pitch bleeds from a gashed tree, congealing in amber icicles. On the roots of a fallen fir, a pageant of inky-cap mushrooms dine for a day, then self-destruct, dissolved in their own dark juices. On cue, skunk cabbages, pungent pioneers of spring, poke skyward like golden minarets. Lacking true flowers, mosses and liverworts yet brighten a bog. This is a world where water calls the tune and moving water plays it. "The sound is everywhere," Miss Winters observes, "dripping on banks, leaping between mossy stones. Little wonder these mountains are called the Cascades."

85

spotted me at about the same time and hurried downstream to find a more private place to drink. Shyness is typical of the animals I've met that are truly wild.

While my clothes and equipment dried in the sun, I enjoyed a leisurely trail breakfast of pancakes and syrup. Later, when I shouldered my pack, a marmot sounded his high-pitched whistle — as if giving me a starting signal. I made a brief search, hoping to catch a glimpse of him, but he was too well hidden in the talus.

Many people think it unusual for a 24-year-old woman to hike alone. Traveling solo, I often see wild creatures that would flee from a chattering group. On my back I carry my shelter and food enough for the length of my stay, and a sense of freedom fills me. I grew up in an outdoor family and have learned enough about terrain, weather, and my own capabilities not to be unduly afraid nor to risk my neck foolishly. Sometimes I must pass up a climb — to the top of Glacier Peak, for example — that I would have attempted in experienced company. But, on the positive side, alone I can set my own pace, relax, and enjoy the beauty of nature without social distractions. Often I stop to thank all I can see just for being there.

The forest fell away as I climbed above 5,000 feet on a new section of the Pacific Crest Trail. The headwaters of Milk Creek's east fork flow from a horseshoe basin abloom with lupine, fragrant phlox, heather, and dozens of other species that thrive in the heights just below the snowfields. For a while I rested in this sweet meadow watching bees and velvet-winged butterflies. Then, leaving my pack at trailside, I scrambled up rocky Vista Ridge on the flank of Glacier Peak.

On all sides rugged Cascades peaks, white-tipped above an antiquity of a forest, unite in one of the grandest mountain panoramas I have ever seen. Towering a thousand feet above its tallest companions, adorned with 18 of some 200 glaciers in the Wilderness Area, the great dome is dazzling under the slanting sun.

From my high perch atop a boulder I can feel the earth as a planet beneath me, an island spinning in space. I am aware of my size.

The wilderness is my church, my school. In its solitude I grow to understand the simplicity and order of nature. Everything that happens is of importance — the sun rising and setting, streams leaping down hillsides, clouds tumbling endlessly, the pollen from a buttercup being transported on the legs of a bee. I have seen a young rabbit carried away by an owl and understand that death is as important as birth. In solitude, my energies merge with those of the earth. Peace descends upon me like the purple blanket that robes Glacier Peak as the sun settles and shadows stretch from deep valleys to the sky. I am a child, taking time to learn.

On hand for the early show — Glacier Peak preened and regal at Image Lake — a marmot lazes on a front-row rock. The scenic lake basin, prime target of a 15-mile trail pilgrimage, grew so popular that tents intruded on the view. Visitors now must camp away from lakeside; fragile alpine plants are making a gradual recovery. Opposite: Shielded from storms and enriched by the decaying rootwad of a fallen patriarch, a seedling fir takes its place in the sun.
KATHLEEN REVIS JUDGE. OPPOSITE: ENTHEOS

Near the rim of the Waterpocket Fold in Capitol Reef National Park, sandstone eroded grain by grain yields a natural Mount Rushmore.

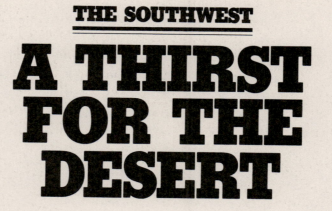

THE SOUTHWEST

A THIRST FOR THE DESERT

Edward Abbey

Why love the desert? A bitter, bleak, barren, blasted sort of country, fit only for creatures like the sidewinder, scorpion, tarantula, and Gila monster: How can humans live in, let alone love, such a place? When I asked this question of an old-time hard-rock prospector, a man who had wandered most of his life across the cactus lands of Arizona, he said he liked the desert because "them other so-and-so's don't." And would say no more. Pondering his reply, I interpreted it as meaning more than simple misanthropy, and have come to accept it as my own reason for preferring the desert to any other home.

Beauty has nothing to do with it; beauty can be found anywhere, even in cities. The desert is merely distinguished, as that prospector implied, by its relative scarcity of life—not only human but plant and animal. Where life is difficult it seems to acquire a higher value. Thus it is austerity and emptiness—qualities which make the desert repellent to most—which make it appealing to some of us.

Unfortunately it is no longer so empty; little of the desert land of our Southwest remains "wilderness" in the exact meaning of the word. Much more than high mountain or forest, desert is vulnerable to motorized invasion. Four-wheel-drive vehicles and trail bikes have exploited this vulnerability. There are other dangers: Subdividers, mining corporations, dam and highway builders, and electric power combines threaten to overwhelm the desert with insatiable demands.

I would not consent to publicize some of the untouched or little-touched places that remain—places I love too much for my own peace of soul—except to try to head off the dangers. Suddenly a man realizes that the age of universal iron and steel, smog and clamor, glass and plastic and aluminum, is almost upon him. It seems as if our children may someday read of the American wilderness—desert or any other kind—as we read of lost Atlantis. In order to save it we need all the help we can get, even at the risk of making widely known what is now little known.

Some fragments of the desert already have been declared permanent wilderness: for people only, machines not welcome. Others may also be saved in the National Wilderness Preservation System if enough public support is forthcoming. As a fanatic on the subject, I hope even to see certain areas set aside as *absolute wilderness*, with all human visitation, by any means—even on foot—forbidden. I believe the earth exists for other purposes than humanity's alone.

Geographers generally divide the desert of the Southwest into four subdeserts: the Great Basin, centered in Utah and Nevada but extending as far north as central

In Capitol Reef's jagged wonders man can read earth's story back to Permian times of 250 million years ago. Sketches trace the sequence in a northern slice of the park—the small figures extending beyond park boundaries to the Aquarius Plateau in the west, the Henry Mountains in the east.

Upheavals, climatic changes, and repeated inundations by ancient seas over hundreds of millions of years left deposits of sand, mud, and debris more than 10,000 feet thick. After the Cretaceous sea receded, a great force—perhaps, geologists say, faulting in the basement rock—created a 100-mile-long, S-shaped wrinkle, flexing the land downward to the east; we know it as the Waterpocket Fold. Later, molten rock pushed up the Henrys and

Oregon and southwestern Wyoming; the Sonoran, spilling from Mexico into California and Arizona; the Mojave, which spreads over parts of California and Nevada and includes Death Valley; and the Chihuahuan, located mostly in Mexico but lapping into New Mexico and western Texas. While sharing many characteristics, each region has its unique features—differences in topography and plant and animal life which follow from variations in elevation and climate. The Great Basin, of which the spectacular canyon systems of Utah form a subsection, is distinguished by the predominance of saltbush, sagebrush, piñon, and juniper as plant cover; the Sonoran by the abundance of giant and other cacti; the Mojave, smallest of the four, by the many-branched Joshua tree, which grows nowhere else; and the Chihuahuan by such plants as sotol, yucca, and lechuguilla.

On the ramparts of mountain chains scattered among the desert areas stand forests of pine and groves of oak, nourished by moisture that the peaks entice from passing clouds. It was in such an area, along the Mogollon and Diablo ranges of New Mexico, a part of the Gila National Forest, that the first national wilderness was set aside in 1924 largely through the efforts of conservationist Aldo Leopold.

From the fragments of wild desert that remain, I have chosen three to write about, not necessarily the biggest nor perhaps even the most beautiful, but places of great interest to me: Capitol Reef National Park in Utah, Cabeza Prieta Game Range in Arizona, and Death Valley National Monument in California. I call them "canyon country," "cactus country," and "final country"; to me Death Valley is a kind of ultimate among American deserts—the last word.

Cretaceous sea covers central North America—70 million years ago.

Lava Flow

Folding—50-70 million years ago. Lava from igneous activity—20 million years ago.

Henry Mountains

Present—erosion at work. Ice-age glacier ground up some of the lava rock.

Sulphur Creek

Chimney Ro

Torrey

Frem

Canyon Country. Rock—the incredible mass of highly colored, queerly weathered rock—is the chief attraction of the quarter-million acres of Capitol Reef National Park and the adjoining canyonlands. Blazing sunlight and dazzling thunderstorms, deep stillness and secret pockets of flowers and life: these are essentials but not the essence of this region's fascination.

When I made my first trip to Capitol Reef, it was those spooky, unimaginable shapes of stone that caught and held my attention. Now, some two decades later, they still delight me with their color, texture, and infinite yet logical variety of form. Domes, pinnacles, turrets, spires, arches and bridges, pits, pockets, potholes, plunge pools, goblins and hobgoblins, cracks and crevasses and canyons, buttes, cathedrals, caves, grottoes, alcoves, humps, hills, holes and hollows, slick walls and sheer cliffs—there is, as far as I know, no other place on earth where time and weather have created so curious and so intriguing an assemblage of landforms.

From a distance of 20 to 30 miles to the east, Capitol Reef and the Waterpocket Fold, the 100-mile-long geological structure of which the reef is a part, resemble a mountain range. But as you get nearer you begin to realize that this is a very odd mountain range. The peaks turn out to be sheer, rounded humps of monolithic sandstone. The valleys reveal themselves as severe gashes in the rock—slits and slots, usually much deeper than wide, with perpendicular, sometimes overhanging walls and sandy or boulder-strewn floors. The reef and the fold then seem more like a wall, a barrier rising as much as 2,000 feet above the surrounding country. In fact, to early travelers the word "reef," borrowed from seafarers, meant such a barrier. This is a

spread over parts of the plateau; some found its way to the fold. But full-scale erosion had begun when the land was tilted, and continues today—exposing richly hued layers from various geologic periods. The layers are shown here as a single color for each era of sedimentation.

The uplifted areas eroded more rapidly; hence surface layers on the west are older than those across the valley.

In the deepest canyons are Cutler sandstone and Kaibab limestone. Petrified wood is in the Chinle formation; the Morrison holds fossils of reptiles that lived 140 million years ago. Variations in the hardness of rock produced weird shapes. Rounded domes of Navajo sandstone are the "capitols" of Capitol Reef.

PAINTING BY WILLIAM H. BOND

Hickman Bridge

Fremont

Visitor Center

WATERPOCKET FOLD

Capitol Gorge

Pleasant Creek

🟨 Cretaceous (Dakota, Mancos, Mesaverde)	🟫 Early Triassic (Moenkopi-Chinle)
🟩 Late Jurassic (Carmel, Entrada, Curtis, Summerville, Morrison)	⬜ Permian sediments (Coconino/Cutler-Kaibab)
🟫 Triassic-Jurassic (Glen Canyon group— Wingate, Kayenta, Navajo)	🟫 Older layers resting on Precambrian "basement" rock

wall with few openings; it is crossed by only two roads, the paved highway through the park and a dirt track known as Burr Trail. To geologists the fold is a monoclinal flexure, a warping of the earth's crust, in this case tilted down on the east but leveling off horizontally in the west. The Waterpocket Fold is perhaps the finest specimen of this phenomenon in North America.

The precipitation here—a little snow in winter, thunderous but limited storms in summer—adds up to no more than an average eight inches a year. This may seem like a wholly inadequate force to create such fantasies in stone as appear in Capitol Reef, but it is the same sparse rainfall which keeps the land so bare of plant life, leaving it highly vulnerable to erosion. Anyone who has witnessed a flash flood roaring down a canyon, the water dark with silt and debris, can easily understand the power of water and the defenselessness of mere rock.

To get the feel of this country, to taste its atmosphere and sample its spirit, you must leave your car and go up into the hills of golden stone, up into that never-never land of petrified cities, secret waterpockets crawling with fairy shrimp and mosquito larvae, and into those mysterious little canyons which lead nowhere, where no human has ever gone before, for all you know. You must follow those dim trails which take you out of civilization's web, beyond all that is safe and familiar, out of sight, out of mind, out of reach.

On that first trip into Capitol Reef, in what now seems like an epoch ago, when I was still innocent of trouble and the park roads were still innocent of asphalt, I did not venture much beyond the end of the trail. For lack of time, I would have said. But there was also an element of timidity. I didn't much like the looks of that crazy landscape north of Hickman Bridge or south of Capitol Gorge. Today things have changed; wilderness is vanishing at a rate which accelerates from year to year. Nothing to do, then, but plunge at once into the heart of what is left, embrace it if you can, try to save it—if only for the record.

So, one recent April, a friend and I went jeep-riding south of Burr Trail, into the southern reaches of the park, the wildest and emptiest quarter. The scenery is essentially the same as that in the northern three-quarters—the contorted monocline of sandstone, the vertical escarpment on the east, the trickling stream on the canyon floor, the ineffable sky above. Only the bugs seem much worse, no doubt owing to the many pools of stagnant water collected in the waterpockets. Bugs are more numerous and aggressive here, I think, than anywhere else in the canyonlands. The gnats work the day shift, the mosquitoes the night (Continued on page 101)

Contorted and denuded, Utah's rock deserts long discouraged exploration. Beyond the sunlit Navajo sandstone on the Waterpocket Fold loom peaks uncharted till 1869. "Unknown Mountains," Maj. John Wesley Powell dubbed them. Today, the Henry Mountains honor Joseph Henry, first Secretary of the Smithsonian Institution.

The arid land bears witness to the role of water as a prime mover and shaper. Water bore the sediments that became Moenkopi sandstone, and carved the layers into such fantasies as the Egyptian Temple in Capitol Reef (below). Tranquil, sky-hued Willow Creek, flowing beneath a seeping fissure in the Escalante region, masks water's destructive potential. Coyote Bridge reveals it; this span, over another Escalante stream, was gouged by flash floods.

The rite of spring—or a spell
of rain—garbs the austere
desert in Cinderella beauty.
On May evenings monarchs of the
Sonoran hillsides wear crowns
of creamy white. Only a few
saguaro buds in each cluster
bloom at a time, wilting in the
next day's heat. The saguaro
is Arizona's state flower.

Five-spot mallow—each petal
splotched with carmine—often
brightens somber lava buttes;
some call it Chinese lantern
because of its globular form.

Another flower of eventide,
the white trumpet of sacred
datura adds a vesper note
to desert washes and roadsides.
This poisonous, narcotic plant,
also known as thorn apple
or western jimsonweed,
was used in Indian ritual.

Radiance beams amid the
spines on members of the
large cactus genus Opuntia:
the magenta-crowned beavertail
(below), the tree cholla
(at right, above), which grows
up to ten feet tall, and a
prickly pear, its curved joint
topped by a golden nugget.

Spiking rocky slopes, agaves
raise their flower heads high—
on 15-foot stalks in some
species. Daisy-like desert star
and purple mat, or nama, keep
low profiles (opposite).
In lush years purple mat spreads
a broad, vivid carpet; in dry
years the plant is tiny, with
few leaves and perhaps only
a single bloom. For a close look
at such ground-hugging plants
you have to bend low—hence the
nickname "belly flowers."

99

shift, in such devotion to your blood that you tend to forget the rattlesnakes and scorpions which might otherwise provide all the amusement anyone could wish.

The rangers had warned us about the jeep trail, about the sand too deep and soft, about the quicksand too soupy and quick for even four-wheel-drive vehicles. We had disregarded their advice and so spent many a hot and weary hour shoveling, jacking up the jeep, and laying out flat rocks to make a roadway where no roadway was meant to be. It is quite possible to bury a four-wheel-drive vehicle inextricably and forever in those apparently bottomless bogs on the canyon floor.

Why the jeep anyway? No good reason—merely sloth. We could have gotten there as quickly and more healthfully afoot, the way more visitors will travel these parts when wilderness proposals for Capitol Reef are enacted. Even since my visit jeeps have been restricted to maintained roads, and rangers plan to ban all vehicles beyond the end of a proposed scenic drive extending two-thirds of the way to the park's southern tip.

Somewhere beyond Bitter Creek Divide, Tarantula Mesa, Fountain Tanks, and the mouth of Muley Twist Canyon (the names are part of the poetry of this weird land), south of Halls Divide and Halls Creek Canyon and the Red Slide, we gave up the struggle against the sand. We drove high on the slickrock and made camp on a little gravelly flat in the midst of miles and miles of sculptured, floraless sandstone. We had hoped by climbing also to escape the gnats and mosquitoes; in that hope we were disappointed, but at least we gained a fine view. We stayed there, meditating and slapping insects, for several days.

One day I went for a walk alone. I carried an old Army combat pack containing a canteen, some cookie crumbs left over from a previous hike, two oranges, and a snakebite kit. I intended to climb to the top of the fold and be back in time for supper. Nothing ambitious; just a good walk on the rock. According to the topographic maps the summit was only a couple of thousand feet above our campsite.

I made good progress at first, and as long as I kept moving even the gnats let me alone. Then came difficulties. You are walking over this naked sandstone, good footing, no loose gravel, no problems, you think, and then you come to the rim of an abyss. Have faith in friction, you remind yourself, hoping to descend. But the pitch of the rock, steeper and steeper, makes you stop. The crevasse is too wide to leap; nothing to do but go around it. On the fold the shortest distance between two points is often a highly meandering line.

About noon by the sun, I reached a high point on the monocline and was able to see the world beyond the canyons. Mountains bulked in all directions—northeast the Henrys, eastward the Abajos, south the blue dome of Navajo Mountain, southwest Kaiparowits Plateau, on the northwest Boulder Mountain and the Aquarius Plateau. In between these were arrayed gorges, badlands, solitary buttes, and mesas glowing in sullen colors through an ocean of heat waves. Nearby shimmered Lake Powell, perhaps an hour's flight for a raven, but a one- or two-day hike on human feet.

Way off northeast, beyond the Henrys, lay the Robbers Roost country, where Butch Cassidy and the Wild Bunch briefly holed up during the midpoint of their free-enterprising career. Art Ekker of the Robbers Roost Ranch can still show you their century-old hideouts. Southward, on public lands between my perch and the fifty-mile-long Kaiparowits Plateau, meandered the gorges of the Escalante River and its tributaries, a near-perfect wilderness—and one long threatened by exploitation.

The way up had included many detours. I decided to take a shortcut going down, that is, to attempt to proceed directly from where I was to where I wanted to be.

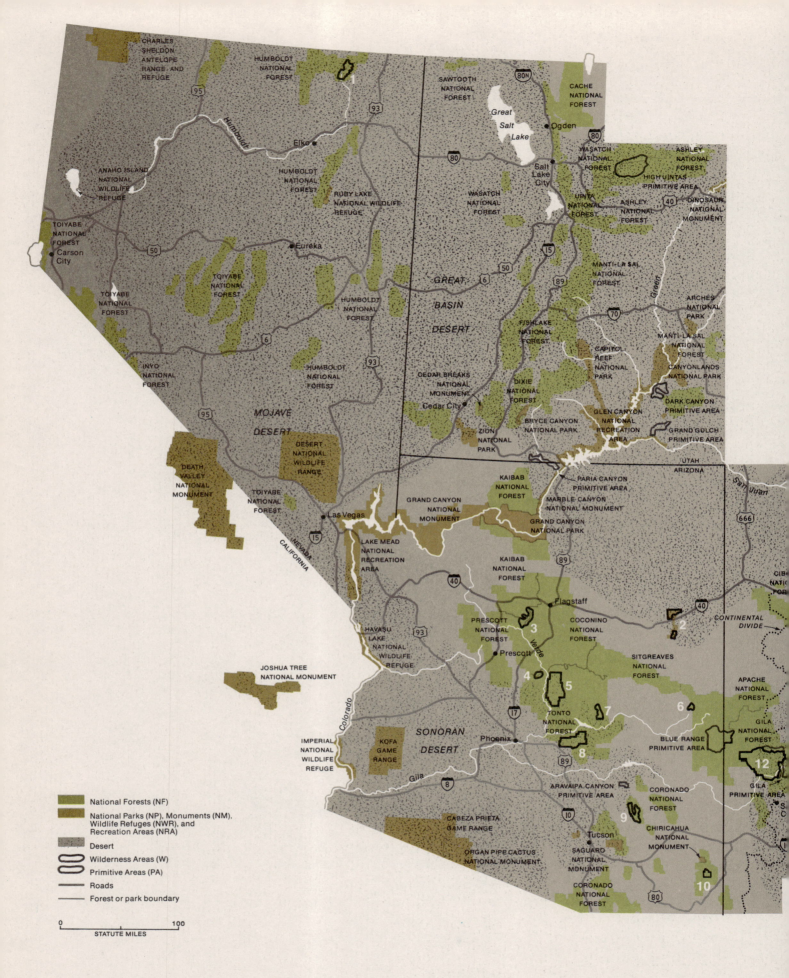

CHARLES
SHELDON
ANTELOPE
RANGE AND
REFUGE

HUMBOLDT
NATIONAL
FOREST

SAWTOOTH
NATIONAL
FOREST

CACHE
NATIONAL
FOREST

Great
Salt
Lake

Ogden

WASATCH
NATIONAL
FOREST

ASHLEY
NATIONAL
FOREST

HIGH UINTAS
PRIMITIVE AREA

Elko

Salt Lake
City

ANAHO ISLAND
NATIONAL
WILDLIFE
REFUGE

HUMBOLDT
NATIONAL
FOREST

RUBY LAKE
NATIONAL WILDLIFE
REFUGE

WASATCH
NATIONAL
FOREST

UINTA
NATIONAL
FOREST

ASHLEY
NATIONAL
FOREST

DINOSAUR
NATIONAL
MONUMENT

Green

TOIYABE
NATIONAL
FOREST
Carson
City

Eureka

TOIYABE
NATIONAL
FOREST

GREAT

BASIN

DESERT

MANTI-LA SAL
NATIONAL
FOREST

ARCHES
NATIONAL
PARK

TOIYABE
NATIONAL
FOREST

HUMBOLDT
NATIONAL
FOREST

CAPITOL
REEF
NATIONAL
PARK

MANTI-LA SAL
NATIONAL
FOREST

CANYONLANDS
NATIONAL PARK

INYO
NATIONAL
FOREST

HUMBOLDT
NATIONAL
FOREST

FISHLAKE
NATIONAL
FOREST

CEDAR BREAKS
NATIONAL
MONUMENT

DARK CANYON
PRIMITIVE AREA

MOJAVE

DESERT

DESERT
NATIONAL
WILDLIFE
RANGE

Cedar City

DIXIE
NATIONAL
FOREST

GLEN CANYON
NATIONAL
RECREATION
AREA

GRAND GULCH
PRIMITIVE AREA

DEATH
VALLEY
NATIONAL
MONUMENT

ZION
NATIONAL
PARK

BRYCE CANYON
NATIONAL PARK

UTAH

ARIZONA

San Juan

TOIYABE
NATIONAL
FOREST

Las Vegas

KAIBAB
NATIONAL
FOREST

PARIA CANYON
PRIMITIVE AREA

MARBLE CANYON
NATIONAL MONUMENT

666

LAKE MEAD
NATIONAL
RECREATION
AREA

GRAND CANYON
NATIONAL
MONUMENT

GRAND CANYON
NATIONAL PARK

NEVADA

CALIFORNIA

KAIBAB
NATIONAL
FOREST

89

HAVASU
LAKE
NATIONAL
WILDLIFE
REFUGE

Flagstaff

CONTINENTAL
DIVIDE

CIB
NATIO
FOR

JOSHUA TREE
NATIONAL MONUMENT

PRESCOTT
NATIONAL
FOREST

3

COCONINO
NATIONAL
FOREST

2

Colorado

Prescott

Verde

4

5

SITGREAVES
NATIONAL
FOREST

6

APACHE
NATIONAL
FOREST

IMPERIAL
NATIONAL
WILDLIFE
REFUGE

KOFA
GAME
RANGE

SONORAN
DESERT

TONTO
NATIONAL
FOREST

7

GILA
NATIONAL
FOREST

Phoenix

8

BLUE RANGE
PRIMITIVE AREA

12

Gila

89

ARAVAIPA CANYON
PRIMITIVE AREA

CORONADO
NATIONAL
FOREST

GILA
PRIMITIVE AREA

S. C.

CABEZA PRIETA
GAME RANGE

9

Tucson

CHIRICAHUA
NATIONAL
MONUMENT

ORGAN PIPE CACTUS
NATIONAL MONUMENT

SAGUARO
NATIONAL
MONUMENT

CORONADO
NATIONAL
FOREST

10

80

Legend:

National Forests (NF)

National Parks (NP), Monuments (NM), Wildlife Refuges (NWR), and Recreation Areas (NRA)

Desert

Wilderness Areas (W)

Primitive Areas (PA)

Roads

Forest or park boundary

0   100
STATUTE MILES

THE SOUTHWEST

Numbered sites are established Wilderness Areas. All but two lie in national forests, one in a national park, another in a national wildlife refuge. Unnumbered entries are units officially considered for wilderness. Bureau of Land Management (BLM) Primitive Areas are regulated in much the same way as Forest Service Primitive Areas and lands in the Wilderness System. A figure after the name is wilderness acreage only, not total acreage of the park, refuge, or primitive area. Pages cited offer fuller description; page 337 lists contacts for obtaining details on particular areas.

NEVADA

1 Jarbidge W. 64,827. Rugged, remote, mountainous. Fish in 9,300-ft.-high Emerald Lake. Mule deer, blue and ruffed grouse plentiful. Steep trails.

Charles Sheldon Antelope Range and Refuge. Arid mesas in high sagebrush desert.

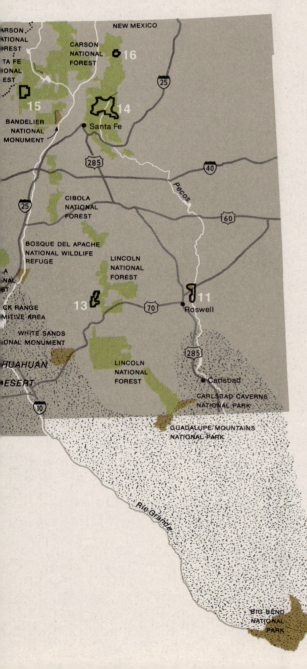

Ruby Lake NWR. Marshlands at foot of Ruby Mountains. Trumpeter swans, sandhill cranes.

Anaho Island NWR. 240. Lies in Pyramid Lake. Nursery for white pelican colony. No public use.

Desert National Wildlife Range. 1,443,100. Desert bighorn sheep. Trails, water scarce.

CALIFORNIA

Death Valley NM. See pages 104 and 113.

Joshua Tree NM. 325,000. High desert country, Joshua trees.

UTAH

High Uintas PA. 322,998. Highest mountains in Utah, to 13,498 feet. More than 250 lakes. Rugged alpine scenery.

Dinosaur NM. White-water rivers, deep gorges in fossil-rich canyon country.

Arches NP. Striking, eons-old stone formations. Pygmy forest of piñons, desert junipers.

Canyonlands NP. Deep, narrow canyons, high desert plateaus.

Dark Canyon PA (BLM). 74,317. 26 miles long. Beavers, coyotes.

Grand Gulch PA (BLM). 27,480. Canyon 60 miles long. Water limited; springs far apart. Summer storms cause flash floods.

Glen Canyon NRA. Majestic canyons above Lake Powell. Includes part of Escalante slickrock wild lands.

Capitol Reef NP. See pages 90 and 105.

Bryce Canyon NP. 16,303. Colorful pinnacles, canyons.

Cedar Breaks NM. 4,370. Mountain juniper, identified as cedar by Mormon settlers, surrounds the "breaks" or badlands; also 1,600-year-old bristlecone pines.

Zion NP. Color-rich limestone and sandstone canyons. Many trails. Some pristine areas in Kolob Canyons region.

ARIZONA

Paria Canyon PA (BLM). 8,726 in Utah, 18,789 in Arizona. Rarely visited 45-mile-long canyon. Four- to six-day backpack trip ends at Lee's Ferry. Beware of flash floods.

Grand Canyon NP and NM and Marble Canyon NM. 512,870. Though most of the canyon is due for wilderness designation, the Colorado River remains open for motorized boats and rafts.

Lake Mead NRA. Wild canyons near crowded boaters' resort.

2 Petrified Forest NP W. 50,260. Rainbow Forest in the south contrasts with Painted Desert in the north. Fossils, Indian ruins. Home of prairie rattlesnake and its archenemy, the roadrunner.

3 Sycamore Canyon W. 47,757. Miniature Grand Canyon; many geological layers exposed. Varied biotic communities.

Havasu Lake NWR. 17,116. Partly in California; proposed Needles Wilderness. Towering pinnacles and secluded backwaters shelter prairie and peregrine falcons.

4 Pine Mountain W. 20,061. Forests; mesas. Canyon walls contain Indian relics. Remote; few visitors.

5 Mazatzal W. 205,346. Mountainous. Deep canyons. Little water; travel difficult.

6 Mount Baldy W. 6,975. Streams lace forest slopes.

Blue Range PA. 177,239. Partly in New Mexico. Rugged scenic beauty. Box canyons.

7 Sierra Ancha W. 20,850. Timbered peaks; canyons. Rough; some places inaccessible.

8 Superstition W. 124,140. See page 119.

Kofa Game Range. Rugged desert mountains and wide arid plains. Bighorn sheep, wild burros.

Imperial NWR. 14,470. Partly in California. Desert uplands cut by Colorado River. Sparse vegetation includes the hardy creosote bush.

Cabeza Prieta Game Range. 744,000. See pages 105 and 106.

Organ Pipe Cactus NM. Named for a cactus rare in United States. Sonoran Desert. Stark mountains, dry washes, rocky canyons. Trails and scenic roadways.

Aravaipa Canyon PA (BLM). 5,580. Thousand-foot cliffs. White settlers massacred 85 Apaches here in 1871.

9 Galiuro W. 52,717. Desert mountain country. Dense brush limits off-trail travel.

Saguaro NM. 32,300. Home of largest cacti in U. S.

Chiricahua NM. 6,925. Rhyolite towers and "balanced" rocks.

10 Chiricahua W. 18,000. Pine-clad peaks. Haunt of Cochise and Geronimo.

NEW MEXICO

Carlsbad Caverns NP. 30,210. Spelunkers' wilderness. Connects by Guadalupe Escarpment to Texas' Guadalupe Mountains NP. 46,850.

White Sands NM. Moving dunes of white gypsum granules reach heights of 50 feet.

11 Bitter Lake NWR W. 8,500. Grasslands harbor wildlife.

Black Range PA. 188,179. Proposed Aldo Leopold W. Trail traverses rough forest land.

Gila PA. Semi-arid region of Mogollon Mountains.

12 Gila W. 433,690. First federal Wilderness Area. Paradise of high mountain forest, trout streams, abundant game, miles of trails. Diverse geological formations.

13 White Mountain W. 31,283. Bonanza for the botanist—five life zones, 6,000 to 11,400 feet.

Bosque del Apache NWR. 32,500. Once the "Groves of the Apache." Desert vegetation, Indian ruins.

14 Pecos W. 168,332. Many lakes, streams; 100-ft. waterfall. Truchas Peak for the climber.

Bandelier NM. 21,110. Steep canyons, high wooded mesas.

15 San Pedro Parks W. 41,132. Meadows dot evergreen forest on flat mountaintop.

16 Wheeler Peak W. 6,029. Tundra covers 13,160-ft. Wheeler Peak, highest point in state.

TEXAS

Big Bend NP. 533,900. Vast desert, mountains, deep canyons. Carry drinking water.

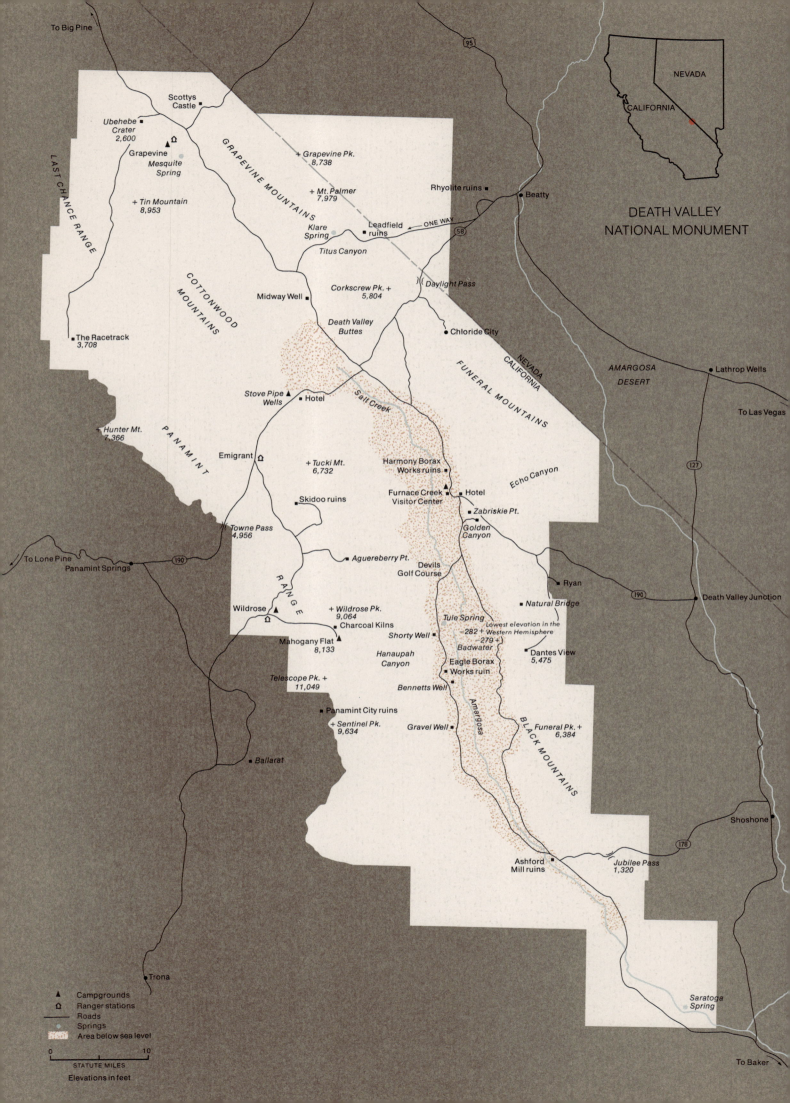

DEATH VALLEY
NATIONAL MONUMENT

NEVADA

CALIFORNIA

To Big Pine

95

Scottys
Castle

Ubehebe
Crater
2,600

Grapevine

Mesquite
Spring

+ Grapevine Pk.
8,738

Rhyolite ruins

Beatty

+ Mt. Palmer
7,979

+ Tin Mountain
8,953

Klare
Spring

Leadfield
ruins

ONE WAY

58

Titus Canyon

The Racetrack
3,708

Midway Well

Corkscrew Pk. +
5,804

Daylight Pass

Death Valley
Buttes

Chloride City

NEVADA

CALIFORNIA

AMARGOSA
DESERT

Lathrop Wells

Stove Pipe
Wells

Hotel

Salt Creek

To Las Vegas

127

+ Hunter Mt.
7,366

Emigrant

+ Tucki Mt.
6,732

Harmony Borax
Works ruins

Echo Canyon

Skidoo ruins

Furnace Creek
Visitor Center

Hotel

Zabriskie Pt.

Towne Pass
4,956

Golden
Canyon

To Lone Pine

190

Panamint Springs

Aguereberry Pt.

Devils
Golf Course

Ryan

Natural Bridge

190

Death Valley Junction

Wildrose

+ Wildrose Pk.
9,064

Charcoal Kilns

Tule Spring

Lowest elevation in the
−282 + Western Hemisphere

Shorty Well

−279 +

Dantes View
5,475

Mahogany Flat
8,133

Badwater

Hanaupah
Canyon

Eagle Borax
Works ruin

Telescope Pk. +
11,049

Bennetts Well

Panamint City ruins

Gravel Well

Funeral Pk. +
6,384

+ Sentinel Pk.
9,634

Ballarat

Ashford
Mill ruins

Jubilee Pass
1,320

178

Shoshone

Trona

Saratoga
Spring

▲ Campgrounds
⚲ Ranger stations
— Roads
• Springs
Area below sea level

0   10
STATUTE MILES
Elevations in feet

To Baker

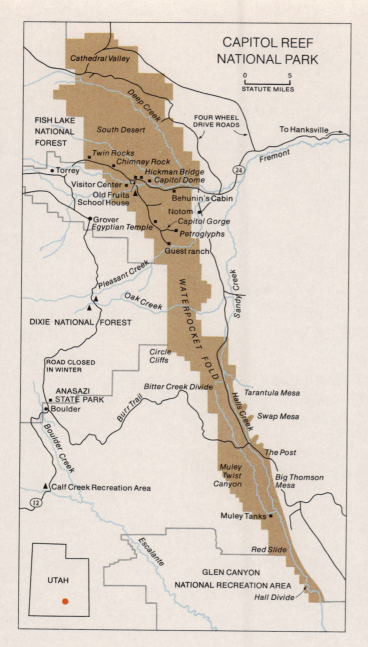

CAPITOL REEF NATIONAL PARK

0   5
STATUTE MILES

Cathedral Valley

Deep Creek

FISH LAKE NATIONAL FOREST

South Desert

FOUR WHEEL DRIVE ROADS

To Hanksville

Fremont

24

Twin Rocks
Chimney Rock
Torrey
Hickman Bridge
Capitol Dome
Visitor Center
Old Fruita
School House
Behunin's Cabin
Notom
Grover
Capitol Gorge
Egyptian Temple
Petroglyphs
Guest ranch

Pleasant Creek

Sandy Creek

Oak Creek

DIXIE NATIONAL FOREST

WATERPOCKET FOLD

Circle Cliffs

ROAD CLOSED IN WINTER

Bitter Creek Divide

Halls Creek

Tarantula Mesa

ANASAZI STATE PARK
Boulder

Burr Trail

Swap Mesa

The Post

Big Thomson Mesa

Boulder Creek

Muley Twist Canyon

12

Calf Creek Recreation Area

Muley Tanks

Escalante

Red Slide

UTAH

GLEN CANYON NATIONAL RECREATION AREA

Hall Divide

DEATH VALLEY

Its sparse vegetation watered by two inches or so of annual precipitation, its floor a 200-square-mile salt pan, Death Valley invariably summons extremes of language. "The Creator's dumping ground," a forty-niner called it.

Yet thousands find pleasure and much to ponder in 3,000-square-mile Death Valley National Monument. From campgrounds and inns at Furnace Creek and Stove Pipe Wells, hikers head for the Panamints, Grapevines, and Cottonwoods. Many take pack stoves —wood-gathering is banned and backcountry camping restricted —as well as plenty of water. Some journey down to Badwater and see in the pool the image of 11,049-foot Telescope Peak, the monument's highest reach.

Candidates for wilderness status, 16 roadless tracts, from 17,000 to 337,000 acres, harbor many of the monument's 21 unique plant species as well as pupfish descended from Ice Age species.

Roads (many ungraded) reach old mines and ghost towns like Chloride City. Borax, of 20-mule-team fame, is still mined; Death Valley is one of four Park Service sites where law permits mining.

Ideal visiting months are November to April. Summer temperatures top 110° F.; in such heat a hiker may sweat a quart an hour. Many summer trekkers go from 8,133-foot Mahogany Flat to Telescope's cool summit. Rangers urge caution in the lower reaches due to heat and flash floods.

CABEZA PRIETA

Stretching for 56 miles along the Mexican border, Cabeza Prieta Game Range alternates low mountain chains and basins of sand and lava. "Forests" of tall cacti and palo verde, mesquite, ironwood, and the ubiquitous creosote bush shield a dozen threatened animal species.

Summer heat and military air-to-air gunnery training hold down travel in Cabeza Prieta. Entry is restricted on shooting days; permits are required.

Much of 860,000-acre Cabeza Prieta is proposed for wilderness, but the jeep trail that grinds along part of old El Camino del Diablo will remain open to vehicles, with campsites at Papago and Tule Wells. Dead wood may not be gathered within two miles of the trail. Two shorter but also rugged routes may be driven: the Chico Shuni (no permit required) and Charley Bell Trails.

CAPITOL REEF

The Fremont River's verdant little valley attracted a few Mormon settlers in the 1870's to the area around what is now Capitol Reef National Park, and some 80 years later uranium and oil prospectors arrived to hack and drill. But the rewards were meager, and so this 254,241-acre string bean of water-hewn rock remains little scarred by man.

Petroglyphs tell of occupation by prehistoric Indians. Spring offers wild flowers and perhaps the sight of a golden eagle hunting food for its nestlings; fall brings warm days and cool nights, ideal for camping. Catchments which may hold runoff for weeks gave a name to the park's dominant feature, the Waterpocket Fold; trails ascend its wall and reach such curiosities as Hickman Bridge. "Dry camping"—tote your own stove and water—is necessary in the backcountry. Inquire about conditions before taking the jeep trails spoking north to Cathedral Valley and south along the Waterpocket Fold.

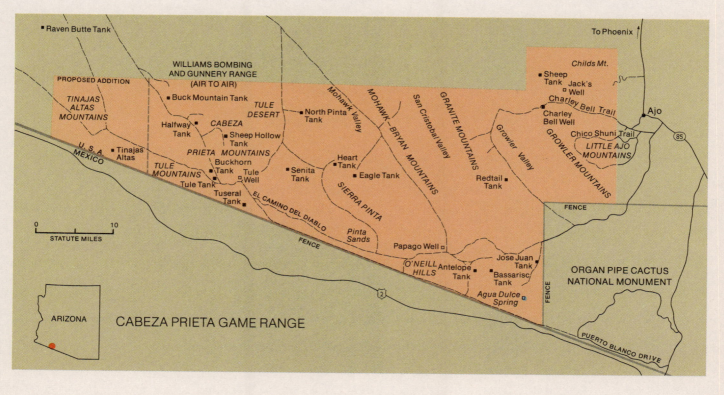

Raven Butte Tank

To Phoenix

WILLIAMS BOMBING AND GUNNERY RANGE (AIR TO AIR)

Childs Mt.

PROPOSED ADDITION

TINAJAS ALTAS MOUNTAINS

Buck Mountain Tank

TULE DESERT

Mohawk Valley

MOHAWK-BRYAN MOUNTAINS

San Cristobal Valley

GRANITE MOUNTAINS

Sheep Tank
Jack's Well
Charley Bell Trail

Ajo

Halfway Tank

CABEZA

North Pinta Tank

Charley Bell Well

85

U.S.A.
MEXICO

Tinajas Altas

Sheep Hollow Tank

PRIETA MOUNTAINS

Chico Shuni Trail

GROWLER MOUNTAINS

LITTLE AJO MOUNTAINS

TULE MOUNTAINS

Buckhorn Tank

Tule Well

Senita Tank

Heart Tank

Eagle Tank

Growler Valley

Redtail Tank

Tule Tank

Tuseral Tank

EL CAMINO DEL DIABLO

SIERRA PINTA

0   10
STATUTE MILES

Pinta Sands

Papago Well

FENCE

FENCE

O'NEILL HILLS

Antelope Tank

Jose Juan Tank

Bassarisc Tank

ORGAN PIPE CACTUS NATIONAL MONUMENT

2

Agua Dulce Spring

FENCE

ARIZONA

CABEZA PRIETA GAME RANGE

PUERTO BLANCO DRIVE

Night-blooming cereus

Barrel cactus

Ocotillo

I should have known better; I did know better. But I tried anyway. When the sun went down, I was still trying, sucking on my last orange and looking for a way out of a box canyon. When the moon came up, around midnight, I was crouched in a cave trying to keep warm, a big fire in front of me, a little fire behind, no coat, no blanket, only frigid sand beneath. A long night, but educational. In the morning, I found a way out, but it wasn't easy. I got to camp in time for lunch.

Cactus Country. From the canyonlands of Utah to the cactus forests of southern Arizona, from the Great Basin to the Sonoran Desert, from 4,000 or 6,000 feet above sea level to only 700 to 3,000, it's downhill all the way—a nice trip in autumn or winter but something else in summer. Although tastes differ. I have friends, genuine desert rats, who like the southern desert best in summer, when the tourists have been driven out, when the temperature hangs around 105° F. by lunchtime, when the Gila monsters and cone-nosed bugs and giant hairy scorpions rattle about like happy kids all night long.

Being only a humble desert mouse, I prefer to see the hot parts in the milder months. Thus it was in February that three friends and I ventured into one of the largest areas of mostly primitive Sonoran Desert this side of Mexico: the Cabeza Prieta Game Range, 860,000 acres big.

This place is difficult of access for two reasons. First, only jeep trails lead into it. While three of these will remain open to vehicles under the Fish and Wildlife Service's wilderness plan, bear in mind that a "jeep trail" may be defined as any pair of wheel tracks which gets you into trouble, creates demoralizing repair bills, and generally goes nowhere. Second, Cabeza Prieta has to some extent been appropriated by the Air Force and Marines for aviation training, including air-to-air gunnery practice. A northeast corner is some eight miles from an air-to-ground target area. Nearly all the game range is closed to visitors on shooting days—about a third of the year. Entry permits must be obtained from Luke Air Force Base at Phoenix and the Marine Corps Air Station at Yuma.

Cabeza Prieta was established as a wildlife range in 1939 to protect desert bighorn sheep, about 250 of which scramble over its rock and sand. It also protects the Sonoran pronghorn antelope, an almost extinct subspecies. An international herd of pronghorns ranges the borderlands; most of the animals remain in Mexico, but about 60 spend a good deal of time in the game range. Some have also been seen in neighboring desert land. Cabeza Prieta became part of a vast Arizona target range in World War II. At first glance the two uses seem to conflict. Wildlife managers, however, do not feel their mission has been compromised. They point out that gunnery practice overhead tends to discourage too many visitors, conserving the meager water supply and fragile vegetation for the animals.

In two jeeps we entered Cabeza Prieta from the east, via the adjoining Organ Pipe Cactus National Monument. At the boundary fence stood a bullet-riddled metal sign with the likeness of a bighorn sheep. Close by was an Air Force warning sign, also well shot up. Nothing personal: merely an old Western tradition.

We crossed a dusty expanse where little grew save creosote bushes, but presently climbed into a more interesting zone of plant life. Here were groves of the saguaro cactus, many 40 to 50 feet tall, eccentric figures with gesturing arms, suggestively human, each unique and individual, all burnt by the sun, beaten by storms, punctured by woodpeckers, and invaded by bacteria and beetles, yet very much alive, assertively existent. A pleated trunk allows this cactus to expand and contract, accordion-style, when it takes in water after a rain or loses it during drought. It may live as long as 200 years—pretty good for a column of woody ribs and succulent pulp encased in something like watermelon rind. The saguaro is the Big Daddy of cacti in the United States, a plant so conspicuous that it has become in the American mind a symbol for all our deserts, though it grows only in southern Arizona, extreme southeast California, and the northwestern part of Mexico.

It is only one cactus among many in this arboreal desert. There are numerous kinds of cholla, for example, including the teddy-bear, so named for its deceitfully plush and cuddly appearance when seen from a distance. There is the aptly named organ pipe and its relative the senita, also called the "old man" cactus because of the gray, whiskerlike spines on the tips of its branches. Many forms of prickly pear are found here, and such smaller but often beautifully flowering cacti as the hedgehog, the many-headed barrel, the fishhook, the night-blooming cereus, and a form of pincushion cactus only three to ten inches high when mature.

We made lunch at an old miners' camp called Papago Well, reduced now to ruins and wreckage. To the southeast rose the Agua Dulce (Sweet Water) Mountains. The remains of gold and silver mines can still be found in those peaks, and perhaps more interesting, Agua Dulce Spring, the only known seep in Cabeza Prieta. It was one of the few reliable water sources along the old trail from Mexico to California.

El Camino del Diablo, it was called: the Devil's Highway. That trail, or rather group of trails, was pioneered by Spanish missionaries and soldiers centuries ago. It was followed later by American traders, colonists, and gold-seekers. Extreme heat, the scarcity of water, and unfriendly Indians gave the route its sinister reputation, maintained well into the age of the automobile. An entire family, it is said, was found dead in the shade of their broken-down car in the 1930's. Their water containers were empty; even the radiator had been drained.

This sort of thing rarely happens anymore, for paved highways now bypass Cabeza Prieta. In order to perish in this cactus wilderness in these Safety First times it is necessary to make a little extra effort, to go where there is no need to go, to bring too little water, to get lost, to wait for midsummer, to shoot yourself in the foot practicing the quick draw, or to get hit on the head by a spent projectile. It's not easy.

We encountered traces of the Devil's Highway as we headed toward a plain of lava. Rusted sardine cans and sherds of auto tires, those were to be expected. But more impressive was our first grave: an iron cross driven into a hump which held the remains of a prospector named O'Neill. Later, we came upon a mound of stones, and at its head the name Nameer and the date 1871 spelled out in black rocks. Now and then we saw more recent evidence of man: the wreckage of aluminum-painted wooden target drones and an occasional scatter of .50-caliber machine gun shells. There's not much of this type of litter in the Cabeza Prieta wilderness, however, and even these traces of unseemly bric-a-brac could be removed.

We spent one afternoon on that lava field, a grand, arid barrenness swept by a hot wind. At times we ground along in low-range, four-wheel drive. An old volcano rose on the south, sand dunes on the southwest, treeless mountains in all other directions. A few vultures soared above, the only moving life in sight. Even the creosote bushes and some scrubby little cholla—

A little drench, a lot of drought—a harsh challenge to survival, but desert plants have ways to meet it.

The succulents hoard water; after a good rain their roots soak up much more than the plant can use immediately. The cereus stores the excess in a turnip-like tuber; stem succulents like the barrel cactus—and the saguaro—fill spongy cells in their fluted, expandable trunks. To reduce transpiration—the loss of moisture through breathing pores—cacti have evolved in leafless form. Photosynthesis in cacti takes place in the green stem covering.

The ocotillo covers its slender, spiny stems with leaves, but sheds them during drought. A perennial, it can grow new ones whenever there's rain in the warmer months.

Shallow, wide-spreading roots enable the prickly pear to collect a bit of moisture from even a light sprinkle. The mesquite tree sends roots both shallow and deep— as deep as 60 feet to find sources of life-giving water.

DRAWINGS BY GEORGE FOUNDS

Mesquite

Prickly pear

almost nothing else grows there—looked not dormant but dead, waiting for the resurrection of the summer rains. Slowly the heights of the Sierra Pinta turned past on the northern horizon, granitic rock dappled with light and shade, dark brown and rosy pink, the two-tone effect which inspired the Spanish to name this range "painted mountains." A grim desolation, a place transparently beautiful, a place wild as the wind or bitter as death: There are, to paraphrase the poet Wallace Stevens, 14 ways of looking at a desert. You choose.

At 1500 hours, for this was military country, we noticed the gibbous moon hanging in the blue sky. Fat moon in the afternoon. I remember the time because it was then that the tailpipe fell off one jeep and the transmission locked in the other. We took a half-hour break to make repairs on our weary machines.

Onward. We finally reached the end of the volcanic plain, approached and moved among the outlying hills of the Sierra Tuseral, and made camp before sundown in the middle of a broad and lovely wash where great mesquite and ironwood trees towered above clean, bright, untrampled sand.

There is no better fuel than a few chunks of the heartwood of dead ironwood. Hard as the name implies, heavy as stone, centuries in the making, it provides a slow, passionate, smokeless fire, ideal for cooking. Throw your meat on the coals, aborigine-fashion, turn it once, pluck it free, and sink in your fangs—you'll think you're back home in Eden. What's more, the coals will remain hot all night; you can use them in the morning to light your breakfast fire.

That was a splendid evening. At sundown the Sierra Pinta off to the northeast lit up suddenly with what seemed to be an interior illumination, as if some troll had thrown a switch deep in the bowels of the mountains. The sun went down and the lavender twilight took over, softly and sweetly, followed in due course by the brilliant reappearance of the moon. Nobody could sleep; we sat through most of the long winter's night telling stories and singing songs, giddy on moonshine, starshine, and the penultimate case of beer.

We rose the next day at the crack of noon. There was some feeble stirring about, an attempt at breakfast, then a desperate plunge westward around the Tuseral Mountains to Tule Well, an old way station on the devil's route through hell. There's a crossing of trails here, a shack, a well with live windmill pump and storage tank, and an old cast-iron sign warning travelers from across the border to register with U. S. Customs. In all it's a plausibly habitable spot—though, of course, no one lives here. We lingered long enough to wash up (Continued on page 113)

Portfolio Notes

OPPOSITE: *Featherlike shoots of salt grass, one of the few plants able to live in the fierce heat and saline soil on Death Valley's floor, rise from an underground stem near the lowest point in the Americas.*
FARRELL GREHAN

PAGES 110-111: *Wind-hewn from wind-borne sands, a finishing touch of beauty added by slanting sunrays, dunes crest like breakers near Stove Pipe Wells in Death Valley. Water tumbling from the distant Grapevine Mountains molded the old mud hills in the middle ground and rumpled the land with a fan of debris.*
FARRELL GREHAN

PAGE 112: *Where creature comforts are few, nature shapes its creatures to suit. Bighorn sheep, largest of desert mammals, can store heat in the daytime and radiate the excess at night. These two have just filled their bellies at a tank in the Cabeza Prieta Game Range. Man lends a hand here, with pump-driven wells and water trucked to rock basins. Like most of its kin, the voracious collared lizard slakes its thirst from fluids in its food—insects and other lizards, which it hunts by day. Saguaro flowers grow at the stem tips and open at night—accommodating the long-nosed bat seeking nectar and pollen. The cactus wren nests amid cholla spines, a fortress most predators avoid—though not the slithering black racer bent on a meal.*
UPPER: GALE MONSON. LOWER: M. W. LARSON, ENTHEOS, AND OTIS IMBODEN, NATIONAL GEOGRAPHIC PHOTOGRAPHER

and refill water bags and canteens before driving on through the Cabeza Prieta Mountains, so named for a "black head" of volcanic rock which forms one of the highest peaks. Crossing the wild, flat, hot, dusty expanse of the Lechuguilla Desert, we came to our last campsite, at the foot of the Tinajas Altas Mountains.

Tinajas Altas means "high tanks"—in this case, seven natural stone catchments where rainwater may remain for weeks or even months after summer storms, supplying foxes, mountain lions, desert bighorn sheep, pronghorns, and coyotes. The Jesuit missionary Eusebio Francisco Kino, traveling this inhospitable country to seek out its Indians and also to find a route from Mexico to California, recorded the location of these tanks in 1699. Later travelers always stopped to drink, water their horses, fill their casks, maybe shoot a bighorn, and maybe sometimes endure—if they lived that long—a bit of ambush, Indian-style.

We climbed the bold granitic slickrock to view the highest tank, a basin half full of dark green water, a bouillabaisse rich in tadpoles, beetles, mosquito larvae, toads, flies, fleas, worms, drowned centipedes, and pale gnawed bones of obscure origin. We each took a hearty drink, filled our canteens, and crawled back down the rock, glad to know such hidden places still exist. Another day and night we spent in that magical spot. Then we took the long jeep trail north to the highway, caught the traffic's current east, and floated home to Tucson.

Final Country. From 4,316-foot Daylight Pass, northeast entrance to Death Valley, the highway descends through Boundary Canyon and Hells Gate into the inferno at sea level and below. Below, below: beneath a sea not of brine but of heat, of shimmering waves of light and wind as fierce as a volcano's breath. The glare on the floor of Death Valley is stunning. Yet also exhilarating. The air seems not clear like glass but tinted, golden toward the sun, smoke blue and blue-black in the shadows. The colors, I believe, are present in the air itself—the hues of sky, sand, and hills reflected by billions of dust particles.

At ten in the morning on a June day the thermometer reads 114° F. Later in the day it will become much hotter. (A temperature of 134° was recorded in 1913.) But with the humidity close to zero the heat is not immediately unpleasant, nor even uncomfortable. Like the dazzling light, it is intoxicating at first. Then you begin to notice a malignant note in that silent symphony of radiation.

A hard place to love, this graben. (Death Valley is not, you see, a proper valley but a depression formed by faulting, a collapsed trench up to 16 miles wide.) This lower-than-sea-level desert is bitter as alkali, rough and harsh as tangled iron, miserly with life in any form. Speeding by car along the valley floor, you will see nothing much but vast salt beds left by evaporation and immense fans of gravel and rock spreading down like glaciers from the mountains.

Yet there is life: not much of anything but a little of each. Around the sand dunes are clumps of arrowweed and a few mesquite trees—some dead, others looking dead, all doing their utmost, it seems, not to attract attention. Salt grass grows on the flats, creosote bush, desert holly, brittlebush, and prickle poppy on the alluvial fans. Higher up, at about a thousand feet of elevation, you find the first poor stunted cactus specimens—cholla, prickly pear, and a barrel cactus. Of the 550 square miles below sea level, nearly two-fifths consists of the harsh salt on which very little grows; in the area between the salt pan and sea level, botanists have counted about 140 species of plants. This is a little less than a fourth of the number that grow in the entire 3,000 square miles of the national monument.

Driving across the valley, I stop at Stove Pipe Wells Village, named for a nearby watering place known to prospectors who traveled this way at the turn of the century and before. Inside the gas station a few humans are huddled beneath the cold-air blower. Some of Death Valley's mammals—ground squirrels and pocket mice, for example—are able to survive the summer heat only by burrowing deep. The human inhabitants endure by building artificial burrows; not adaptation but insulation is the principle.

Through a shield of glass, I watch desert sparrows outside. They are crawling in and out of the grills of parked cars. What are they doing? They are eating tourists: bugs and butterflies encountered elsewhere and rushed down to the valley smashed and annealed to hot metal. Like Yellowstone's bears, these birds have learned to make a good thing off passing trade. They also perform a useful service; it is a long, hot climb out of Death Valley and a clean radiator is essential for the trip.

It's good, once, to get a taste of Death Valley as it is in the summer. But only a mad dog would go for a walk then. Better to wait until fall or winter to explore afoot in all save the highest reaches of the monument's mountain ranges. Then there is much to explore. Death Valley has many roads—too many—but most are dirt tracks, and this net lies but lightly on the land. In between are numerous areas, well over 1.5 million acres in sum, which offer to the traveler who is willing to leave his car a sense and a vision of what Death Valley is really like—of what it was before man came, of what we hope it will be for millenniums to come. Many of these areas may be protected in the wilderness preservation system.

Once on a time we lived in Death Valley. My wife was a schoolteacher. I was school bus driver, janitor, and official resident philosopher. Probably the best job I ever had. During that year I wandered freely; I have returned often in the years since. Sometimes I made notes on paper, sometimes merely on my mind. What follows are selections from the happiest hours of my Death Valley days.

The Panamint Mountains, October. In autumn you can escape extreme heat in the Panamints, the valley's western wall. But no matter how high you climb it seems impossible to leave the influence of aridity and anti-life. At 7,000 feet in this latitude you might well be in a forest of yellow pine with meadows and streams. Instead you see a monotony of dun-colored hills supporting shrubs and junipers. The trails make walking easy, but you have to carry water.

Between 7,000 and 9,000 feet you pass more junipers and a fair growth of piñon pine. Higher, toward the 11,049-foot summit of Telescope Peak, appear thin stands of limber pine and the massive, all-enduring bristlecone pines—perhaps the oldest living things on earth. Scientists cored one that had lived more than 4,600 years.

I pass three wild burros. Descendants of lost and abandoned prospectors' stock, they range through the Panamints, multiplying freely, competing with the native bighorns for forage. They stand about a hundred feet off the trail, watching me hike by. Unafraid, they merely blink their heavy eyelashes like movie starlets when I halt to stare back. But they trot away when I attempt to approach.

The bray of the donkey is well known. But these little beasts can make another sound, and it is startling. In what appears to be lifeless terrain you suddenly hear a great dry cough seemingly close behind your shoulder. You spring about ten feet before daring to look around. You see nothing. Then, hearing a second cough, you scan the hills and discover, far above, a gray or black burro.

I stand by a cairn on the summit of Telescope Peak, looking out on a cold, windy,

Braying burros recall the days when prospectors tried—few successfully—to strike it rich in Death Valley. Some 1,500 burros roam the monument, many in the Panamint Range, displaying traits that made their forebears ideal beasts of burden on the arid wastes. They seem little bothered by extremes of temperature and find sustenance even in such spiny fare as the barrel cactus, shunned by most browsers.

and fantastic earth. Rugged peaks fall off southward into the haze of the Mojave Desert. On the west are the Panamint Valley, the Argus range, more mountains, more valleys, and finally the snow-clad Sierra Nevada. The Sierra is the reason no forest worthy of the name clothes the Panamints; it blocks the sea winds and almost all the moisture. One of those Sierra pinnacles is Mount Whitney, highest point in the 48 contiguous United States. To the north and northwest rise the Inyo and White Mountains, almost as high as the Sierra. East of Death Valley are the Black Mountains, the Amargosa Valley, and wave after wave of still farther mountains. A dirty smudge on the horizon locates Death Valley's inevitable counterpart and complement, Las Vegas—Glitter Gulch—the only sizeable city within 100 miles of the monument.

Hanaupah Canyon, January. A hard place to love? A few single-blanket prospectors who wandered these funereal barrens seemed to find love possible. Could it have been only sudden wealth they were after? Not likely. Not in the case of Shorty Borden, I think. He devoted eight months of his life in 1932 to building by hand a nine-mile road to his lead and silver diggings in Hanaupah Canyon in the west-central part of Death Valley. Then he discovered it would cost him more to transport his ore to a smelter than the ore was worth.

Where the salt flats approach the base of the eastern mountains, 279.8 feet below sea level, stands a clear pool known as Badwater. Surrounded by beds of snow-white alkali, it seems devoid of life. Not so. A species of fairy shrimp survives in that briny pond. According to legend, Badwater is poisonous, containing arsenic. Again, not so. But one cupful of that emetic water, potent with Glauber and other salts, would turn the strongest stomach. I tasted a mouthful but spat it out.

From this spot, not far from the lowest point in the Western Hemisphere, I looked one day across the pale lenses of the valley floor to the brown fan of Hanaupah Canyon, up to the canyon's entrance, and from there, higher and higher to the cornices of frozen snow on Telescope Peak. One would like to transit that interval sometime. I have been part of the way. (The trail I once took to Telescope's top went by another direction.) I hiked far up Hanaupah to Shorty Borden's deserted camp.

I saw there that loveliest of desert things, a flowing stream of sweet, cold water, and drank about a gallon. There are no trees beside the stream, but plenty of low willows, wild grapevine, and other water-loving vegetation. Beyond the springs which feed the stream, the canyon is dry until you come to the place where the canyon forks. Explore either fork and you will find water again: on the right a little waterfall, on the left small cascades in a chute of polished andesite with moss, ferns, and flowers clinging to the walls. Almost no one ever comes here.

Echo Canyon, December. Roaming into Echo Canyon, which penetrates a proposed wilderness unit northeast of the monument headquarters at the oasis of Furnace Creek, I probed deeply into the intricacies of the Funeral Mountains. These were not named for their proximity to Death Valley, but for their shape and coloration: escarpments of smoldering red bordered with charcoal; crags, ridges, and defiles edged in black and purple. This is a primeval chaos of faulted, uplifted, warped, and folded dolomites and limestones, of conglomerates and fans of mud,

Nearly extinct in the United States, its desert habitat whittled by fences, highways, and urban sprawl, the Sonoran pronghorn antelope is confined largely to the 860,000-acre Cabeza Prieta Game Range. An estimated 60 are found there, a few more in adjoining Organ Pipe Cactus National Monument and on nearby lands. Perhaps 500 roam in Mexico, where no refuge exists. Unlike crag-dwelling bighorn sheep, pronghorns inhabit the lowland areas where their favored shrubs and grasses are more plentiful.
DRAWINGS BY GEORGE FOUNDS

sand, and gravel. Here is also evidence of volcanism: walls of andesite embellished with elegant mosaics of rose and yellow quartz. Fool's gold—pyrite—glitters in the black sand. Mica-bearing shales glint under backlight. Veins of pegmatite zigzag and intersect like an undeciphered script across the face of a cliff.

Nowhere in Echo Canyon can I find a trickle of water. But it must be present, at least in minute amounts, under the surface, for here and there grow saltbush, spruce bush, desert trumpet, barrel cactus, and the indomitable creosote bush. You may see a few tiny lizards and the hoofprints of bighorn sheep. Sit quite still for an hour and you may also see a small gray bird flit past. That was the bird that lives in Echo Canyon—seemingly, the only one.

The echoes are good. At certain locations on a still day, one clear shout will create a series of overlapping echoes that go on and on toward a diminuendo so faint that the human ear cannot detect the final vibrations.

Tramp far enough up Echo Canyon and you will come to the ruins of a mining camp with deep shafts, a wooden tipple, and a rolling mill largely intact. The inside walls of the cabin are papered with pages from the *Literary Digest*. Half buried in sand are a child's tricycle, a broken shovel, and the remains of a Model-T Ford.

Returning through twilight, later than planned (as always), I descend the narrow gorge between flood-polished walls, the gorge itself like the stem of a wineglass in relation to the valley above and the alluvial fan below. The somber overhanging cliffs are riddled with grottoes—the eyesockets of skulls, where bats hang in clusters upside down, waiting for nightfall.

Out on the dunes, April. Death Valley's winter, much too lovely to last, is long over. The days are windy, already hot. I go for a walk on the dunes in the vicinity of Stove Pipe Wells. I bear for the highest, following the curving crests of lesser dunes that lead toward it. I pass a few mesquites decked out in new leafery, bright green on black. No other perennials are deep-rooted enough to survive in all this sand. On the last half mile, in deeper sand, there is no plant life whatever, but one can see the prints of birds, mice, lizards, and beetles.

Late in the afternoon I reach the summit of the highest dune, 200 feet above the valley floor. From there I get a clear view of the north end of Death Valley and the mountains which wall it in—almost half a million acres proposed for inclusion in the wilderness system. Nearer at hand I see what appears to be a true pond of water, not a mirage. That requires investigation.

Glissading down the great hill of sand, climbing another and descending the far side of that, I come to the margin of the pool. The shore is jellylike, a mass of quivering quicksand. I wade through it to taste the water. It is fresh, with hardly a taste of salt—fit to drink. This water must have been left from a recent rain. Filling my canteen, I struggle through the quicksand to firm ground.

A few mesquites grow here. I decide to spend the night. I scoop a hole in the sand, build a fire, and sear a piece of beef. Mesquite, like ironwood, is an excellent fuel, burning slow and hot and imparting a nutty flavor to your meat.

I eat my supper by the dying coals. The sun goes down. A few stray clouds catch fire, burning gold and vermilion. These Death Valley mountains that look during the day like burnt and mangled iron become at sundown soft, radiant, full of dream and promise. And the crescent dunes, so harsh by daylight, acquire another aspect now, divided by a hard, clean, sharp edge into sides of purple shadow and luminous gold. Above the rim of the darkening west floats the evening star.

Long live Death Valley. Long live the wilderness.

An eastern-style oasis in the Chihuahuan Desert, South McKittrick Canyon in Guadalupe Mountains National Park nurtures bigtooth maples, chinquapin oaks, hop hornbeams. Ancestors of these species flourished here in west Texas thousands of years ago, before climatic change slowly turned the region to desert; relicts survived in the deep, moist canyons.

The 77,500-acre preserve contains most of a V-shaped plateau of uplifted limestone more than 200 million years old. Its great fossil reef— one of the most extensive in the world—includes El Capitan, a 2,000-foot sheer cliff visible for 50 miles. At the edge of a 46,850-acre tract proposed for wilderness preservation rises 8,751-foot Guadalupe Peak, tallest in Texas.

WALTER MEAYERS EDWARDS, NATIONAL GEOGRAPHIC STAFF

TRAIL RIDERS OF THE STORIED SUPERSTITIONS

Robert Laxalt

We rode into the cruel country when spring was crossing southern Arizona, when the hollows held the heat of approaching summer and the high bluffs carried the lingering bite of winter past. With parched throats, cracked lips, and legs stabbed by cactus spines, we penetrated a land as hostile as it is strangely alluring—the Superstition Wilderness.

Awaking from freezing nights, we rode through scorching noondays, drawn ever deeper into the Superstition Mountains, which stand like aloof and inscrutable judges of the long parade of humanity that has left its mark on this region: the ancient Salado cliff dwellers . . . Coronado's conquistadors in search of the golden cities of Cíbola . . . the Apaches, for whom the mountains were sacred and offered a refuge in war with white soldiers . . . Spanish and Mexican gold-seekers . . . prospectors and desert rats, men pursuing legends, making legends.

We are the latest to pass, riders and backpackers who escape from civilization and trek the 140 miles of trails scratched through the 124,140 acres of the wilderness. Our party, organized by the Wilderness Society, numbered 25: outfitters, guides, wranglers, and 19 paying horsemen, most of us with some riding experience.

Unlike those who had gone before, we were in search of an intangible. For me, a moment of understanding came during a rest stop in a high mountain pass. I sprawled on the ground and watched a puff of cloud cross an endlessly blue sky. As I wearily turned to get up, I saw beside me a tiny hedgehog cactus in bloom—life, at once fragile and tenacious, struggling in a harsh land. For Agnes Schlosser, a fellow rider, the lure was the untamed land. "I am going to ride or backpack every wilderness I can before I get old," she told me. She is in her seventies.

Behind a sun-grazed curtain of rock Superstition Wilderness looms—a stark stage for dramas that began in hope and ended in despair or in death. Here Indians conjured gods—and miners like the fabled Dutchman conjured gold. New players ride the stage today, seeking the wealth of adventure.

Some aim for Miners Needle, a beacon that lured men toward the Dutchman's phantom mine. In the three rocky fingers that beckon on the horizon, a dot of blue reveals the Needle's eye.

A sure-footed horse, leading a trip from
JF Ranch, plunges down a brushy slope.
Improved trails and old, unmarked paths
crisscross the Superstitions. Rangers
warn: Stay on the beaten track to avoid
getting lost. Water holes dot the land;
some may run dry, some are hard to find.
Map and signpost preserve the memory
of wilderness characters, old and new:
Peralta of the famed Lost Dutchman
Mine; Ed Piper, who sought it until,
a legend himself, he died in 1962.

The death in the fangs of this young
diamondback rattler helps sustain
the desert's web of life. By eating rodents,
snakes check plant-eaters' numbers.

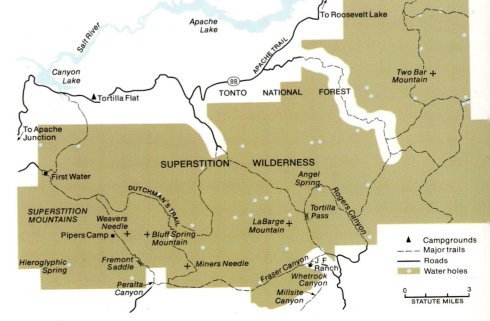

▲ Campgrounds
- - - Major trails
—— Roads
Water holes

0   3
STATUTE MILES

The beginning of the trip, from a cow camp at the edge of the northern boundary of the wilderness, was disarmingly easy as we followed a dry creek bed flanked by low-growing mesquite and scrub oak. Then big Bill Crader, our leader, veered his sorrel gelding up a trail that led through narrow, twisting defiles. As we brushed through clusters of spiny cactus, our route dipped sharply down into ravines. The arid ground and air seemed to suck the moisture from my body. We mounted to ridges on nearly invisible paths, our lunging horses scrambling for footholds in tiny crevices. These small mixed breeds could slide along rock slabs like skaters or thread a 12-inch ribbon of trail like mountain goats. And they did it without dislodging boulders upon the serpentine line of riders below.

We returned to our base camp just before dusk, knees weary from absorbing jolts. Our horses, unsaddled and corralled, rolled over and writhed in the dust to ease their itching backs. Each of us found what he hoped was a soft spot in the thickets for a sleeping bag. Then we gathered for a dinner of pork chops broiled over coals by Bill Crader's wife Rowean. Our camp lay just outside the wilderness. Drought had fouled the water holes at interior campsites which Crader normally used. You could still find clear springs and streams in the Superstitions, but the terrain around these oases was unsuited to a party as big as ours. So while we rode each day, the wranglers would transport duffle and gear to the next layover site at the wilderness border, set up camp, and await the trail riders.

After dinner the first night we sat around a campfire of pungent mesquite logs and began getting to know each other—and what was in store for us. I wondered how much truth there was in Bill Crader's words of greeting: "Outside of centipedes, scorpions, little water, and trigger-happy prospectors looking for the Lost Dutchman Mine and Jesuit treasure caves, you haven't a thing to worry about."

I trod warily through cactus to the promontory where veteran guide John Dahlmann stood, his long frame outlined against a backdrop of sky and mountain. We had all paused here at Tortilla Pass for lunch and rest, the horses tied to bushes and the brittle branches of scrub oaks. The land we looked upon was the heart of the wilderness, carved out of the southwestern corner of Tonto National Forest. The forest itself is a vast domain—nearly the size of Connecticut—encompassing cactus-studded desert, pine-covered mountains, cattle and sheep pastures, and a chain of lakes that lure water-skiers, fishermen, and picnickers. But no one would find a lush picnic spot in the terrain that John and I now scanned—especially in this

LOWELL GEORGIA

"The mine...is marked by the Weaver's Needle"

In the last message of a man seeking the Lost Dutchman Mine, in the sight of a compass—and in the spotlight of a rising sun—Weavers Needle appears, a landmark become legend. The paper quoting its name was found amid the bones of a man shot to death in 1931 near the 4,500-foot monolith. A volcanic core

LOWELL GEORGIA

visible 40 miles away, the rock dots many treasure maps, which use it or its pointing shadow as "X."

The Needle is named after Pauline Weaver, son of a pioneer and his Cherokee wife. Weaver did find gold — but not here. Geologists say nearby rock bears few minerals; ore around the Needle assays at about 25 cents per ton. But men keep trying. The "Danger" sign, marking a claim on the wilderness border near Superstition Mountain, warns off the curious.

Prospectors, forbidden mechanized equipment, must use methods "as compatible as possible" with preservation of the environment. Under the Wilderness Act, no new claims may be filed after 1983. But the Needle, once the site of many claims, will not be scarred again: It has been closed to mining.

Artist Ted De Grazia (right), who carries a rock hammer and a sketchbook into the desert, has found a little ore — and a lode of inspiration for his paintings of the Southwest.

Framed by a cave mouth, riders wind up a switchback trail to the top of Peralta Canyon. The realm of rock bristles with relics of its volcanic creation. Particles blasted from the earth formed a sheet of rock that cracked as it cooled. When erosion cut along the joints, columns remained to become the Pima Indians' "Frozen People."

To cholla cactus, dubbed the "untouchable" of the plant world, horsehide proves little tougher than a pincushion.

Barbed spines dig so deep that pliers are used to yank them.

A giant saguaro, limbs laid low by bacterial rot, towers over a horseman. In rainy season the disease spreads swiftly from a wound, can kill a plant in a week. At other times the saguaro heals itself. When the Gila woodpecker digs a nest hole in the pulpy flesh, scar tissue grows, forming a permanent cavity that shelters the builder—or tenants such as elf owls and mice.

To human desert dwellers saguaros supplied fuel and "apples," eaten raw or stewed. Fermented, the fruit makes an intoxicating drink. Today, along Superstitions trails, mindless visitors hack and gouge these titans—perhaps pursuing the hoary fantasy that sighting through a hole in a cactus will lead them to treasure.

harsh year, without the late summer rains and balmy springtime that can mantle the desert in green and put flowing streams in nearly every canyon bottom.

The light reflecting off the upper Sonoran Desert was painfully brilliant. In the distance loomed wrinkled mountains and massive rocks. More than 30 million years ago the land was relatively flat. Then a volcanic spasm left a gigantic caldera. Around it explosions spewed a layer of ash and broken rock 2,000 feet thick. In torrid clouds the layer spread for miles around, covering the area with volcanic glass that cooled to form great sheets called welded tuff. Later the land rumbled again, and magma from deep within the earth filled the caldera and created a dome —the mass that would become 5,057-foot Superstition Mountain, the highest point in the range. The violence continued intermittently. After a final outburst came 15 million years of relative quiet, when water carried off loose ash and bedded it down, and boulders crumbled into rocks and sand and soil.

This is the saga read from the rocks by geologists. The Indians living in this land read a tale of a great flood that left in the mountains a high-water mark, a white layer of rock. When Spanish conquistadors saw the soapy seam and heard the Indian myth, they named the region *Sierra de la Espuma*—the Mountains of Foam. And from the tales and myths, from an Indian belief that a Thunder God dwelt here, from yarns told at campfires on black nights—and from fears of what the mountains held —came their modern name, the Superstitions.

Looking at the maze of boulder-strewn canyons below me, I tried in vain to fathom this haunted, contorted land. "This country doesn't make any sense to me," I said to John. "We've been out here three days now, and I still can't see a pattern to it."

The chill breeze that whipped through the pass flapped the wings of John Dahlmann's chaps and whisked away the smoke from his cigarette. "You're dead right about that," he said. "Most of those ravines lead nowhere. They turn and twist into each other and usually end up in box canyons. That's why so many people get in here and can't find their way out." John shook his head. "I've ridden backcountry from Alaska to Mexico, and I'm here to tell you this is one of the meanest and driest of them all. But there's something about these mountains that pulls like a magnet on people. They keep coming back, and I'm no exception."

Along Millsite Canyon, which borders the wilderness preserve, we came upon a cluster of mine shafts. The timbers that had braced their entrances had crumbled under the weight of rock and earth. The tailings of refuse rock outside the shafts were meager, a sure sign of quickly abandoned searches.

"They were hardly worth going to," Bill Crader said in his Texas drawl. "The Superstitions are full of holes like that. I don't like to take the pleasure out of things, but I've yet to see any gold that came from the Superstitions."

Bill Crader doesn't believe the Lost Dutchman exists—not here, at any rate. But who can sit around a campfire in the Superstitions and not rekindle the legend of the Dutchman? The tale, as convoluted as the land that produced it, begins in the 1860's with the arrival in Arizona of Jacob Waltz, or Walzer, a German-born prospector. The Dutchman—anyone German, or *Deutsch*, was "Dutch"— supposedly had befriended a descendant of Don Miguel Peralta, whose domain included the Mountains of Foam when Spain ruled the Southwest. Peralta, said an older legend, had found a fabulous gold mine. But, the story goes, mining ended after Apaches ambushed a gold-laden mule train bound for Sonora.

The Peralta descendant—wounded in a gambling fray and nursed to health by Waltz, according to one account—showed his appreciation by taking the Dutchman

to the mine. Waltz was said to emerge periodically from the mountains leading a burro loaded with gold-bearing quartz. Though he settled in Phoenix and became a chicken farmer, he reportedly disappeared into the Superstitions now and then to replenish his hoard. And, it was said, men who followed him never came back.

When Waltz died in Phoenix in 1891, he left as a legacy only a legend. But it was real enough to send countless men into the mountains in search of what they called the Lost Dutchman Mine. More than 30 of them have died on their quest—some by suicide, some by accident or exposure, and some by murder.

In Apache Junction, the starting point for most gold hunters (and the rendezvous for our trek), you can inevitably find someone with a treasure map. A little man with suspicious, darting eyes showed me what he claimed was a copy of the original map leading to treasures hidden by the Jesuits, who left Spanish territory in 1767. The map was crisscrossed with trails and bore the drawing of a Jesuit in a peaked hat pointing a crucifix to the treasure caches. "I've found them caves, and there's seven hundred million dollars in gold chalices and jewels in 'em!" he said. Looking more furtive, he added, "But I can't move until I get legal protection." When I asked him where the caves were, he wrenched the map away.

On the trail we heard pathetic stories of obsessed prospectors and desert loners who had followed their maps and dreams. One man, I was told, searched for more than 50 years, leaving the mountains only to earn enough money to buy provisions and head back. Another said he lived on rattlesnakes and lizards. At a rubble-covered grave near Rogers Canyon, John Dahlmann told us the man buried there had run naked through the night shooting at stars. And Bill Crader told of another man crushed by the cave-in of a mine after 18 years of vain searching.

Even experienced, cautious guides and trail-trained horses cannot protect you from all the hazards of the Superstitions. One day, while traversing a hillside of loose shale in Whetrock Canyon, my horse lost her footing and dropped out from under me. Having been through that kind of experience from boyhood, I vaulted out of the saddle on the uphill side. The mare began to roll, but I had kept

Climbing out of the past, Rowean Crader, wife of the trail riders' guide, emerges from a cave that shelters Rogers Canyon cliff dwellings. Here, about A.D. 1300, lived Salado Indians, ancestors of today's Pueblos, who in a harsh land found much: mesquite beans and saguaro fruit, clay for pots, yucca for sandals. Pima Indians, more recent residents of the region, personified the tall stone columns below as people who survived a great flood sent by a wrathful supreme force.

Drought bares the rumpled bed of Hieroglyphic Spring, named for its riddles in rock. Such petroglyphs are often found near springs. This one, says archeologist Emil W. Haury, could represent the sun. But, he adds, "Who knows what was in the mind of the maker?" In digs at nearby Snaketown, Dr. Haury's Arizona State Museum team unearthed a village of the predecessors of the Salados, the Hohokam. Sharp sticks their tools, they dug miles of canals to irrigate fields of corn, beans, and squash. Their culture lasted from several centuries before Christ to A.D. 1400-1500.

her reins and dug my boot heels into the shale to keep her from going all the way down. When I got her to her feet, she was quivering like a leaf.

Photographer Lowell Georgia fared worse. His saddle's latigo, a long strap that tightens the cinch, snapped and he was hurled against a boulder. He mounted again when the strap was fixed and rode until his side began to swell. Later he discovered he had torn the muscles of his hip.

"At least we didn't have to ride out for a helicopter to haul you away," Bill Crader heartily told Lowell. Like many other volunteer searchers, Bill has helped carry the living and the dead out of the wilderness. To avoid the need for such services, new-comers venturing into the heart of the Superstitions must pay special heed to the rules of safety: Leave word with someone about your plans. Stick close to major trails. Carry more water than you think you'll need. Pocket a snakebit kit. And bring tweez-ers—and pliers—for pulling out cactus spines.

I soon learned that just about everything that grows in the Superstitions, even a lily, has a spine or a hook. My first lesson came early in the trip when I made the mistake of walking through some high bushes. I was well into the thicket before I realized that the gray stems were covered with tiny, curved prickles that hooked into my flesh. At the price of scratched arms I had discovered an unfriendly shrub called catclaw.

From then on I was cautiously fascinated by every bush and cactus along the trail: ocotillo, its tentacles tipped by red flags of flower; sotol, looking like a miniature palm tree, whose prickly leaves gave Indians hemp for sandals and clothing; Spanish bayonet, its candlestick stalks centered in a bed of spiny leaves; prickly pear with its paddle-shaped stem joints; giant saguaros towering 30 feet; barrel cactus wrapped

in a mail of spines. And cholla, with its chained joints, one of which attached itself to my leg with barbed points that were a long time working themselves out.

The plant that affected me the most was the stately agave, or century plant. Its dead leaves, resembling starfish arms, littered the slopes. Some agaves spend a lifetime producing a single blooming stalk—and then die. But a solitary cluster of flowers in the Superstitions is infinitely more precious than a garden in a verdant land.

When our trek was nearing its end, we followed a rough trail to 3,900-foot Bluff Spring Mountain. Here have been found relics of crude smelters and *arrastras*, primitive mills in which ore was pulverized between slabs of stone. The Peralta miners and perhaps the Dutchman himself may have worked them. From here he could have seen, as we did, the pinnacle landmarks of Miners Needle and Weavers Needle. Our trail followed the edge of a canyon whose floor lay about 1,000 feet below, nearly straight down. Indian cliff dwellings pitted the rock faces on the opposite wall. In Rogers Canyon we had explored similar honeycombs whose ceilings were blackened by the soot of countless fires. Here lived the Salado Indians, who had disappeared from the Superstitions by the 15th century.

Pima Indians, who dwell nearby, no longer harvest crops in the Superstitions, but we found the Frozen People of Pima legend still standing on the heights above Peralta Canyon. The supreme power, angered at the ways of earthlings, had sent a great flood to punish them. Those who climbed above the waters were turned to stone. The formations of weather-sculptured tuff truly looked like grotesque giants, some hunched, brooding and frowning, others convulsed in agony. They evoked in me a chill that the heat of the desert could not dispel. But I looked back one last time as we passed out of the canyon. As long as the Frozen People stand, I knew, these mountains will be possessed, in some mute, disturbing way, by superstition.

129

Bristling victors of another day's duel in the sun, jumping chollas stand watch as darkness brings respite to a scorched wilderness. In painful encounters desert travelers swore the prickly joints leaped from the plant— hence the name. Actually, the joints just detach easily. Though the spines fend off browsers, pack rats eat cholla joints and pack them away to fortify gigantic nest mounds.

In the gold of a sunset or in the ruby jewel of a hedgehog cactus lies the treasure of the Superstitions. Riches? So far, only the fool's gold of dreams, and nuggets of wisdom such as this: "The mines men find are never so rich as those they lost."

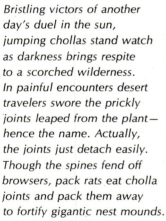

LOWELL GEORGIA

130

The Salmon, legendary "River of No Return," cuts a burnished trail through the brooding gorges of Idaho's Bitterroot Mountains.

RAMPARTS OF THE ROCKIES

Frank Craighead, Jr.

Fifteen miles from the nearest highway my horse splashed through a small stream, treading sharply angled rocks that spoke of a newly cutting brook, young in geological terms. I dismounted to examine Two Ocean Creek where it tumbles along the very spine of the Rocky Mountains—the Continental Divide. Just downstream within the shade of large spruces the creek divides. One fork flows west, becoming Pacific Creek, the other east as headwaters of Atlantic Creek.

Golden willow leaves tumbling down Atlantic Creek travel no farther than Yellowstone Lake, but in increased volume the waters exit through the deep and colorful canyon of the Yellowstone River, eventually to join the Missouri and Mississippi.

Pacific Creek races to rendezvous with the swift-flowing Snake River for the journey across Idaho, through Hells Canyon, into the Columbia, and thence to the Pacific.

At this unique spot in the Teton Wilderness, fur trapper Osborne Russell in 1835 jotted the first accurate description of Two Ocean Pass, noting in his journal that here "a trout of twelve inches . . . may cross the mountains in safety." As a long-time resident of Wyoming I have cast many a fly to its native cutthroat trout on both sides of the Rockies—superb! Dipping my cup, I thanked Two Ocean Creek not only for the drink of cold, clear water but also for the trout's route of passage.

Two Ocean Creek originates almost in the center of the high primeval country stretching from the Cabinet Mountains in northwest Montana to the San Juan Mountains in southwestern Colorado. Within the four-state area of Montana, Idaho, Wyoming, and Colorado lie 50 actual and proposed wilderness preserves, totaling some 8½ million acres. Coniferous forests are the hallmark of this vast region of the Rockies. Water is the single most valuable natural resource. The terrain is rugged, the scenery superlative. Here elk, moose, mule deer, mountain sheep, mountain goats, grizzly bears, black bears, and cougars still roam.

In the first half of the 19th century, the mountain empire which encompasses these wild remnants was penetrated and explored by trappers seeking beaver skins. Plews were in demand for making beaver hats, and the animals were so thick they got in each other's way, Lewis and Clark had reported. After that epic expedition of 1804 to 1806, men such as John Colter, Manuel Lisa, Major Andrew Henry, Wilson Price Hunt, John Hoback, John Frémont, Joe Meek, Hugh Glass, Jim Bridger, Jedediah Smith, William Sublette, and their trapping companions threaded the mountain passes and plumbed the recesses of steep-walled canyons. On foot or by horse they became familiar with every stream large enough to sustain beaver. In bullboats, in hewn dugouts, and on log rafts they braved the currents and rapids of the larger rivers. No big segment of the Rockies was unknown to them; remote indeed was the area their moccasins did not tread. Frequently battling Indians and competing with other trappers, these men lived a life that was rough, uncertain—and habit-forming.

In a few years the drama of the beaver trade mounted to a climax and then, like the populations of this fur-bearing rodent, abruptly declined. But the trappers were a breed so imbued with the spell of the wilderness and the elemental challenge in their way of life that few ever returned to a "civilized" existence.

Rather, civilization moved west on the heels of the mountain man; in fact, the homesteader was guided by him. Cities since have mushroomed in the fertile valleys of the Rockies. Rails, roads, and air lanes crisscross the area. Rivers have been dammed and many of them polluted. Cattle and sheep replaced the bison. Elk, mountain sheep, and grizzly bear have been eliminated from river bottoms and edges of the plains, and limited to habitats in the high mountains.

But in those remnants of a wild empire that stand relatively unmodified, we today can still find beauty and solitude; have a taste of living fully, intensely, and freely in the moment; sense the thrill of exploring the unknown; and have the inexpressible satisfaction of being part of an untamed environment.

As wildlife biologists, my brother John and I for years have been using the wilderness country of the Tetons, Yellowstone, and the central Rockies as an outdoor research laboratory as well as enjoying the matchless opportunities for recreation.

Teton Wilderness, in the heart of a five-million-acre expanse of mountain scenery, was the first part of the Rockies I became acquainted with. Astride the Divide, it is a region of snow-capped peaks, rugged canyons, cold lakes, and clear, fast streams. As in most Rocky Mountain wildernesses, winters are long and cold, snows deep, and spring an almost instantaneous happening.

The vast Yellowstone-Teton Wilderness complex is noted for its excellent trout fishing, its abundance of big game animals, and its variety of other wildlife. The combination of dense timber and open meadows of sagebrush and grass provides the habitat of what is probably the largest single congregation of grizzly bears left in the contiguous United States, an estimated 250 animals. The great silvertip was already being forced out of its natural domain at the time of the beaver trade; in modern times extermination became a definite threat. Trying to find methods to stabilize the dwindling population, we conducted extensive studies of the Yellowstone animals, monitoring the den life and meanderings of scores of grizzlies.

Once in the northern reaches of Yellowstone, I was examining the remains of a large bull elk. I was probing the partly eaten carcass to determine whether it was a grizzly kill or had attracted the bear as carrion. Glancing toward the timber several hundred yards away, I saw a big grizzly loping toward me. Abandoning camera and tripod, I picked up my pack and slowly backed away. The grizzly advanced rapidly; occasionally he rose on his hind legs attempting to pick up a scent, then dropped down and plunged forward. The nearest tree was a quarter of a mile away and I had no chance of reaching it, so I continued to back slowly, the grizzly closing the distance. I had retreated less than a hundred yards when he reached the carcass. Certain that his objective was to defend his food, I expected him to continue the apparent charge. But he caught my scent. Abruptly he wheeled and raced back over his tracks, running as only a grizzly can when he goes all out. Thankful for the animal's natural inclination to avoid man, I retrieved my camera and gave up my interest in his stinking food cache.

One of the largest concentrations of elk in the nation is found in the Teton-Yellowstone area. The southern, or Jackson Hole herd, in summer roams the high country of the Teton Wilderness and southern portions of Yellowstone National Park. In late October and early November as winter snows begin to accumulate, elk bands migrate down through the wilderness studded with hunting camps, bound for winter haven on the National Elk Refuge near Jackson, Wyoming. Hunters from all parts of the country converge on Jackson Hole each fall to collect trophies of elk, as well as deer, moose, mountain sheep, or bear.

Many residents also hunt, some largely as an excuse to tramp and camp in the out-of-doors, others to get meat. For some, man's age-old urge to provide from nature lives on in the present, though the necessity may no longer exist.

I have a favorite spot in the Teton Wilderness where I have hunted elk and mule deer year after year and where I have taken my children and watched them learn to hunt. We usually backpack up to our base camp on the afternoon before hunting season opens. Invariably on our arrival in early evening, we are greeted by a small group of mule deer: fawns, does, and a few bucks. The little meadow where we camp has grown up in coarse coneflower, probably due to previous overgrazing by game animals, and in some spots to excessive trampling. A small mineral stream from which we get our drinking water trickles out of the hillside, runs less than a hundred yards, and disappears in a seep or spring. Obviously it is the mineral water, not the unpalatable coneflower, that attracts the deer.

My delight at being welcomed each year by these gentle creatures of the forest has influenced my hunting habits. I have not shot a mule deer in this special area, although the opportunities have been legion. Here we prefer to hunt elk, usually in the early morning while they are feeding in the open parks.

Resting at camp, we sometimes sit motionless and lure the overfriendly gray jays to chunks of butter or bacon held in our hands. Often at night lying under the stars I listen enthralled to a coyote orchestra—a few howling animals sounding like fifty. Once they came so close we thought they might enter our camp. No sooner had their barks and yips died away than we heard the distant hoot of a great horned owl. We answered the hoots, and eventually our silent-flying caller landed on the spire of an Engelmann spruce towering up at the foot of our sleeping bags. We felt a kinship with all wild things. Another night, light snow flurries dissolved in fog as the moon rose. Soon all about us was an eerie glow of filtered moonlight and drifting fog. The stillness of night was broken by the shrill bugling of a bull elk. We slept with high expectations for the morning hunt.

A grove of mixed timber protects our tents from wind and the direct assault of snow and rain. But only the fir and spruce are alive; all the lodgepole pines are now dead from attacks of the Rocky Mountain pine bark beetle. Within a year or two the brown needles will drop. The trees will no longer furnish resinous cambium for the spring diet of grizzly and black bears or seeds for the red squirrel but will harbor insect food for flickers and other woodpeckers. My sense of wonder grows at the intricacies of nature.

Born on the crest of a continent, unique Two Ocean Creek in Wyoming's Teton Wilderness spills east and west. Rising from a nameless little lake, the creek wanders southward along the Great Divide for some three miles, then splits and filters through a marsh filled with noisy frogs. Pacific Creek, here shown branching to the right, feeds the Snake River watershed; Atlantic Creek joins the Missouri-Mississippi drainage, ultimately to mingle with its namesake ocean via the Gulf of Mexico.
DRAWING BY GEORGE FOUNDS

The effects of beetle devastation, here as in other infested wildernesses, raises a question: Should man attempt control where the timber is not harvested, or should he allow nature to take its course? The chemical ethylene dibromide, mixed with diesel oil and sprayed on infested trees, will kill beetles beneath the bark, but the treatment may not halt the outbreak. After attempted control of pine bark beetles in the Teton area, Forest Service researchers concluded that the eventual survival of lodgepole pines will be about the same whether or not the infested stand is treated. Further, it is evident that insect control measures are a manipulation of wilderness conditions by the managing agencies. The result, even when control is effective, is often the temporary maintenance of a preferred stage of plant succession or the encouragement of changes that would not naturally occur.

A basic characteristic of wild places and of life itself is change. The fundamental force behind all change is, of course, solar energy. Radiant energy trapped by the chlorophyll of the lowly lichen on the mountain peak, as well as by needles of the towering fir or spruce, is converted into the chemical energy of food molecules, which, in turn, is utilized by animals and other plants.

Fire, wind, flood, disease, and other more subtle forces affect the natural succession of plants in an ecosystem. The sequence of ecological change, however, proceeds in an orderly and predictable manner. On rocky peaks and in glacier-scoured basins, the first plants to establish themselves are foliose and crustose lichens. Existing on elements from the air, minerals from rock, and energy from the sun, lichens decorate the surfaces of solid stone with their reds, yellows, oranges, greens, and other hues. In time, the action of plant excretions on the host rock produces a meager soil in which mosses can grow. Mosses, in turn, accumulate humus that provides seedbeds for grasses, sedges, and eventually shrubs and trees. Some plant types are quite transient, others more stable. Each so alters the environment through its life activities that growth conditions become less favorable for it and more favorable for succeeding plant forms. Thus a wilderness of rock and lichens evolves step by step toward a climax forest, one in which young trees can grow in the shade of parent trees. In the Rocky Mountains the climax forest, the most advanced vegetation that can grow in the existing climate, is composed (Continued on page 145)

Portfolio Notes

OPPOSITE: *Stunted trees struggling for a toehold hug the shattered gables of the Bitterroot Mountains. The range forms the backbone of the largest national forest Wilderness—the Selway-Bitterroot—sprawled across more than a million acres of Idaho and Montana. This granite outcrop looms near 10,157-foot Trapper Peak in Montana, one of the highest summits in the range.*
FARRELL GREHAN

PAGES 138-139: *Prairie Reef rises a sheer thousand feet above the forested floor of Bob Marshall Wilderness in Montana. Some 7 miles west of this layered stone reef looms another: the Chinese Wall, stretching 12 miles along the Continental Divide. In their Cambrian limestones are imbedded fossils of sea creatures half a billion or more years old.*
FARRELL GREHAN, PHOTO RESEARCHERS

PAGE 140-141: *Sunrise stalks a quartet of elk in Yellowstone's Hayden Valley,*
casting their long shadows from a ridgetop strewn with sage. Most of the park's elk seek cool, high pastures in summer; a few stay behind to forage on bottomland grasses, rewarding wildlife watchers on the Grand Loop drive. The valley, along with many of the park's geysers and other thermal features, is proposed for wilderness preservation in ten tracts totalling nearly three times the size of Rhode Island.
SAM ABELL

PAGE 144: *Lonely hunter of the highlands, a mountain lion pauses for streamside refreshment in the Idaho Primitive Area. Called cougars, catamounts, pumas, or panthers, these big cats haunt the crags and canyons of some of the continent's remotest wilds. Except in mating season, mountain lions lead solitary lives. Of an estimated 4,000 to 6,500 that still prowl the West, about 200 live in this region of thrusting peaks and unspoiled forests.*
MAURICE HORNOCKER

Rockies denizens: Cow moose and her calf share a moment of serenity at the sun-spangled edge of Rainey Lake near Yellowstone's north boundary.

Shrilling defiance, a female golden eagle soars past her eyrie near Livingston, Montana. She protests the invasion of her domain by naturalists who have come to study her ways.

Bighorn sheep cock a wary eye on the stony slopes of the Salmon. Hunters once thought the agile bighorn escaped foes by plunging from cliffs—and landing safely on its horns.

An audacious coyote saunters past a Yellowstone grizzly absorbed in burying a bull elk carcass to dine on later.

of such shade-tolerant species as Engelmann spruce, alpine fir, white fir, and western hemlock. Each plant type has distinctive birds and animals that are associated with it, and as the habitat changes, the wildlife changes. When an indigenous animal species is unable to adapt to slow environmental changes or sudden ones, such as fire, it declines in number or is replaced by species more adaptable to new conditions. The balance of nature is not a static condition but a dynamic progression or regression of plant and animal populations.

The spectacular Teton peaks, pilot knobs that guided early explorers and mountain men, rise above glaciated canyons and cirques, alpine meadows, forests, and blue-green lakes of the Teton Range. These jagged mountains, formed by a fault block of Precambrian igneous and metamorphic rocks, are the youngest of the Rocky Mountain chain, some nine million years old. The high rocky ridges do not harbor mountain goats, though goats inhabit the Idaho Primitive Area only 200 miles to the west. Nevertheless, the portion of Grand Teton National Park proposed for wilderness designation supports a variety of wildlife that can often be approached closely enough to photograph. Elk migrate in summer to canyons in the northern area. Here pine martens prey on red squirrels, and a wandering grizzly or wolverine may leave a track in mud or snow.

On a recent trip to this uncrowded section of the Teton park, I canoed across the upper waters of Jackson Lake, after waiting impatiently for one of numerous August storms to pass. Angling across so that I would hit the waves squarely, I approached the shore just upstream from the mouth of Berry Creek. Here I spotted two moose on shore and one in the water, with the mountains silhouetted in evening light. I dropped my paddle and picked up the camera. Just then a big beaver astern of the canoe smacked his tail on the water and dived in alarm. The moose retreated and I followed, penetrating the shoreline through a wide beaver channel leading to a stick beaver lodge. Here I beached the canoe, cached some gear, and put on my backpack. The moose having vanished, I watched a mother otter and two young ones frolic. They swam one behind the other, surfacing and diving in a fluid motion which made them appear as one large sinuous reptile moving through the water. I kept expecting the mother to surface with fish in her mouth, but apparently there were no trout for either man or otter in this alluring channel.

For an hour or so I explored the shoreline, slogging through sedge, pushing through willows, detouring around beaver channels. Then I headed up Berry Creek. With darkness approaching, I stopped and caught two cutthroat trout for my supper, hooking the first one on my second cast. While these and a kettle of soup cooked, I spread my sleeping bag not far from the bank and rigged a tarp so that I could pull it over me if a storm rolled in. One more precaution: Though bears were not common, I had seen grizzly signs in other years, so I checked out the lower branches of a nearby cottonwood to make sure I could climb it if I felt the need. Then, with rushing water as my dinner music, I ate and turned in, under a blanket of stars.

After a sunrise breakfast, I headed up the Berry Creek Trail. In the early light which sometimes plays tricks with vision and perspective, I saw a small band of elk, one of which—a cow—was wearing a white collar. No trick this time. It was an animal banded by the Wyoming Fish and Game Commission in its efforts to record the feeding and migration routes of various elk bands, data helpful in game management. Recently my colleagues and I, seeking new and more effective research methods, have experimented with the tracking by satellite of animals equipped with radio transmitter collars—the first such application of Space Age technology. Though I do

THE ROCKIES

Numbered sites are established Wilderness Areas. Most lie in national forests, only one in a national monument. Unnumbered entries are units officially considered for wilderness. Bureau of Land Management (BLM) Primitive Areas are regulated in much the same way as Forest Service Primitive Areas and lands in the Wilderness System. A figure after the name is wilderness acreage only, not total acreage of the primitive area, national park, or wildlife refuge. Page reference offers fuller description; page 337 lists contacts for obtaining details on particular areas.

MONTANA

Medicine Lake NWR. Stopover and breeding ground for migratory waterfowl and shorebirds.

Bowdoin NWR. Nesting and feeding area for ducks, pelicans, geese; upland game.

Charles M. Russell NW Range. Grassy river breaks fringed with conifers along the Missouri. 263 bird species.

UL Bend NWR. Flats broken by draws and ridges. Geese, swans, migratory birds. Antelope, elk, mule deer.

Glacier NP. Mountain majesties; 1,000 miles of trails. Glaciers, mountain goats, grizzlies. Some areas hit by outside pollution.

1 Cabinet Mountains W. 94,272. Snow-clad peaks, glacial lakes, waterfalls. Large game. One-day hike into interior. Huckleberries abound in late summer.

National Bison Range. In Flathead Valley. Grasslands, hills, timber. Buffalo, elk, deer, antelope.

Mission Mountains PA. 73,207. Glaciers, lakes. Bears. A few horse trails, but pack in feed.

2 Bob Marshall W. 950,000. See pages 149 and 157.

3 Scapegoat W. 240,000. Grizzlies, wolverines. Scapegoat Mountain, 9,185 feet. Vegetation sparse.

4 Gates of the Mountains W. 28,562. Trails wend narrow limestone gorges. No fishing, but many colorful flowers.

Bear Trap Canyon PA (BLM). 2,761. Nine-mile gorge rises 1,500 feet above Madison River. Superb trout fishing. White-water boating in Thundering Chutes.

Spanish Peaks PA. 65,026. Rugged mountain country. Lakes, meadows, miles of trails. Fine trout fishing.

Beartooth PA. Granite Peak, Montana's highest at 12,799 feet, challenges climbers. Plateaus, deep canyons.

Absaroka PA. Forested high mountain country with alpine meadows. Excellent fishing.

Red Rock Lakes NWR. Breeding site for rare trumpeter swan. Marshes, timbered slopes, terraced cliffs. 185 bird species.

Humbug Spires PA (BLM). 7,041. Rolling hills studded with 600-ft.-tall white granite spires. Bear, deer, moose, bighorn sheep.

5 Anaconda-Pintlar W. 157,803. Rugged mountains; alpine meadows, larch trees. Mountain goats. Excellent fishing.

IDAHO

6 Selway-Bitterroot W. 1,240,618. Partly in Montana. Wild mountain country includes 45 miles of the Selway River; many trails.

Salmon River Breaks PA. Wild river canyon. Mountain sheep, bears, elk. Settlers' cabin ruins. White-water boating; hiking.

Idaho PA. See pages 149 and 150.

Deer Flat NWR. 734. Islands in the Snake River. 162 species of birds. Hunt for ducks, quail, pheasant. Good fishing.

7 Sawtooth W. 216,383. Jagged granite pinnacles; 42 peaks over 9,000 feet high. Mecca for backpackers and climbers. More than 200 alpine lakes; many gorges. Additional acreage under study in adjacent Sawtooth National Recreation Area.

8 Craters of the Moon NM W. 43,243. Stark lava landscape. Ice caves, natural bridges, lava tubes. Trail to Great Owl Cave.

WYOMING

Yellowstone NP. 2,016,181. See pages 134 and 148.

9 North Absaroka W. 351,104. Steep canyons, glaciers, petrified trees, natural bridge. Trail from Buffalo Bill Cody's old lodge to Sunlight Basin.

Cloud Peak PA. 137,000. Named for 13,165-ft. mountain that dominates area. Vertical walls rise 5,000 feet. Anglers can dip into more than 250 lakes and 49 miles of streams.

10 Washakie W. 691,130. Deep canyons, broad ridges above timberline, weird volcanic formations. Petrified forest. Du Noir addition proposed.

11 Teton W. 563,500. See page 133.

Grand Teton NP. 115,807. See pages 145 and 148.

National Elk Refuge. Meadows, marshes, uplands lie in the Tetons' shadow.

Glacier PA. 182,510. Rugged mountain country on east slopes of Wind River Range; granite cliffs scoured by living glaciers. For hardy outdoorsmen.

12 Bridger W. 383,300. Rugged, glaciated west slope of Wind River Range. High trails usually passable by mid-July. Many trails.

Popo Agie PA. See page 163.

COLORADO

13 Mount Zirkel W. 72,472. 12,180-ft. namesake peak in Park Range. Many lakes; good fishing. Large meadows.

14 Rawah W. 27,664. Name means "wilderness" in the Ute tongue. Some areas very rugged. Fish-filled lakes.

Rocky Mountain NP. Varied terrain to 14,200 feet. Alpine tundra; stands of pine and spruce. Elk, beaver, golden eagle.

Indian Peaks. Spectacular high country along Continental Divide. Deer, elk, bear, bobcat, cougar. 90 miles of trails.

Flat Tops PA. 142,230. Grassy lava plateau broken by islands of timber. Grazing ground for deer and elk. Tranquil lakes, rushing streams.

Gore Range-Eagles Nest PA. 87,950. Seventeen peaks over 13,000 feet. Permanent snowfields. Virgin forests.

15 Maroon Bells-Snowmass W. 71,329. See page 180.

Colorado NM. 7,700. Plunging canyons expose geological formations. Spires and domes carved by erosion. Bison herd.

16 West Elk W. 61,412. Stream-slashed canyons. Unusual geological formations such as "The Castles" thrust sheer walls hundreds of feet high.

Black Canyon of the Gunnison NM. 8,780. One of the world's great wild canyons. Monolithic walls rise 2,000 feet above the river.

Uncompahgre PA. Jagged 14,000-ft. peaks; lush mountain meadows, tundra, lakes, waterfalls, glaciated basins.

Wilson Mountains PA. 27,347. 14,000-ft. peaks challenge climbers, Navajo Lake draws backpackers. Game abounds.

San Juan PA. Ragged peaks of the Needle Mountains and the Grenadiers. Forest Service proposes to combine with Upper Rio Grande PA to form the Weminuche Wilderness.

Upper Rio Grande PA. Streams, forests, open parks on slopes of Continental Divide.

17 La Garita W. 48,486. "The Overlook," with 14,000-ft. San Luis and Stewart peaks, lies across the Continental Divide. Accessible July-September.

Great Sand Dunes NM. 32,930. San Luis Valley dunes rise nearly 700 feet at foot of Sangre de Cristo Mountains.

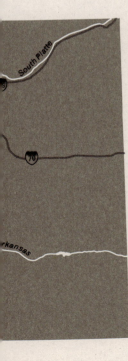

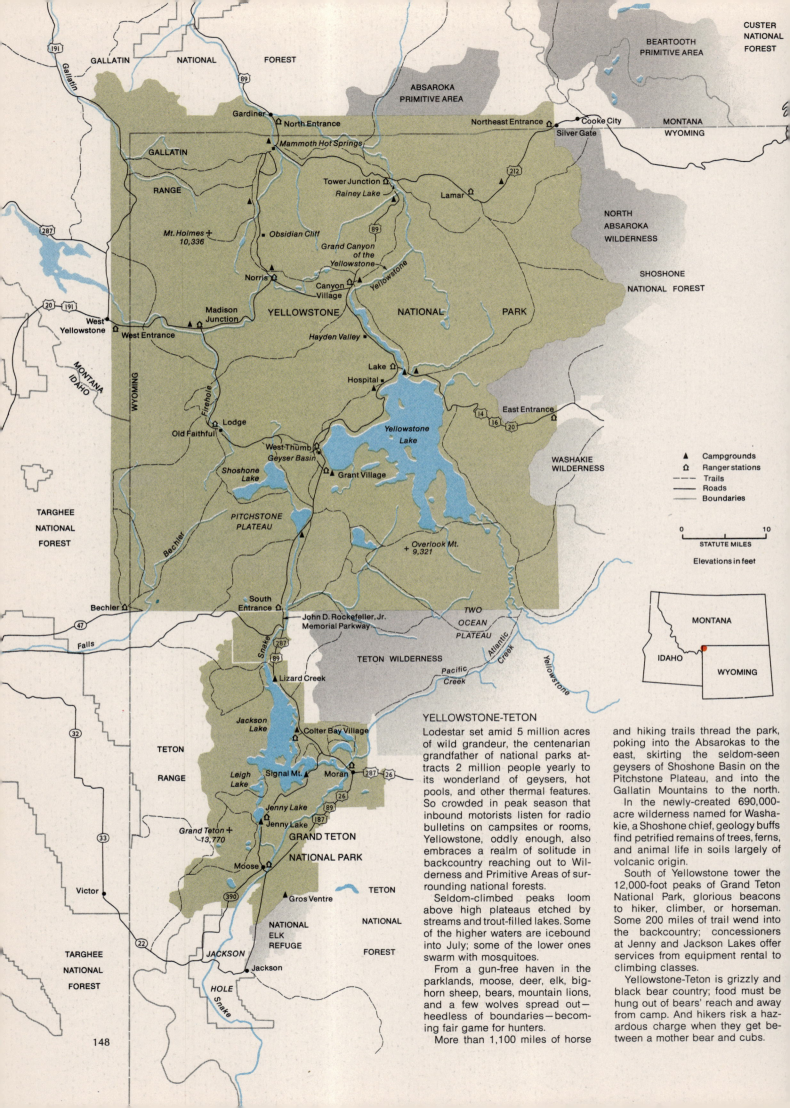

GALLATIN NATIONAL FOREST

191

CUSTER NATIONAL FOREST

BEARTOOTH PRIMITIVE AREA

89

Gardiner
⌂ North Entrance

▲ Mammoth Hot Springs

ABSAROKA PRIMITIVE AREA

Northeast Entrance ⌂ ● Cooke City
Silver Gate

MONTANA
WYOMING

GALLATIN

RANGE

287

Tower Junction ⌂
Rainey Lake
Lamar ⌂

212

NORTH ABSAROKA WILDERNESS

Mt. Holmes +
10,336

■ Obsidian Cliff

89

Grand Canyon of the Yellowstone

Yellowstone

SHOSHONE NATIONAL FOREST

20 191

West Yellowstone
⌂ West Entrance

Norris ⌂

Canyon Village ⌂

YELLOWSTONE   NATIONAL   PARK

MONTANA
IDAHO

WYOMING

Madison Junction ▲⌂

Firehole

Hayden Valley

Lake ⌂ ▲
Hospital

14
16 East Entrance ⌂
20

▲ Campgrounds
⌂ Ranger stations
--- Trails
— Roads
— Boundaries

Old Faithful ⌂ Lodge

West Thumb ⌂
Geyser Basin

Yellowstone Lake

WASHAKIE WILDERNESS

Shoshone Lake

▲ Grant Village

TARGHEE NATIONAL FOREST

PITCHSTONE PLATEAU

▲

Overlook Mt.
+ 9,321

0   10
STATUTE MILES

Elevations in feet

Bechler

Bechler ⌂

South Entrance ⌂

John D. Rockefeller, Jr.
Memorial Parkway

TWO OCEAN PLATEAU

MONTANA

47

Falls

287
89

Snake

TETON WILDERNESS

Pacific Creek

Atlantic Creek

Yellowstone

IDAHO

WYOMING

32

▲ Lizard Creek

Jackson Lake

TETON

RANGE

▲⌂ Colter Bay Village

Signal Mt. ▲

Moran ⌂
287 26

Leigh Lake

Jenny Lake ⌂
26
89
▲ Jenny Lake 187

33

Grand Teton +
13,770

GRAND TETON

NATIONAL PARK

TETON

NATIONAL

Victor

390

Moose ▲⌂

▲ Gros Ventre

NATIONAL ELK REFUGE

FOREST

22

JACKSON

● Jackson

TARGHEE NATIONAL FOREST

HOLE

Snake

MONTANA

IDAHO

WYOMING

YELLOWSTONE-TETON

Lodestar set amid 5 million acres of wild grandeur, the centenarian grandfather of national parks attracts 2 million people yearly to its wonderland of geysers, hot pools, and other thermal features. So crowded in peak season that inbound motorists listen for radio bulletins on campsites or rooms, Yellowstone, oddly enough, also embraces a realm of solitude in backcountry reaching out to Wilderness and Primitive Areas of surrounding national forests.

Seldom-climbed peaks loom above high plateaus etched by streams and trout-filled lakes. Some of the higher waters are icebound into July; some of the lower ones swarm with mosquitoes.

From a gun-free haven in the parklands, moose, deer, elk, bighorn sheep, bears, mountain lions, and a few wolves spread out—heedless of boundaries—becoming fair game for hunters.

More than 1,100 miles of horse and hiking trails thread the park, poking into the Absarokas to the east, skirting the seldom-seen geysers of Shoshone Basin on the Pitchstone Plateau, and into the Gallatin Mountains to the north.

In the newly-created 690,000-acre wilderness named for Washakie, a Shoshone chief, geology buffs find petrified remains of trees, ferns, and animal life in soils largely of volcanic origin.

South of Yellowstone tower the 12,000-foot peaks of Grand Teton National Park, glorious beacons to hiker, climber, or horseman. Some 200 miles of trail wend into the backcountry; concessioners at Jenny and Jackson Lakes offer services from equipment rental to climbing classes.

Yellowstone-Teton is grizzly and black bear country; food must be hung out of bears' reach and away from camp. And hikers risk a hazardous charge when they get between a mother bear and cubs.

IDAHO PRIMITIVE AREA

High, wild, and remote—the Idaho Primitive Area sprawls across 1¼ million acres of four national forests. Its rugged, 10,000-foot battlements rise from canyons, meadows, and forests dark with pine and fir.

On its northern edge the Salmon River gnaws at a mile-deep chasm, part of a 180-mile gorge deeper than the Grand Canyon.

Beyond lies the Salmon River Breaks Primitive Area, an even wilder realm that, with the Idaho area, is sought as wilderness.

The Salmon and its Middle Fork form a 230-mile, thrill-filled white-water course. Called "River of No Return" by pioneers who recycled or sold their boats downstream after the one-way haul, the main Salmon today is "returnable," its currents conquerable by powerful —and noisy—engines.

But on the Middle Fork, a protected wild river, motors are not allowed—a ban that conservationists hope to extend to the Salmon. Some 30 commercial outfitters, plus private groups, run float trips down the Middle Fork, typically an 8-day, 110-mile excursion from Dagger Falls. Mountain goats and bighorn sheep brave canyon ledges—also good habitat for rattlesnakes. Antivenin serum and snakebite kits should accompany each river party.

Because 4,000 people run it from June through August, starting times and campsites are reserved in advance to avoid congestion.

Anglers, backpackers, and horsemen travel freely over some 2,000 miles of trails in the Idaho Primitive Area. Some fly in to remote airstrips; others hike or ride from trailheads at places like Big Creek, Dagger Falls, or Bighorn Crags.

BOB MARSHALL

Wilderness to Bob Marshall was "the song of the hermit thrush at twilight . . . and the melody of the wind in the trees." Both are heard in the Wilderness that bears his name—a 950,000-acre sweep of snowy peaks, jutting cliffs, and forested valleys spreading into two national forests. West of it lie the Mission Mountains, a proposed 73,207-acre wilderness of spectacular crags laced by old Indian trails. Turbulent streams tumble into lakes named Gray Wolf, Frigid, and Angels Bathing Pool. Though a few riding trails traverse the range's eastern walls, rough terrain and sparse forage favor use by backpacker and climber.

By contrast, Bob Marshall Wilderness is ideal for both foot and horse traveler. From May to October more than 5,000 thread the 700 miles of trails. Good horse feed is plentiful. Anglers cast for Dolly Varden and cutthroat trout. Hunting is allowed, except in the Sun River Game Preserve. Users wander where they will and tent wherever fancy chooses.

The new Scapegoat Wilderness, whose 240,000 acres include prime grizzly bear habitat, represents a triumph for citizens who fought for the tract for 22 years.

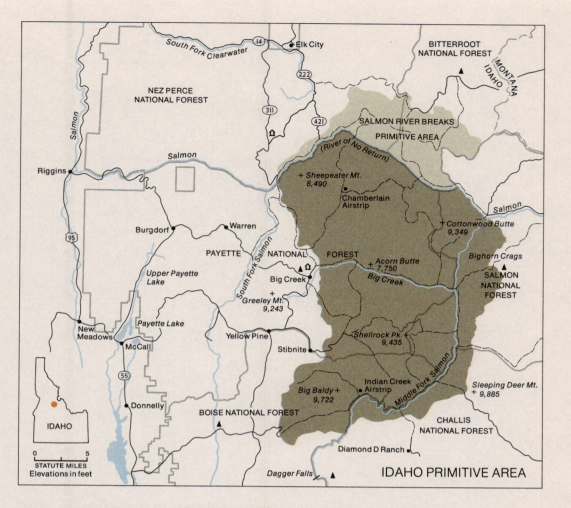

IDAHO PRIMITIVE AREA

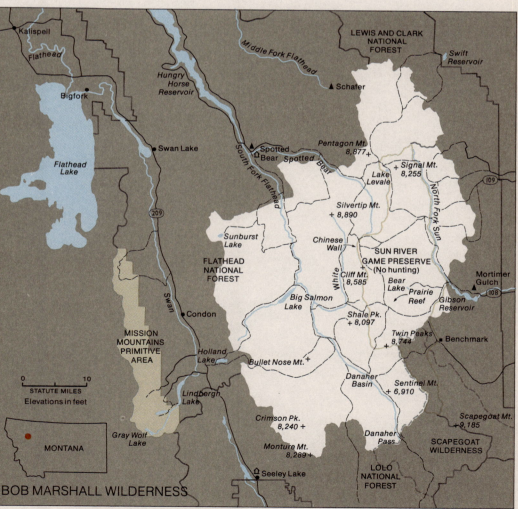

BOB MARSHALL WILDERNESS

not find the scenery of this area as spectacular as canyons to the south, I was intrigued by the steep-walled gorge through which Berry Creek runs for nearly half a mile. I stopped occasionally to fish and to watch families of ruffed grouse, eventually arriving at the willow meadows where Berry and Owl creeks converge. The meadows are cut with beaver dams, channels, and holes that the fisherman must avoid while moving along the bank, eyes riveted on a floating dry fly. Uncommonly lucky, I soon had caught all the trout I could use. While cooking them beside a patch of mountain gentians, I felt as much in my element as the moose bedded down in nearby willows or the red-tailed hawk on the topmost branch of a pine.

This was a short trip into wilderness but a good one, providing me the chance to hike, fish, and camp; to observe mountain plants, birds, and mammals; and to find solitude. For I did not meet another person.

W ild water, foaming, roaring, gnaws at the canyon walls as it tumbles 2,600 vertical feet in less than 100 miles. In rubber rafts and kayaks, my brother's family and mine had come to test our skills on the Middle Fork of the Salmon River, running "free of impoundments and generally inaccessible except by trail" through a mountain labyrinth that includes the Idaho Primitive Area.

August 26: Awoke at 6:45 a.m. Fortified ourselves for the trip with a breakfast of eggs, bacon, trout, and—for variety—tried the freshwater mussels used by early Indians. Found them tough. Picked wild cherries and hawberries before shoving off.

Grassy slopes, mountain mahogany, ponderosa pine, hawthorne, and wild rose bushes slipped by. We saw and heard many chukars, an introduced game bird that feeds on exotic cheatgrass and, in turn, provides food for golden eagles.

We hit Tappan Falls about 3:00 p.m. Because the water was low and because knifelike rocks edge the falls, we decided to portage some of our camera gear. While carrying a hefty load, Charlie almost stepped on a rattlesnake, the second of the day—Derek had encountered one earlier in the afternoon. Cautiously retracing their steps, the boys guided the first lightly laden raft toward the falls. On this rough section of river, so the tales go, many hunting parties rafting downriver had met disaster. When the rubber raft plunged over Tappan's six-foot drop, it folded in the middle. Both Derek and Charlie disappeared momentarily. They came up shouting with excitement, minus their hats, precariously balanced in a gyrating raft completely filled with the waters of the racing Middle Fork.

Farther downstream, with darkness settling, I headed my kayak into the middle of a rapids and, because of poor visibility, shot over a large rock submerged in the roughest part of the white water. The front end of the kayak nosed straight down into the swirling caldron. I was certain I was going to flip end for end, but the craft righted itself. Or perhaps I instinctively had made the right moves even though I could see little of the water ahead. Five days later we climbed a hill to Veil Falls to see some Indian paintings of mountain sheep and golden eagles. Dry weather had reduced the waterfall to a fine spray misting over the edge of the amphitheater. A nearby mineral lick attracts mountain sheep— in the old days probably the most numerous big game in the region— but none were present when we arrived. The Shoshone, or Sheep-eater, Indians lived in these canyons as recently

Tail thrusting powerfully, a cutthroat trout lunges toward a fly—and perhaps a sizzling end in a buttery skillet. Named for crimson slash marks below the jaw, these speckled beauties are native to high Western lakes and cold, swift streams; the species divides into several races and interbreeds with the rainbow trout. Although a 40-pounder has been landed, cutthroats may run under a pound in fast water. They readily strike flies as well as other lures and live bait, but are scarce in some places. On the Salmon's Middle Fork they may be fished only on a catch and release basis. Whether for the flesh—succulent and sweet—or only for sport, cutthroats lure many an angler deep into the wilderness.

as the late 1800's. But bone chips, tools, and mussel shells found in rock shelters along the cliffs confirm the presence of man much earlier — some artifacts date back 8,000 years.

During the Sheep-eater campaign of 1879, when the last of the Shoshone Indians were hunted, subdued, and removed, Captain Reuben F. Bernard and his men, traveling from the Boise Valley, dropped down the Middle Fork by way of Loon Creek. "Within a distance of 10 miles," Bernard recorded in his diary, "we have come from 10 feet of snow to roses and rattlesnakes." Though he managed to cross the tortuous gorge of the Middle Fork, Bernard called it "Impassable Canyon."

A short distance from Elk Bar, I saw a large male chinook, or king salmon, battered and completely exhausted from his long fight against the current. Deep holes and pools of the river, as well as the tails of the rapids, provide good steelhead and salmon fishing. Nearly one-third of the chinook redds, or spawning nests, found in the Salmon River drainages are in the Middle Fork and its tributaries.

From March through July the salmon migrate from the Pacific up the Columbia and Snake Rivers to ancestral waters such as the Middle Fork where they spawn and die. The young spend one or two years in these fresh waters before returning to the sea. The steelheads, really oceangoing rainbow trout, move up the Salmon River in fall and winter and spawn in the Middle Fork and its tributaries in spring. Today the salmon and steelhead must fight their way up so many fish ladders to reach spawning grounds that one more dam on the Columbia, the Snake, or the Salmon might end their migrations forever.

My experiences fishing for steelhead I will not soon forget, but it was even more of a thrill to watch my teen-age nephew Johnny's bout with a steelhead on Big Creek, which flows into the Middle Fork. When he set the hook it was like a detonator, exploding the pool into action.

The huge fish stripped out line and leaped several feet into the air in a vigorous effort to shake the hook. Unable to give line fast enough, Johnny headed down the left bank. A smooth, sheer rock outcrop interrupted the bank. On reaching the obstruction, Johnny jumped into the stream, wading waist deep toward the far shore where a long gravel bar would allow farther travel downstream. Part way across, he staggered but regained his footing on the slippery rock bottom, still managing to keep a tight line on his fish. Fifteen minutes later and several hundred yards downstream, a weary but proud Johnny worked a 32-inch steelhead into shallow water.

My introduction to the Idaho wilds came in 1952 when I served as consultant to an Air Force school at McCall, teaching crews of the Military Air Transport Service how to survive and travel to safety following a crash or bailout. After two weeks of base instruction, small crews and instructors took off on ten-day treks into trailless stretches of wilderness, using only maps and compass to navigate. Our packs contained the rations and survival gear normally available to airmen. In winter we traveled on snowshoes. Of the many adventures, hard times, and interesting sidelights, it is the common everyday winter stimuli and experiences that I recall most vividly — the swish-swish of snowshoes in an otherwise soundless void; the slow, plodding travel in deep powder through a muffled world of white and gray; the beatitude of flakes falling without the whisper of a breeze.

Roly-poly pika, impish harvester of the heights, gathers food for winter's long siege. It lives at altitudes up to 12,000 feet, making its home amid tumbled rocks that offer a haven from stooping hawks. The size of a guinea pig, the pika is related to the hare — though, with its frequent bleating, much noisier than its silent, long-eared kin. As summer wanes, the pika scuttles about collecting sedges, grasses, and flowers which it piles into half-bushel stacks to cure. It may hoard up to 50 pounds of hay to feed on when the snow lies deep upon its mountain world.
DRAWINGS BY GEORGE FOUNDS

151

Solitude and the numbing cold seemed like fellow travelers. The silence was broken when we stopped to set up shelter for the night. A note of cheerfulness would be added by the call of the gray jay, the friendly forest resident that appears from nowhere and acts as though he's a charter member of the camp group.

To our trainees we pointed out the numerous tracks and runways that reveal the presence of snowshoe rabbits and red squirrels. A snare, made of a short loop of frozen cord or fine copper wire, set at the entrance to a red squirrel burrow or snowshoe rabbit runway often will provide a hungry man with enough nourishment to continue his travels. The slow-moving spruce grouse—or fool hen—can often be flushed from stands of spruce and fir. If necessary, under survival conditions, grouse can be clubbed. Hopefully, winter survival techniques will not be needed for military purposes in the future. But for the outdoorsman, the hunter, and the ski tourer, training in meeting emergencies can mean the margin between survival and death. Being prepared breeds both confidence and caution.

Ecological studies—of plant succession, fire history, water and air quality—carried out in near-pristine areas help us to deal more knowledgeably with similar problems in environments greatly modified by man, and also are of direct use in helping to maintain quality habitat for wild creatures. The Idaho Primitive Area and Selway-Bitterroot Wilderness region has served as laboratory for studies of the mountain lion, the bighorn sheep, and the Rocky Mountain goat, and of the effects of mining and lumbering on spawning streams of steelhead and salmon.

A recurrent problem is too many elk. Once plentiful on the plains, elk thrived on grass. But as settlers claimed the rich valleys and meadowlands, elk were spared only the higher, timbered country. Very adaptable animals, they could winter on mountain maple, serviceberry, willow, red dogwood, and other woody plants. New growth that followed forest fires provided improved range, and numbers of large predators were destroyed; elk populations multiplied. Offhand, abundant game seems to be a hunter's dream. But research shows that when overpopulation occurs, the range deteriorates; herds show a preponderance of older animals, fewer calves are produced, and the adults tend to be smaller and in poor condition. Antler development also is retarded. The result: an inferior population destined to subsist on scanty rations, to be killed by severe winters. A normal balance of wild predators helps prevent overpopulation; another partial solution is to disperse hunters into remote areas so they can help keep the growing herd in check.

During the fall rutting season the bugling of the bull elk can be heard at any hour, though it seems more common around sundown and sunrise. The shrill whistle starting low and rising to a high pitch, ending in grunts and sometimes a stomping of hoofs, is a wild, thrilling sound to wilderness travelers. (Continued on page 157)

Portfolio Notes

OPPOSITE: *Nature turns jade to sapphire on the flanks of the 13,167-foot mountain that gives its name to the Cloud Peak Primitive Area in Wyoming's Bighorn Range. Meltwater laden with pulverized rock—glacial flour—greens Glacier Lake's shallow upper bowl. Surface water, clearing as suspended particles settle, overflows into the deeper basin below.*
ED COOPER

PAGES 154-155: *Brawling through Yellowstone Park's southwestern reaches,* a fork of the Bechler River throws itself at the feet of a hiker at Ragged Falls. A 30-mile trail leads through the cascade-strewn Bechler Valley, crossing lush meadows and hot-and-cold-running streams.
SAM ABELL

PAGE 156: *Daybreak dances where climbers tread with care. Mountaineering students whet climbing skills on the northeast ridge of 14,130-foot Capitol Peak, one of five "14'ers" that preside over Colorado's Maroon Bells-Snowmass Wilderness.*
DAVID HISER

One fall night at the head of Chamberlain Creek, the bugling of a bull elk woke me just before dawn. Turning over in my sleeping bag, I returned his call. He answered, and I repeated. As we continued, each of his calls came from a position closer to my bed. Finally, just as dawn was breaking, I saw white-tipped antlers emerge from the timber. The bull stood motionless, less than a hundred feet away. Apparently he had not detected human scent, as he did not seem to be alarmed. For several minutes I watched him in the growing light; then he turned abruptly and vanished into the pines. Answering a bull's bugling, which he may take as a challenge from a rival male, can sometimes lure him close enough to be photographed.

That autumn there was a bumper crop of nuts of the whitebark and limber pine, and the grouse, Clark's nutcrackers, gray jays, chipmunks, and red squirrels converged on pine-clad ridges to gather the nutritious seeds. Golden eagles also may congregate where grouse are feeding. As I walked along such a ridge one day, grouse exploded into flight at my approach, winging across a narrow wooded valley. Simultaneously I heard a shrill whistle overhead, similar to that of a descending bomb. A golden eagle, his wings folded tight against his body, was dropping in a near-vertical stoop, wind shrieking through his primaries. He pulled out of the stoop just at treetop level as the grouse plummeted into a thicket. A golden eagle streaking down on a frightened grouse is not an everyday sight but one that the hiker in this wilderness abounding in diverse wildlife may one day hope to experience.

"While sitting on a ledge partway up the Chinese Wall in Montana's Bob Marshall Wilderness, I heard my cousin Craig cry out. I looked up to see a brilliant meteor rush silently past, leaving a red smoky trail. A moment later came the muffled sounds of exploding rock. That night, lying under a screen of stars with the northern lights glowing, I realized how ancient man must have felt when most of the earth was wilderness. The meteor and stars and aurora seemed to be part of what wilderness implies—something unique, fragile, and beautiful."

A memorable episode it was for my son Charlie, who thus conveyed impressions of his first visit to the 950,000-acre wilderness. With Craig and my daughter Jana, he had approached from Great Falls, driving west across the flats toward buttes and knobs. On the horizon, clouds and peaks blended into a hazy range of giant earth-sky mountains. From the Benchmark station in Lewis and Clark National Forest they hiked five miles through lodgepole pines, picking up the West Fork of the South Fork Sun River at the wilderness boundary, and thence upstream.

"In the 15 or so miles that we trailed the stream toward its source in a bowl beneath the massive limestone cliff called the Chinese Wall, we saw much evidence of past fires: mountainsides in all stages of regrowth," Charlie continued. "Ridges separated thick green forests from the naked skeletons on slopes where fires had burned to a peak and died. Here and there huge trees, killed by fire but refusing to fall, stood guard over seedlings growing from the blackened earth. Forbs and grasses grew in abundance. Pink and yellow monkeyflowers added color to stream banks, and the white-flowered beargrass, a lily, was conspicuous along the trail. At one rest stop I extracted fibers from the beargrass leaf as former Indian inhabitants of the area did, and twisted them into a tough line suitable for fishing. Just afterward we topped a rise to be greeted by the Chinese Wall. We camped beneath the cliff that night in a meadow fringed with beargrass and wild onions on one side, gnarled forest on two others, and the bouldered talus of the wall to the west."

"I felt like we were in a fortress," Charlie commented later, "nestled up against cliffs so vast they put our camp in shadow by early afternoon."

The Bob Marshall Wilderness, within the Flathead and Lewis and Clark National Forests, brackets 60 north-south miles of the Continental Divide in western Montana. Three-fourths of the area is forested, the remainder divided between grass and brushland and barren, rocky terrain.

In the past large fires periodically burned over parts of the forest. Most were touched off by lightning but man was responsible for some. The biggest on record, in 1910, burned an estimated 25 percent of the present-day Wilderness. Wildfire, when uncurbed by man, is as much a natural agent as wind or rain, influencing the entire character of wild areas: fauna, flora, scenic views, water runoff, water quality, and in consequence the recreational opportunities and esthetic values.

Forest Service policy for several decades has been to suppress all fires within its jurisdiction. Thus in the Bob Marshall Wilderness the visitor can study both the effect of early fires on the ecosystem and what happens when fire is treated not as a sometimes-useful force of nature but as an enemy. In this part of the Rockies, the first year's growth following fire is usually herbaceous vegetation. This is followed by shrubs—an excellent source of food for deer and grouse. Elk also seeking shrubs in winter find ample browse in these areas. The combination of open parks and heavily forested retreats, along with a large elk population, provided optimum habitat for the grizzly bear, an omnivorous feeder. As herbivores, grizzlies depend on tuberous plants and grasses of the open country; as carnivores, they feed on elk, deer, and small mammals. Other wildlife is varied and abundant.

Plant succession following the early fires has now progressed past the shrub stage into the timber stages—primarily lodgepole pine. Fires favor the lodgepole because its cones usually require heat to open and release the seeds. Complete protection from subsequent fires is helping to create more uniform cover of timber with fewer open parks and decreased browse and other resources required by wildlife. The diversity and numbers of wildlife tend to decline as the forest grows into a climax stage, which some protected areas of the Bob Marshall have already reached. This forest type is desirable in limited quantity but does not afford scenic views and is not easy to travel through without well-maintained trails. Nor does it provide good sites for camping or forage for saddle horses and pack stock.

Should complete fire protection continue, changed recreational opportunities will in time make the Bob Marshall—or any other wilderness—much different from when it was first set aside. Is rigid fire protection in keeping with wilderness objectives? Many ecologists think not. Their recommendations for keeping pristine conditions in wilderness areas have included simulating the processes of nature by periodic controlled burns as well as permitting wildfires in small, preselected areas to burn. A trend now apparent is to do as little managing as necessary, allowing fuller play to natural forces.

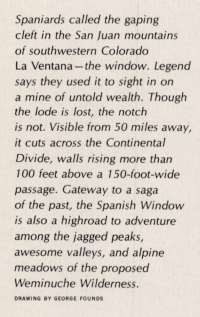

Spaniards called the gaping cleft in the San Juan mountains of southwestern Colorado La Ventana—the window. Legend says they used it to sight in on a mine of untold wealth. Though the lode is lost, the notch is not. Visible from 50 miles away, it cuts across the Continental Divide, walls rising more than 100 feet above a 150-foot-wide passage. Gateway to a saga of the past, the Spanish Window is also a highroad to adventure among the jagged peaks, awesome valleys, and alpine meadows of the proposed Weminuche Wilderness.

DRAWING BY GEORGE FOUNDS

High is the word for the Colorado portions of the Rocky Mountains included in or proposed for the National Wilderness Preservation System. Some sections lie along the Continental Divide. In the state's southwestern corner the San Juan Primitive Area, which includes the famed Spanish Window, boasts an *average* elevation of some 10,000 feet. The most rugged of its high peaks rise in the Needles Range; three—Mount Eolus, Sunlight Peak, and Windom Peak—tower above 14,000 feet, flinging a bold "I dare you" at the expert mountaineer. Much of the southern portion of the nearby Uncompahgre Primitive Area consists of sparse alpine tundra lying above 12,000 feet.

Though the trip was years ago, I still have vivid recollections of my first trek into the treeless alpine zone of the Colorado Rockies, a region much like the San Juan and Uncompahgre. Here desiccating winds sweep over a surface broken only by boulders; the land is snow-clad most of the year. But it was summer with the sun like a warm sweater on my shoulders. The intense white light of midday cast a sheen on moss campion, dryads, dwarf paintbrush, forget-me-nots, arctic gentians, and snow buttercups that brightened patches of soil. Elatedly I jumped from one lichen-encrusted boulder to another, for I was young and this was a new world for me to explore. I felt free, exhilarated. I wanted nothing so much as to go on indefinitely hiking through this magic kingdom of Lilliputian plants, learning the ways of rosy finches and saucy Clark's nutcrackers, watching the golden eagle soar purposefully above a marmot sunning on a rock—with an escape crevice nearby. Each day brought new sights and new stimuli.

I was hiking one day over a stretch of boulders splotched with gray lichens when suddenly at my feet a rock the size of a coconut started to walk. I blinked. When I looked again, all was motionless. Maybe the scarcity of oxygen affects the eyes. Maybe I'd been out in the sun too long. Again the stone moved, and this time I caught the glint of light on the dark eye of a white-tailed ptarmigan. With slow, methodical steps this plump grouse-like bird padded across the tundra. When it stopped, it blended with the surroundings so perfectly that it was impossible for me to distinguish bird from rock. When I glanced down to check my camera setting, and when a slight shifting of nearby "rocks" drew my gaze to other members of the ptarmigan family, I simply could not relocate the original one until it moved again. Such excellent camouflage is undoubtedly of survival value to a vulnerable creature living in a region devoid of cover. The golden eagle hunts over this same habitat, for I had sighted one earlier in the day. But even its keen, discriminating eye apparently could not separate a motionless ptarmigan from the surrounding mottled gray rocks.

As I moved on, scrambling down a rough talus slope, a strident, hard-to-locate *ennk —ennk* called my attention to another member of this alpine community. The pika, like the ptarmigan, is hard to see when immobile. It was only when he scurried over the rocks that he became visible.

This is a land of hot summer sun and intense ultraviolet radiation when skies are clear, but even the shade of a passing cloud produces chill, and nights are cold. Continual freezing and thawing of water disintegrates rocks, and heaves and molds soil. The temperature range, short growing season, scarcity of moisture, and meager soil tend to limit the number of plants and animals. Only about 300 kinds of plants and a few dozen year-round bird and mammal species live in the alpine zone. Because of the simplicity of flora and fauna, the various parts of an arctic ecosystem can readily be identified. An ecosystem might be defined as a complex of plants, animals, and non-living components so enmeshed and interdependent that the system operates as a unit. In size, an ecosystem may vary from a small seepage area at the base of a perennial snowfield to a vast boulder-strewn fell-field. Low matted plants grow in the shallow soil between boulders, and it is in these micro-meadows that pikas make "hay" while the summer sun shines. Stems, leaves, and flowers of plants cut and precisely piled by this small member of the rabbit family make an aromatic hay—survival fare for winter. Under the turf, pocket gophers tunnel, consuming the roots of plants. Gophers, in turn, become food for nocturnal hunters such as owls, and for weasels and coyotes that move to high altitudes in summer. Because of their underground lifestyle, pocket gophers seldom fall prey to hawks and eagles as do pikas and marmots.

Days are long on the ramparts of the Rockies, I discovered. But when the sun drops behind distant peaks, the air chills suddenly and I would hike down to scrubby timber. In the lee I would rig a tarp shelter and build a fire for the night.

Heading down toward timberline on what proved to be my last day in this alpine world, I stopped to examine a clump of miniature willow trees—no more than an inch and a half tall but perhaps 50 or more years old. The white fluff on the disproportionately large catkins—willow "down"—makes excellent tinder. As I gathered a puffy palmful from these tiny trees I could not help but marvel at the adaptations that enable plants to live and grow in this harsh, high world: curled and wax-coated leaves to reduce moisture loss, succulent leaves to store water. Hairs on nearby plants such as alpine forget-me-nots and snow buttercups not only absorb warmth from the sun but catch precious moisture—dew, rain, or snow.

A distant murmur of thunder brought me to my feet. Almost before I realized a storm was imminent, lightning jagged the sky and the thunder escalated to an ominous roar. Knowing that this exposed, treeless area was no place to be just now, I dashed for a rocky, cliff-bordered ravine that led precipitously to lower ground. The wind picked up speed. Dark clouds rolled in from horizon to zenith. Then hailstones started pelting me. They looked like golf balls and felt like rocks. A scattering turned into a fusillade of icy pellets hitting the ground with such velocity they could maim a man and possibly kill. The earth turning white under my feet, I put my arms over my head and face and made for the cliff face, hoping to find a sheltering crevice. I was now in a changed and isolated world with no link to the balmy valleys far below. Increasing speed, I slipped on the hail-covered downgrade. A twinge of pain grabbed my knee as I stumbled, but I plunged on to find the meager shelter I needed.

The storm passed almost as quickly as it came. I hobbled down to my cached pack. The willow fluff, now a damp wad in my pocket, seemed a fragile token of another planet. One "where man himself is a visitor who does not remain," I might have said, but at that time did not have the words. A slightly hurt, wiser, more appreciative wilderness visitor than when I came, I donned an extra shirt under my windbreaker and began the long, painful trip down.

I n an early morning flight over the rugged Gros Ventre Mountains in Teton National Forest, I once was awed by the beauty of the horizontal rays of the rising sun striking Pyramid Peak through light clouds. I could imagine it as a giant laser beam and the boulders strewn in wild array below as chips from the disintegrating mountain. There must have been sunrises like this in the days of the mountain men. But in those days, men had neither the power to sunder a mountain nor the machine to rise above and view it suffused in the sun's glory.

It is good to have wilderness in the Rockies, places to find moments of intense involvement—stimulants and tonics we all need in the course of a lifetime. Man strives eternally for freedom and finds it expressed, at least temporarily, in the expanse and order of a wilderness environment.

Like silvery spears upraised, quaking aspens salute the sky in Maroon Bells-Snowmass Wilderness. The lightest breeze sets leaves aquiver, stirring whispers to delight the ear. One of the glories of the Colorado Rockies, "quakers" grow up to 90 feet tall, their golden leaves translucent under the autumn sun. Beavers dine on the smooth, whitish bark and build dams of trunks and limbs. Indians brewed a spring tonic tea from the aspen's sweet inner bark.
DAVID HISER

160

slicked-back hairs of the synthetic fur allow smooth forward movement but protrude to arrest energy-wasting backslide. On less strenuous grades, a special wax rubbed on ski bottoms discourages slippage.

Against a backdrop of dark forest, we shuffle ahead like white-daubed characters in an impressionistic painting. Our packs and the grade deny us the graceful kick and glide of the day-tripping cross-country skier. As the hours pass, the shoulder straps cut deep and the first rest stop is a luxurious relief.

Threading thickets of lodgepole pine and crossing flat, open meadows, we are engulfed in primordial quiet—the whisper of snowfall, the sigh of wind through pine needles. Around us loom snow-covered hills whiskered with trees. Far ahead, dark peaks jut like shark fins above the sea of forest.

At the noon break I drain the last of my two plastic bottles of water—unwisely. When we stop to camp at frozen Pete's Lake in late afternoon, I am dog-tired and cotton-mouthed. The burner on my little gasoline camp stove sputters determinedly, but the dry snow fluff scooped into the cooking pot melts into drinking water with agonizing slowness. What amounts to a simple, unconscious act in my urban existence—getting a drink of water—has become an all-important, hard-sought necessity in the wilderness. The needs to keep warm, stay dry, and eat when the body cries for fuel also mushroom in importance.

Bundled like Yukon sourdoughs, expedition members dip into a pot of macaroni and cheese—cooked with a quarter of a pound of margarine. A diet heavy in starches and fats provided calories needed to stoke body furnaces against the cold. Each two-person tent team cooked for itself, but mealtimes often saw pairs sharing dishes potluck-fashion. Despite voracious appetites and ample food, most of the participants lost weight.

One team member packed pots and the single-burner stove, the other the nylon tent and collapsing aluminum poles. The heavy loads each carried prompted such expedients as bending to rest packs on

DAVID HISER

ski poles at stops. Trampling sideways on skis leveled and firmed tent sites, cut risk of a surprise plunge through snow crusts in a sleeping bag.

Loose but multilayered clothes combated cold. "Pick boots big enough so you can still wiggle your toes inside three pairs of wool socks," instructors advised. "Warm chest, warm extremities" was another adage; the body tries to protect a skimpily clad trunk by retaining blood at the expense of heat circulation to arms and legs.

Weary travelers switched to felt "bunny boots" around camp and inside tents at night, letting hiking boots worn while skiing dry out for the next day's trek.

"I think you have to endure hardships like these to sharpen your appreciation—to make life more intense," says Laurie Low, student at the University of Colorado at Boulder. "I gain self-confidence finding I can do things I never thought I could do."

At Pete's Lake we have climbed 2,500 feet. There we enjoy the first of the expedition's two campfires. The comfort of gazing into a crackling blaze—wilderness TV—is usually forsaken in NOLS attempts to avoid "civilizing" an area. To heal our fire's black blemish, pine needles and other forest-floor debris are scattered over the cold ashes the following morning. Litter is unthinkable. Food wrappings of plastic or paper are carried until they can be burned. No food cans or jars accompany us in the woods. Foil packaging and fuel containers that can't be destroyed are packed out again. The entire group shares a single latrine dug into the snow; those who prefer toilet tissue over the suggested snowball must put a match to it. Such devotion to wilderness purity grows contagious. For two days I carry a used tea bag in the pocket of my bright red parka, uncertain about its disposal, until someone suggests scattering the tea leaves and igniting the bag.

"Bright garb makes a person more visible in winter," Paul Petzoldt had told me in Lander, "but in summer we're starting to encourage wearing drab colors. That way, people will be less noticeable and can walk or camp within a few hundred yards of each other and never lose the important feeling of being alone in the wilderness."

169

Wilderness grocery, a food cache yields provisions for the final ten days of the trek. Supplies packed in before the onset of winter go into parcels in the open air assembly line.

Ice fishing added a welcome item to the diet; instructor Hunker pulls a brook trout from the Middle Fork of the Popo Agie River. A tough 20 minutes of ice-ax hacking produced the hole in the river's covering —and bruised student knuckles. Fishermen could see bottom in the swift, chest-deep stream.

Author Grove took 45 minutes with bucktail spinner to hook the first fish. Its entrails smeared on the spinner added attractiveness, and a catch of 16 more came rapidly. One cook boiled heads and tails with water and powdered milk to make a fish chowder.

curry-flavored rice, macaroni and cheese, plus fresh fish caught through a hole chopped in the foot-thick ice covering the Popo Agie River. Hot cups of Jell-O or fruit drink top off the menu. I take my turn as chef, with dubious results. "Not bad," mused a victim of my culinary bout with powdered eggs one morning. "Not bad, but they don't taste at all like eggs."

A full moon in a clear sky bathes the winter nights with milky glow, keeping gab-fests going outside the tents until hours past our usual 9 p.m. sack time. Bob Simon, a talented 18-year-old from Cleveland, Ohio, burlesques old show tunes and dance routines, triggering belly laughs that warm both body and spirit. The tedium of getting ready for bed also delays sleep. Held to a cramped sitting position in the two-person tents, I wrestle off my boots, windproof pants and parka, padded vest, and one of my three sweaters. Padded booties replace the three wool socks on each foot, but the loose socks accompany me into the sleeping bag along with damp gloves so body heat will help dry them overnight. Also zippered in, to prevent the contents from freezing, are the two water bottles. Head enveloped in the hooded top, I close the bag to a breathing hole the size of a silver dollar.

The expedition, until now a collection of friendly strangers, finally becomes a close-knit group. Nicknames underline the familiarity. Californian Jeff Kopf with his pointed orange cap, tapered red beard, and snapping eyes becomes known as the "Wizard." Handlebar mustache and military bearing give Jeff Parker, a quiet Minnesotan, the title "Duke," and chatty, vivacious Mary Bolton, a midyear graduate of Radcliffe, is the "Duchess." Long, lithe photographer David Hiser unfolds his legs to rise from an evening cooking circle, and the cry rings out, "Spiderman!" I didn't qualify as a man of distinction: no nickname.

On the sixth day the daily rotation of leaders gives me the task of guiding the group for the final leg to the foot of the high mountains. Four steep slopes stairstep us to the highlands, a bleak, nearly treeless world of knifing cold. Strong winds rip unfettered across the frozen Deep Creek Lakes—Upper, Middle, and Lower. I raise my head to check our direction and an icy whip lashes my face, snatching my breath. Breaking trail in fresh snow up the four successive climbs drains my legs. Finally, the pull of the pack straps and the alternating push on the ski poles saps my arms as well. As we top the last pass, my left arm numbs, then hangs limply while the pole, looped to my wrist, drags behind.

In deep snow amid the fringe of lakeshore scrub pine, we dig pits to level our tents and shelter our camp stoves from the wind. With our hands warming around a tin cup of hot chocolate, 18-year-old Greg Steltenpohl and I chuckle over the contentment we feel in what, by civilized standards, should qualify as a miserable setting. We are warm, despite the tent-rattling gale that races through the camp. We are tired, but pleasantly so, after the hard climb.

With the hot drink sending a sweet fire down our throats, Greg grows philosophic: "Back in civilization, you find entertainment, but it's mostly mental. Here it's also physical, and it's easier to understand a simple pleasure like keeping warm." Another wilderness sage, likewise inspired by the thaw, puts it a different way: "You can enjoy this because you don't have to analyze why you enjoy it. Out here you don't have to question anything, you only perceive."

The next day, windstorms and low clouds put off our assault on Wind River Peak. For roomier quarters while waiting, we cross the lake to dig caves in the 30-foot drifts of hard-packed snow under a towering cliff. Five hours of tunneling produce three subsurface dwellings with ceilings domed to resist collapse. It is a cozy

Sand lovegrass and gleaming prairie sandreed bask in a summer sunset at Valentine National Wildlife Refuge, Nebraska.

WHERE HAVE ALL THE PRAIRIES GONE?

Robert O. Petty

I stand upon a hill in South Dakota looking west across the Missouri River. It is late June of a year that has brought more than the usual rainfall to this part of the country. The rugged bluffs of the old Missouri Escarpment beyond the river are deceptively lush. Later their grasses will wither and turn brown and the distant hills will stand in sharp contrast to the green pastures and cornfields on the east bank. For me this windswept knoll near the city of Pierre is a special place, a vantage point from which I can see the meeting of eastern and western life and can marvel at the abrupt transition from the freshly minted glacial soils of the north and east to the older, weathered lands to the southwest.

I have driven here, across the long sweep of grass country, from Indiana, where I teach ecology at Wabash College. And once again I have felt that vivid awareness of the sheer immensity of land and sky that can grip and overwhelm the mind. These plains and prairies embrace more than a third of the conterminous United States, about a million square miles from Indiana's gently rolling farmlands to the Rocky Mountains' outlying hills, from the crisp balsam morning air of northern Minnesota to the musty, bird-pierced stillness of the east Texas delta lands.

Traveling through this region today, one might conclude—a bit too quickly—that here surely is a place where the wilderness was defeated utterly, where nearly every horizon beyond the stark geometry of the heartland cities has been shaped by man into a patchwork of domesticated landscapes. Even so, it is still possible to feel a sense of aloneness and find the promise of an undiscovered place upon this vast meeting ground of life and history that we call the Middle West.

What wilderness means, in a sense, is how it was taken away; relentlessly, a chip, a shot, a furrow at a time by ingenious tools—the felling ax, the crosscut saw, barbed wire, Sharp's carbine, the Winchester Repeater. For our story especially, one of the most ingenious of all was John Deere's sod-breaking steel plow, tempered to a hardness that could rip the ancient root tangles of giant bluestem turf and flip it into long black furrows. Generation after generation the ax bits rang across the winter fields, and pungent blue smoke drifted into the hollows as gigantic logs were rolled together and burned. Section by quarter section the federal land auctions of the last century swept out of the dwindling eastern forest onto the lonely prairie. Settlers at first thought that land which could not grow trees was infertile, but they quickly

THE MIDLANDS

Numbered sites are established Wilderness Areas; unnumbered entries are units officially considered for wilderness designation. A figure after the name is wilderness acreage only, not total acreage of the national park or wildlife refuge. Pages cited offer fuller description; page 337 lists contacts for obtaining details on particular areas.

NORTH DAKOTA

Lostwood NWR. 5,577. Prairie pocked with glacier-formed potholes. Breeding ground for waterfowl. Shelters migrating whooping cranes; peregrine falcons, western burrowing owls.

Theodore Roosevelt National Memorial Park. 28,335. See pages 188-189, 191-192.

Chase Lake NWR. 4,155. A major colony of white pelicans nests here, along with ducks, gulls, and cormorants.

SOUTH DAKOTA

1 French Creek W. 3,200. In Custer State Park. Five-mile-long scenic gorge in the Black Hills. Horse trails. Campsites.

Badlands NM. 58,924. See page 191.

Sand Lake NWR. Controlled flooding of James River Valley makes ideal habitat for birds. Spectacular spring migration of blue and snow geese.

MINNESOTA

Tamarac NWR. Lovely realm of tree-bordered lakes where wild rice attracts waterfowl. Look for ruffed grouse and beaver.

Agassiz NWR. Marsh-and-thicket remnant of preglacial lake larger than all the Great Lakes combined. Waterfowl, muskrat, moose.

Voyageurs NP. Dense pine forests laced with miles of waterways make this a paradise for canoeist and boater. Timber wolves.

2 Boundary Waters Canoe Area. 1,029,257. See pages 188-189, 207.

Rice Lake NWR. Forested uplands and swamps where Indians harvest wild rice. Mallards and ringnecks; mink, muskrat, an occasional moose and coyote.

Mille Lacs NWR. Nesting sites for purple martins, gulls, and terns on two rocky islands. Administered by Rice Lake NWR.

Upper Mississippi River WL&FR. Extends some 280 miles from Wabasha, Minn., to Rock Island, Ill., along both banks. Island-flecked marshes; 270 species of birds, 50 mammals, 113 fishes.

WISCONSIN

Horicon NWR. Marshland home of waterfowl and fur-bearers. Ducks nest atop muskrat houses. Cries of honking geese fill the air.

3 Wisconsin Islands W. 29. Three small limestone rocks with sparse vegetation. Remoteness and seasonal storms keep them pristine for their chief tenants— gulls, herons, and waterfowl.

MICHIGAN

4 Porcupine Mountains Wilderness State Park. 40,000. Trails lead from Lake of the Clouds through hardwood forests to sheer cliffs and waterfalls. Look for wolf and marten.

Isle Royale NP. 120,588. More than 150 miles of hiking trails, some 70 lakes. See page 204.

5 Huron Islands NWR W. 147. Eight glacier-gouged granite islands covered with gnarled trees and shrubs. Nesting site for herring gulls.

6 Seney NWR W. 25,150. Sedgy marshlands dotted with knolls, tussocks, and pools formed by dikes and beaver dams. Abounds in birds; deer, moose, bear. Refuge limits use.

7 Michigan Islands NWR W. 12. Three widely scattered islands— Shoe and Pismire in northern Lake Michigan and Scarecrow in Lake Huron. Gulls, herons, ducks. Refuge limits use.

Sleeping Bear Dunes NL. 37 miles of nearly pristine shoreline. Sweeping bays, bluffs, white-sand beaches, an island named for a 400-foot-high dune.

ILLINOIS

Crab Orchard NWR. Canada geese and other waterfowl attract visitors and hunters to this paradise of hills, lakes, and forests.

NEBRASKA

Fort Niobrara NWR. Herds of buffalo, elk, longhorns along the Niobrara River. Fossil museum.

Valentine NWR. Located in the Sandhills region, the 71,516-acre refuge encompasses meadows and hills dotted with marshes and lakes. 225 species of birds.

Crescent Lake NWR. Small lakes and grass-covered dunes provide a haven for antelope, deer, eagles. Refuge limits use.

MISSOURI

Mingo NWR. 1,700. Swamplands lying at the edge of the Ozark Mountains harbor 207 bird species, including the bald eagle.

Irish Wilderness. 17,880 acres in Mark Twain NF between Current and Eleven Point rivers. Also called White's Creek.

ARKANSAS

Buffalo National River. 132-mile stretch of unspoiled river ideal for float trips. 200-ft. waterfall at Hemmed-in-Hollow is highest in the Ozarks. Big Bluff, a sheer cliff, rises more than 500 feet.

Upper Buffalo. 10,590 acres bordering the Buffalo National River area. Heavily wooded, many streams, mountains rising to 4,000 feet; few trails.

Big Lake NWR. Open water and river bottom shelter some 200 species of birds including mallards, pintails, teal, egrets. Closed in winter.

White River NWR. Rich bottomland dotted with lakes and bayous. Moss-hung cypress, alligators, coyotes.

Caney Creek. 14,433 acres in Ouachita NF. Seven-mile-long clear creek flows past picturesque rock outcroppings. Deer, bear, wild turkeys, game fish abound.

OKLAHOMA

Salt Plains NWR. Treeless mud flats covered with thin layer of salt. Visitors collect crystals, marvel at 3 million Franklin's gulls. Refuge limits use.

8 Wichita Mountains Wildlife Refuge 8,570. See pages 189, 202.

9 McCurtain County W. 14,087. Forested slopes. Elk, bobcat. Fishing, boating on Broken Bow Lake.

TEXAS

Big Thicket. See pages 199, 203.

LOUISIANA

Sabine NWR. Major wintering area for Mississippi River flyway waterfowl; some 300 species of birds. Alligators.

Lacassine NWR. Egrets, herons, anhingas nest in cypress groves. Ducks, geese find winter haven.

Breton NWR. 5,000. White-sand barrier islands extending in a 48-mile-long crescent off the Mississippi Delta provide shelter for loggerhead turtles and 23 water and shore bird species.

An amended Wilderness Act, according to the Forest Service, would qualify additional areas in the midlands for preservation. Some, long endorsed by citizen groups under the existing wilderness law, are described above. The rest are listed below:

Belle Starr Cave, 5,700, and Dry Creek, 5,500, Ouachita NF, Ark.; Richland Creek, 2,100, Ozark NF, Ark.; Nebo Ridge, 15,500, Hoosier NF, Ind.; La Rue-Pine Hills, 2,800, and Lusk Creek, 11,000, Shawnee NF, Ill.; Big Island Lake, 6,600, and Rock River Canyon, 5,400, Hiawatha NF, Mich.; Sturgeon River, 13,200, Ottawa NF, Mich.; Bell Mountain, 10,200, and Rock Pile Mountain, 9,000, Clark NF, Mo.; Hercules Wilderness, 16,600, Mark Twain NF, Mo.; Kisatchie Hills, 10,000, and Saline Bayou, 5,000, Kisatchie NF, La.; Big Slough, 4,000, Davy Crockett NF, Texas; Chambers Ferry, 4,000, Sabine NF, Texas; Black Jack Springs, 2,600, and Whisker Lake, 2,700, Nicolet NF, Wis.; Flynn Lake, 6,300, and Rainbow Lake, 6,600, Chequamegon NF, Wis.

GUADALUPE MOUNTAINS NP

LOSTWOOD NWR

VOYAGEURS NP

International Falls

AGASSIZ NWR

ISLE ROYALE NP

Lake Superior

THEODORE ROOSEVELT
NATIONAL MEMORIAL PARK

CHASE LAKE NWR

SUPERIOR NF

CHIPPEWA NF

Duluth

5

HIAWATHA NF

Medora
Dickinson

Bismarck

Fargo

TAMARAC
NWR

Ironwood

OTTAWA NF

6

94

Lake Huron

NORTH DAKOTA
SOUTH DAKOTA

RICE LAKE NWR

MILLE LACS
NWR

CHEQUAMEGON NF

NICOLET NF

7

CUSTER NF

SAND LAKE
NWR

3

HURON NF

SLEEPING BEAR DUNES
NL

7

St. Paul

Minneapolis

Eau Claire

Manitowoc

Cadillac

BLACK HILLS NF

Rapid City

Pierre

Lake
Michigan

MANISTEE NF

BADLANDS NM

90

Sioux Falls

MINNESOTA

94

HORICON NWR

1

CUSTER
SP

chadron

FORT NIOBRARA
NWR

Mason City

UPPER
MISSISSIPPI
RIVER
WILD LIFE
AND FISH
REFUGE

Madison

WISCONSIN

Milwaukee

Kalamazoo

Lansing
Detroit

BRASKA
NF

SAMUEL R. MCKELVIE
NF

Sioux City

Ft. Dodge

MICHIGAN

75

Scottsbluff

VALENTINE NWR

NEBRASKA NF

Cedar Rapids

Rockford

ILLINOIS

Chicago

Gary

INDIANA

CRESCENT LAKE
NWR

81

Des Moines

80

Rock Island

69

orth Platte

Platte

Omaha

Lincoln

IOWA
MISSOURI

Peoria

65

Wabash

80

57

Indianapolis

70

NEBRASKA
KANSAS

66

Springfield

74

Topeka

Kansas City

70

St. Louis

HOOSIER
NF

Ohio

70

Lawrence

Jefferson City

Missouri

Evansville

Garden City

Emporia

Arkansas

Verdigris

FLINT
HILLS

Springfield

CRAB ORCHARD
NWR

55

Wichita

CLARK NF

SHAWNEE NF

OKLAHOMA
TEXAS

SALT PLAINS NWR

CLARK NF

MINGO NWR

IRISH WILDERNESS

Eleven Point

Current

Canadian

35

Tulsa

MARK TWAIN NF

BUFFALO
NATIONAL RIVER

BIG LAKE
NWR

Amarillo

8

Cache

UPPER BUFFALO
WILDERNESS

OZARK NF

White
River

OZARK NF

ST. FRANCIS NF

Oklahoma City

Ft. Smith

Arkansas

Red

9

OUACHITA
NF

Little Rock

Helena

87

OUACHITA
NF

CANEY CREEK
WILDERNESS

Hot Springs

WHITE RIVER
NWR

ARKANSAS
LOUISIANA

WHITE RIVER
NWR

National Forests (NF)

National Parks (NP), Monuments (NM),
Wildlife Refuges (NWR), Wild Life and
Fish Refuges (WL&FR), Lakeshores (NL),
Seashores (NS), and State Parks (SP)

Desert

Wilderness Areas (W)

Roads

0   100

STATUTE MILES

Ft. Worth

Dallas

Sabine

Shreveport

KISATCHIE
NF

20

45

DAVY CROCKETT
NF

Neches

KISATCHIE NF

CHIHUAHUAN
DESERT

Pecos

SABINE NF

Trinity

ANGELINA NF

SAM HOUSTON
NF

BIG
THICKET

Baton Rouge

New Orleans

BRETON NWR

Austin

90

LACASSINE
NWR

BEND NP

Rio Grande

Houston

SABINE
NWR

10

San Antonio

Galveston

35

37

Gulf of Mexico

Corpus Christi

Laredo

187

Brownsville

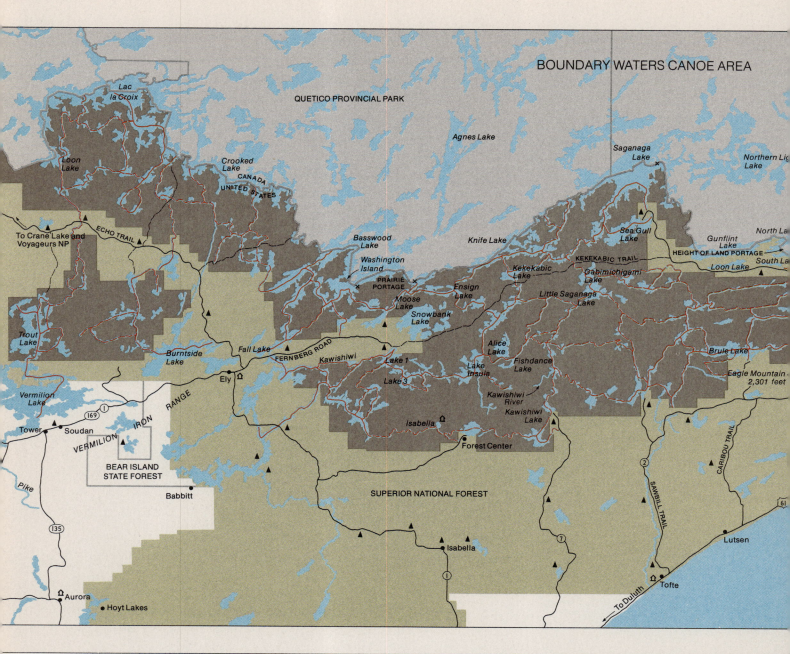
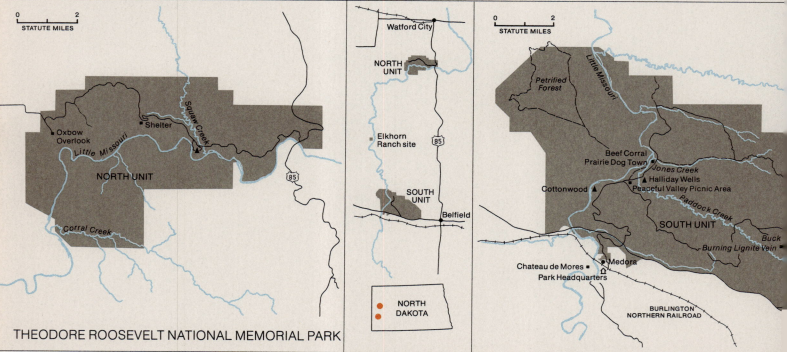

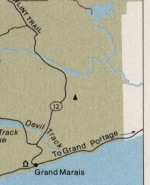

Arrow Lake

CANADA
UNITED STATES

GUNFLINT TRAIL

Devil Track

To Grand Portage

il Track ake

Grand Marais

Lake Superior

MINNESOTA

94

BOUNDARY WATERS

A thousand lakes in a million acres bejewel our only national forest canoe wilderness—the Boundary Waters Canoe Area. A journey deep into the labyrinth is a voyage through time—the solitude, the scenery, the very rhythm of travel evokes the spirit of days when Ojibwa, explorer, and fur trader threaded these waters. Paddle and portage is still the rule—the carry between lakes may be an easy few yards, or a hilly mile or more.

Timber wolves, moose, deer, and black bears roam the forests and bogs; beaver and loons ply the waters—as do anglers lured by walleyes, northern pike, bass, and deep-running lake trout.

For visitors arriving without their own gear, outfitters in Ely, Tofte, Grand Marais, Crane Lake, and other communities offer canoes, camping equipment, even guides. During the summer months boats may jam up at portage points, and campers fill the more accessible of some 1,800 lakeshore campsites.

Along the heavily used routes leading from entry points at Moose Lake, Fall Lake, and Lake 1, rangers limit camping to one night at designated sites. Motors are permitted on about a third of the 1,200 miles of water trails, under an exception in the Wilderness Act.

The 41-mile-long Kekekabic Trail provides backpackers a footpath through the heart of the lake country. In winter increasing numbers trek the frozen wilderness by snowshoe, ski, and—on the approved routes—by snowmobile.

Many travelers venture across the border into more remote wild lands of Canada's Quetico Provincial Park—but a check must be made at Canadian customs stations. Floatplanes, with canoes lashed to pontoons or stowed in cabins, may haul visitors to these checkpoints, though aircraft are banned in the Boundary Waters. Along some 200 miles of border lakes, boaters track the historic route blazed by the voyageurs.

THEODORE ROOSEVELT

"Grand, dismal and majestic," wrote a 19th-century cavalry officer of the badlands of what is now western North Dakota. At sunset, the jumbled hills and pinnacles flanking the Little Missouri River resembled "the ruins of an ancient city."

Today, 70,436 acres of this colorful region are encompassed by three units of Theodore Roosevelt National Memorial Park. Of the total, some 28,000 acres are planned as wilderness.

The largest such tract, 19,000 acres, lies in the North Unit. Here, beyond the tent and trailer sites at Squaw Creek campground, stretch grass-covered tablelands slashed by gullies and ravines. Antelope, bison, and bighorn sheep range the upland meadows; bobcats and coyotes haunt the painted hills; the cries of hawks and eagles echo in the draws.

Two short, easy trails—near the Squaw Creek campground and Caprock Coulee—bring hikers to the edge of the wild lands. The backcountry has few trails and no camping facilities; wood fires are banned. Backpackers and horseback riders may spend the night there, with permits, but should haul their own drinking water.

Roosevelt's Elkhorn Ranch, midway between the North and South Units, is accessible only over a rough, unmarked dirt road; none of its original buildings remain.

In the South Unit, about 9,000 acres lying west of the Little Missouri are slated for wilderness. Old fire roads converted to horse and hiking trails traverse stream-cut plateaus. A square mile of petrified forest lies along the northwest boundary. Camping and other recreational facilities are provided at Cottonwood, Peaceful Valley, and Halliday Wells east of the river.

WICHITA MOUNTAINS

Granite peaks of the Wichita Mountains Wildlife Refuge rise abruptly from the plains of southwestern Oklahoma, dominating rolling, grassy hills, woodlands, man-made lakes, and two wilderness preserves—Charons Gardens and the North Mountain Unit.

Bison, elk, longhorn cattle, deer, wild turkeys, and prairie dogs dwell in the 59,020-acre refuge. Here East meets West, with habitat fit for cardinal and roadrunner, for eastern red cedar and desert mesquite.

The refuge's northern half, including the wilderness unit, is enclosed by a big-game fence and is closed to the public except for occasional tours. Here scientists study the poisonous brown recluse spider, conduct bird censuses, and devise computerized range-management techniques.

The southern portion is visited by about 1½ million people a year. Most come to camp, or to picnic, swim, or fish at Elmer Thomas, Quanah Parker, and other lakes.

Only the most energetic visitors explore Charons Gardens. Water and trails are scarce in this barren, bouldery, 5,000-acre enclave; ticks, chiggers, and rattlesnakes abound. Elk and Twin Rocks Mountains are more than 2,000 feet high; Elk's precipitous southwest face challenges rock climbers. Day trips only are the rule in Charons Gardens; campers stay outside the wilderness at areas such as Sunset, Fawn Creek, and Post Oak that provide fire grates and water.

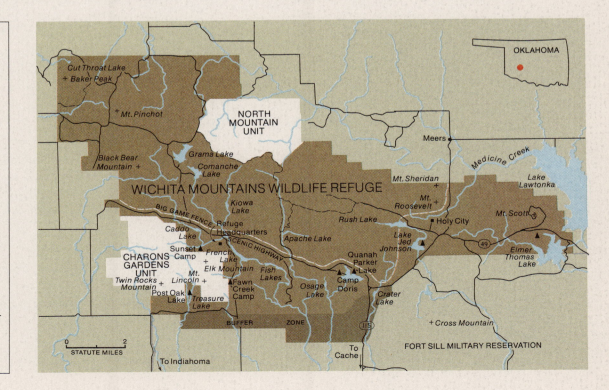

OKLAHOMA

Cut Throat Lake
+ Baker Peak

+ Mt. Pinchot

NORTH MOUNTAIN UNIT

Meers

Black Bear Mountain +

Grama Lake

Comanche Lake

Medicine Creek

WICHITA MOUNTAINS WILDLIFE REFUGE

Mt. Sheridan

Lake Lawtonka

Kiowa Lake

Mt. Roosevelt

BIG GAME FENCE

Rush Lake

Mt. Scott

Refuge Headquarters

Caddo Lake

SCENIC HIGHWAY

Apache Lake

Holy City

Lake Jed Johnson

49

CHARONS GARDENS UNIT

Sunset Camp

French Lake

+ Elk Mountain

Fish Lakes

Elmer Thomas Lake

Twin Rocks Mountain

Mt. Lincoln +

Quanah Parker Lake

Post Oak Lake

Fawn Creek Camp

Osage Lake

Camp Doris

Treasure Lake

Crater Lake

BUFFER ZONE

+ Cross Mountain

115

FORT SILL MILITARY RESERVATION

0   2
STATUTE MILES

To Cache

To Indiahoma

learned that soils which grew such rich wild grass could also grow man's grasses—corn and wheat and oats. Westward, spring after spring, under the arching, stuttered flight of killdeer and meadowlarks, the sunlight spun in the colter discs, flashed from a million plowshares. And the wilderness went under. Not a section, not a square mile of tall-grass prairie was left anywhere east of the Mississippi.

Its potential for man's needs was too great. Perhaps, too, the prairie seemed eternal; a country so big, a sky so wide that the human mind could not encompass it. Some thought it inexhaustible. But in the 1930's the winds churning across the western plains brought us the ultimate harvest of our unthinking—the spring dust storms that turned midday to an orange twilight for a hundred miles beyond our eastern shores.

Trudging out of the eastern forests, pioneers beheld a sea of grass, seemingly endless in its variety and expanse. Hundreds of grasses and flowering plants, some with root systems reaching down 10 or 15 feet, stretched across the virgin prairies and plains. Indian grass, rising nearly eight feet, could conceal a man on horseback. Little bluestem, two to four feet high, throve throughout the Midwest. Buffalo grass, averaging six inches tall, provided year-round forage for bison of the plains.

The rich prairie sod clung like glue to the old wooden and cast-iron plows. Steel plows were the answer. John Deere's "Prairie Queen" came into widespread use in the 1850's; its rolling colter and share of polished steel sliced through tangled roots and sticky soil—and the prairie gave way.

DRAWINGS BY GEORGE FOUNDS

How did these grasslands come to be? Geologists tell us that as the Cretaceous period drew to a close some 60 million years ago, cataclysmic forces wrenched at the earth's crust, buckling and thrusting the Rockies into the sky. The midlands, awash in the waters of a great inland sea, slowly began to emerge. As the shallow sea retreated, a forest rich with deciduous trees took its place for several million years. But as the western mountains continued to rise, they wrung moisture from the Pacific winds, creating an enormous, arid, wedge-shaped rain shadow on their lee side where the forest could not live. To flourish where trees had failed, new plant communities evolved, a biome dominated by grasses and broad-leaved flowering plants called forbs. By simplifying their life cycles, by producing multitudes of seeds, and—most important to survival—by thrusting roots deep into the soil, these hardy plants were able to meet the challenge of aridity.

As plants evolved, so did the animals, building new food chains to take advantage of the great shadeless "windfall" of energy—the sunlight of the open prairie. Turf-running grazers, burrowing insects and rodents, plant eaters and predators—more than 80 species of mammals and 300 kinds of birds in the tall-grass prairies alone—assembled into interlocking ecosystems, adjusting to extremes of temperature, available water, and recurring fires set by lightning.

About a million years ago, the first of several massive ice sheets ground out of the north, blanketing much of the upper Midwest in a great arc bounded roughly by the Ohio and Missouri rivers. These glaciers formed the Great Lakes and much of the Mississippi drainage system, and, by moving and stirring vast quantities of earth, they left deposits that would become some of the richest, most fertile soil to be found anywhere. Then, as the ice receded, chunks of it embedded in the thick deposits melted, leaving a myriad of "kettlehole" lakes to glitter in the Pleistocene twilight.

These, then, were the seemingly boundless plains and prairies that the first human migrants discovered after their journey from Asia thousands of years ago, that awed Coronado and the conquistadors in 1541, and that lay as both a physical and a psychological barrier to 19th-century settlers. Traces of this original wilderness linger today in surprising places. Botanists have found native prairie plants along railroad rights-of-way and in older cemeteries dating from pioneering times. There, in autumn, nod the tufted plumes of Indian grass, switch grass, and big bluestem, the swaying yellow sunbursts of prairie dock, crimson liatris, and a host of others. How ironic that the long steel road which carried the freight of destruction to the prairie should be a refuge for its scattered remnants and that those who turned their lives against a wilderness of grass should sleep in its last few shadows. Many wild corridors also exist along scenic streams and on the old floodplains and terraces of the

John Deere's "Prairie Queen"

Mississippi watershed. Along such streams a narrow border of timber can give a float trip or canoe voyage a wilderness flavor. Whitewater courses on rivers flowing out of the Ozarks are outstanding for such adventure. Even along Lake Michigan's bustling southern tip, a small, state-administered natural area within the new Indiana Dunes National Lakeshore guards a nearly pristine fragment of America's wild heritage—and serves science as a living laboratory of plant succession and history. But in the Midwest, as elsewhere, the major remnants of original or returning wilderness are protected in our national parks, forests, and wildlife refuges.

Indians knew the bizarre, strangely beautiful hills of the western Dakotas as Mako Sica—Land Bad. The first white men here, French-Canadian trappers, called them "mauvaises terres à traverser—bad lands to cross." "Hell with the fire out," growled Gen. Alfred Sully campaigning here against the Sioux in 1864.

Accompanied by my wife Anne, daughter Liz, and sons Bob and Bill, I drove through Cedar Pass on the road to the Sage Creek Basin, heart of a proposed 58,924-acre wilderness unit in the western section of the Badlands National Monument in South Dakota. We would be there three days, tenting at the edge of the wild land and exploring the countryside on foot. We stopped for a while at the top of the pass to look at the lands beyond—a chaos of gnarled beige and pink ridges, steep-walled gullies and canyons, knobs, buttes, and ragged spires. The geology of this region traces back to the birth of the Rockies, when streams gushing from the newly formed mountains cut long parallel grooves in the plain to the east. Eventually the valleys became clogged and then buried in the flood of debris; volcanic ash sifted down from time to time, layering the area with extensive deposits. For 20 million years outwash plains and filled valleys coalesced into a continuous plain of new sedimentary rock. Then, when the land began to rise again—a process still going on—streams burst from the mountains with renewed vigor, carving new channels through the relatively soft overlying rocks and exposing the older formations beneath.

At the Sage Creek campground we left the car and hiked about four miles amid the jumbled maze of washes and gullies. As we crested a hill, a startled antelope sprang away in long graceful leaps, crossing a plain where the wind wove running patterns in the grama and wheatgrass. Western meadowlarks exploded into the air all around us. Later, we came upon a prairie-dog town about half a mile north of our base. The high-pitched barking of a sentry announced our approach, and a scurry of brown fur left the mounds deserted.

As the day ebbed, we pitched our tent in the primitive, waterless campground at road's end. Beyond, the lush June landscape rolled away into hazy green and silver billows of sage and rabbit brush. Thickets of silvery buffalo berry in the draws trailed into sandbar willows. Cottonwoods rattled in the wind. In the distant rock recesses, eastern and western junipers stretched down the hills like marching columns. Farther still, to the northeast, the famed Badlands pinnacles burned with the last reflections of another day. How many rainstorms, how many gusts of wind, how many winters melting into spring have chiseled and shaped this strange and brooding land! Throughout our wandering in this wilderness of gentle wind and sagebrush and sky we encountered no one, nor saw any human trace.

A few days later we arrived at Theodore Roosevelt National Memorial Park in the North Dakota badlands. Here, along the Little Missouri River, Roosevelt ranched and celebrated his joy of wilderness in the 19th-century tradition of trophy-hunting. On these lands three park units combine to capture a myriad of moods from our nation's past, interwoven with the personal history of a towering figure in the conservation

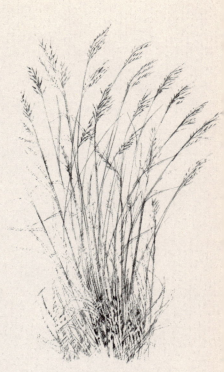

Indian grass

Little bluestem

Buffalo grass

movement. From a ranger I learned that while the park is essentially wild land through-out—"superfine country," the ranger called it—some of the best and most remote areas for backcountry hiking lie in the north unit.

At Cedar Canyon the next morning I took off alone up Caprock Coulee. Though the easy trail serves as a "get acquainted" hike on the wilderness threshold, it offers a spectacular look at the scarred, plateau-top country. Along the trail I made the ac-quaintance of plants I had never seen and met some old friends from back East—stands of green ash, red cedar, and others.

These "relict" colonies growing so far west of their main present-day ranges recall a time when the Dakotas were wetter and cooler than they are now. Climatic changes over the centuries forced plant species to advance or retreat. Those that retreated often left colonies where local conditions remained favorable. Today such stands contribute significantly to the living mosaic of many wilderness tracts.

At the overlook on the Caprock Coulee trail's highest point, the view along the Little Missouri canyon was overwhelming. Around me juts of cap rock, resistant sandstone, rose amid running waves of wheatgrass and June and needle-and-thread grass. Across the ancient valley lay cone-shaped piles of volcanic ash deposited by countless rainstorms, and huge sidewall slabs of rock that had slumped to the valley floor. My mind tried to take it all in, the natural history and the human history that abounds in this place. In the years before Teddy Roosevelt punched cattle here, the Oglala Sioux stalked antelope, deer, and elk on this same plateau. In 1876, General Custer and the 7th Cavalry camped just upstream on their way to the "Greasy Grass" river—Little Bighorn, the white men called it.

For the western Dakotas much of the history of the last century is not happy. It was a harsh country, filled with human conflict—the annihilation of an Indian cul-ture, the senseless slaughter of bison, devastating drought and storm, the further tragedies of overgrazing and economic collapse. In the winter of 1886 fierce bliz-zards wiped out nearly three-fourths of the cattle on the open range, and ultimately drove Roosevelt out of ranching.

Even now the sorrow lingers, reflected in the deserted homesteads, the Indian cemeteries, the scattered graves of settlers. Part of what (Continued on page 201)

Portfolio Notes

OPPOSITE: *Symbol of vanishing wilderness, a lone timber wolf lopes across a frozen stream near Lake 1 in the Boundary Waters Canoe Area. Canis lupus, feared and maligned through the ages, has been hunted, trapped, and poisoned to the edge of oblivion. Only a few hundred survive in the United States outside Alaska—most of them in these remote wilds of northern Minnesota.*
DAVID HISER

PAGES 194-195: *Bison graze a land almost as big as the sky above it in the south unit of Theodore Roosevelt National Memorial Park. Drawn by the "curious, fantastic beauty" of this part of North Dakota, Roosevelt ranched near here in the 1880's. He wrote of hot, dry summers and of winters when "snow-clad plains stretch out into dead and endless wastes of glimmering white."*
THOMAS J. ABERCROMBIE, NATIONAL GEOGRAPHIC STAFF

PAGES 196-197: *Gleaming pinnacles pierce a menacing sky near Cedar Pass in Badlands National Monument, South Dakota. The soft sedimentary rock, scarred by the elements, entombs fossil remains of animals that roamed the earth 25 to 40 million years ago: giant pigs, pygmy horses, saber-toothed tigers, camels, and the rhinoceros-like* Titanothere.
CHARLES STEINHACKER

PAGE 200: *Bathers at Indiana Dunes National Lakeshore thread a "blowout" cleared of vegetation by Lake Michigan's roaring northwest winds. Though roads and developed recreational facilities deny wilderness status to this 8,300-acre world of shifting sand, marsh, bog, forest, and prairie, scientists prize it as a storehouse of Ice Age history whose layered soils and preserved plants weave a tale of more than 10,000 years.*
BRUCE DALE, NATIONAL GEOGRAPHIC PHOTOGRAPHER

Trespassers at the gates of time, canoeists in Texas' Big Thicket probe a primeval world of ooze, moss, and jutting cypress roots called "knees."

This Village Creek bayou offers but a glimpse at the richness of the "biological crossroads of North America." The Thicket nurtures plant life found in southeastern swamps and the arid southwest, in the forests of Appalachia and the woodlands of the coastal plains. Cypress and tupelo,

acid-bog baygalls, stands of beech and magnolia, pine and palmetto flats, patches of prairie—the unique pattern attracts scientists from across the land. Otters, alligators, and a host of other animals dwell here, as do 300 kinds of birds.

An outlaw hideout in bygone days, the Thicket is rich in legend too. "The hell-roaringest place that I ever got into," wrote a visitor. The brush grew so thick, said another, that even the rattlesnakes had

to crawl out backwards.

A ribbon snake, opposite, finds the living easier as it seizes a green tree frog near the edge of a swamp.

The drama of survival involves the Thicket itself. Once it covered more than three million acres. Today, only a tenth remains in scattered parcels linked by wooded waterways. Logging and development go on as conservationists campaign for a national preserve to safeguard the remnants.

199

a man feels here is how this wilderness left its mark on people as, in their various ways, they attempted to possess the land. And a man becomes aware that someday he, too, will rest with yesterday's five billion years. And suddenly the sunlight and the day and the desolate beauty of the badlands take on a new meaning.

Around the turn of the 19th century a strange new sound was heard along the Verdigris River in what is now eastern Kansas. Perhaps a band of Osage hunters stalking elk along the banks heard it—a curious hum that grew louder with each passing minute. Honeybees—"white man's flies"—had swarmed across the broad, smooth-flowing Mississippi some years earlier. Now they had reached the Verdigris, and the Indians knew that the settlers could not be far behind.

Over the next several years these foraging insects, introduced to the New World by early colonists, continued to move westward, 40 miles or so a year, storing honey in hollow cottonwoods along the prairie streams. By 1815 they were a common sight 600 miles west of the Mississippi. The diversity and the long flowering season of the prairie proved a bonanza to the honeybees. And, through enhanced pollination, the flowering plants profited, too. Nitrogen-rich legumes, especially the lead plant and the various clovers, were strengthened ecologically—almost as if in anticipation of the great disturbance that was to come, when they would be called upon to repair the damage wrought by years of overgrazing and drought.

Because of its rareness today, I wanted to visit a true tall-grass prairie, one that would enable me to capture the feeling of vastness that must have gripped the westering pioneers. One of the best and last of these gently rolling vistas can be seen in eastern Kansas in the Flint Hills south of Emporia and just west of the Verdigris, where Osage hunters once roamed.

On a sultry July morning I drove into the Flint Hills with two men from Kansas City, Lawrence Wagner and his father Raymond. With other dedicated men the Wagners nurture the hope of creating a tall-grass prairie national park. From one high hill we gazed across the open grassland that stretched away in every direction to the horizon. I tried to imagine the time on the old Santa Fe or Oregon Trail when, for weeks on end, travelers were totally surrounded by this long look of nature—a treeless expanse unknown to western Europeans. They had seen large pastures and meadowlands, but nothing like this, this endlessness. To see farther than a man could journey in a day! Immigrants had known this feeling only on the open ocean. And here was the sea of grass, waves rolling up to crests and falling away into long, shadowed troughs of more and more grass. The term "prairie schooner" was surely right. A man might ride a Conestoga wagon to St. Louis, but there, psychologically, he boarded a prairie schooner to continue the westward trek.

In the early, pre-pioneering days, large areas along the eastern edge of the prairie remained grassland only because of periodic fires that killed off woody shrubs and trees. Many towns in the region were built on the eastern side of lakes and streams, for in such locations timber groves were protected from fires swept by prevailing westerlies. These groves were coveted as village sites by settlers in need of fuel and building materials and shelter from violent winter storms. Perhaps they were also a haven to a generation reared in the shade of eastern forests. After settlement, when fires were controlled, forests quickly reclaimed large sections of the original grassland. Even today, those who live along the prairie border must burn the grass every few years to keep out encroaching hackberry, elm, and box elder trees.

Late that afternoon, we crossed the Santa Fe Trail not far from where Zebulon Pike had camped in 1806 on his way to the high western peaks. As we approached

Interstate 35 near Emporia, civilization came rushing back: the fences and power lines, signs, buildings, cars, utility poles, pipelines, plowed fields. Amid the din of roaring traffic a single upland plover held to a fence post—the one certainty at its feet. There was pathos in that scene, perhaps because we knew that man's chances to save a meaningful remnant of tall-grass prairie are all but gone. As we pulled onto the highway, we turned for a last look at the mottled plover, but it was gone.

Across the central Great Plains, fresh tender buffalo steak was a penny a pound in 1872, so plentiful were bison in easy range of a Sharp's or Winchester. But the meat was only a by-product of the hide trade. Wagonloads of hides daily rolled to the railheads. At the peak of the slaughter, overkill forced the price of a single hide down to 25 cents. In the 1870's, in western Kansas and Oklahoma, men saw the last of the great herds in their southern range. By 1889 North America's 60 million bison had dwindled to less than 700. In 1905, the American Bison Society was founded in New York City and, two years later, Congress appropriated funds to transfer 15 of the shaggy animals from the New York Zoological Park to the Wichita Mountains Wildlife Refuge.

At nearby Cache, Oklahoma, a few families from the great tribes of the southern Plains—Comanche, Kiowa, Apache—gathered to witness their return. Old men pointed to lumbering wagons that hauled the crated animals the last 13 miles to the refuge. With troubled voices and eyes they recalled other days and told their children of a time long ago when the earth was alive and the bison streamed endlessly from a secret hole in the ground—a bounteous gift from the maker of life.

Today the refuge encompasses two designated wilderness tracts: the North Mountain unit, closed to the public because of continuing ecological studies, and the Charons Gardens section in the south. The refuge shelters 600 to 700 bison— one of the largest herds in the United States—as well as 300 or so Texas longhorns, some 400 elk, and 50 other mammal species. It also contains some of the finest mixed-grass prairielands I have ever seen.

In preserves like this we find that nature is still man's ancient teacher. Many botanists once thought that the Midwest wilderness consisted of three distinct grassland types: the true or tall-grass prairie of the east, the mid- or mixed-grass prairie through the central portion, and the short grasses of the Great Plains. But here in the Wichita Mountains and at other experimental stations where grazing has been controlled, the midgrasses have moved in over the short grasses, which either have become an understory or are relegated to very dry, exposed sites. Ecologists now recognize that, prior to the 1880's, the Midwest had only two major grassland communities. Overgrazing and drought enabled the short grasses to spread far eastward.

As the prairie ecosystem changed, certain creatures—the greater prairie chicken, sharp-tailed grouse, wild turkey, beaver, elk, and white-tailed deer—vanished from upland and streamside. Other wild harvesters took their place: prairie dogs and jackrabbits, mule deer, ground squirrels, pocket gophers, and other rodents. And where grazing damage was severe and combined with drought, sagebrush, shadscale, mesquite, and yucca inherited the sun.

On a sun-drenched day in mid-July, with the crest of Elk Mountain as a landmark, I wandered through the scrub blackjack oak that grows in the dry savanna country of the Charons Gardens Wilderness. Approaching the foot of the mountain, I wound through post oak and eastern juniper to a jumble of enormous boulders, some of them 60 feet across. Scaling the pile,

I looked far to the south across the way I had come and to the plain beyond. The rubble of ancient red granite rock, cast out by volcanic explosions and dated at more than half a billion years, lay scattered down the valley like the bones of creation. My hike, which had begun as an easy stroll, turned into a vigorous climb over boulders and across crevices. Buzzards riding an updraft at the head of the canyon added an ominous note to the scene, reminding me that in Greek mythology Charon was the boatman who ferried the dead to the underworld. As I continued through the notch, I suddenly came upon a small colony of sugar maple trees in a moist, north-facing pocket. The mountain had provided a refuge for this species, too, so far from its eastern forest home. My day was complete.

On my last evening in the Wichitas, as I walked near Osage Lake, a small dark cloud appeared over a rise. It looked like the beginning of a grass fire. I ran to the crest and came upon the largest of all living American land mammals—a bull bison. He was plowing the dust with a hoof. Then he rolled on his side, kicked, and quickly righted himself, turning to me and shaking his head while the dust drifted through the slant of evening light. For a moment I was too surprised to be frightened. A bull bison is impressive at any distance, but at 20 yards. . . . He stared at me from out of that huge shagginess, raised his head suddenly, and lowered it. Then, to my surprise, he simply turned away, walking deliberately as though to some remembered place—a place deep in that special myth we Americans preserve for him.

Man's hand upon the land touched the lives of its creatures, too. The black-footed ferret, never abundant, once ranged the plains from Canada to Arizona. Preying chiefly on prairie dogs, this lithe hunter of the night also took shelter in tunnels dug by its quarry. But the rodents, a nuisance to farmer and rancher, were killed or driven out. With them went the shy, elusive ferret, now considered one of the world's rarest mammals. Scientists hope for its comeback in Great Plains sanctuaries where prairie-dog towns flourish undisturbed.
DRAWINGS BY GEORGE FOUNDS

A young man of the turbulent 1860's, concluding the Civil War was not his war, could simply pack a few belongings, go west, and disappear into the swamplands of east Texas. The Big Thicket was a good place to hide if he was desperate enough and didn't mind a diet of game, fish, and berries. Many a renegade sought refuge in this wild place, some never to be heard from again.

Here in the Big Thicket, between the Neches and Trinity rivers, nature and history and folklore intertwine like a tangle of old vines to create a fugitive memory of a place civilization almost forgot. It is blessed with a richness of life, soil types, climates, and topography that is unrivaled in North America. Here, in an afternoon, one can travel from cypress-tupelo swamps and acid bogs to groves of oak and hickory, and even to patches of big and little bluestem prairie.

At six-thirty in the morning, Geraldine Watson, her son, and I pushed off on a float trip down the Neches River that winds through the eastern edge of the Thicket. We moved through the morning, from early shadows and cool vapors into a bright noonday, drifting in that silent suspension of time a river can create. Gold-headed prothonotary warblers darted in the green blur of branches that were festooned with Spanish moss and bearded lichen. White sandbars, scattered with rosettes of spurge, carpetweed, and, here and there, bright-orange sneezeweed, stretched along the junctions of side streams. It was this sparkling sand, Geraldine said, that had inspired the Indians to call the Neches "Snow River."

We paddled into John's Lake Bayou, back into the quiet water of cypress knees and towering old trees rich in white egrets and kingfishers. Painted turtles plopped from logs, and alligator gar nosed to the surface from time to time, bringing us their ancient message of survival from some dim Paleozoic past.

Geraldine Watson comes from a family of lumbermen. Her father floated the great log rafts down the Neches to Beaumont during the heyday of the big cypress harvest. She clearly loves the poetry of the land she has known since childhood, and now she and others are desperately trying to save it—hopefully as a unit in the national park system. For today the Big Thicket is riddled by oil wells, rice fields, road cuts, and real estate developments. It taunts us with the beauty of a wild land about to die. Its native forests are being replaced by plantations of fast-growing yellow pine at the rate of 35,000 acres a year. Hundreds of acres more have been soaked with oil and brine from wells or cleared for roads and pipelines. Only in corridors along the quiet streams, places like Village Creek, Pine Island Bayou, Big Sandy, Cypress, and Turkey Creek, do remnants of this primeval wilderness still linger— perhaps about 300,000 acres altogether.

That evening, I listened to Geraldine singing ballads as the sun went down. It had grown dark in the east, over toward Jack Gore Baygall, when, reluctantly, I drove off, caught in a haunting resonance of our country's past.

Some of the best north woods wilderness country in the upper Midwest can be found in Isle Royale National Park, a remote 134,000-acre group of islands in the western reaches of Lake Superior. Although copper mining, lumbering, and fire played havoc with the main island in earlier days, its vegetation is making an impressive comeback. Pungent forests of spruce and fir spread along the shore and in the northern part; to the south and along the ridge tops grow stands of hard maple. Known for its wolf and moose populations, the island offers scientists excellent opportunities for studies of plant and animal ecology.

In late August my son Bob and I, along with two friends, flew to Isle Royale for several days of backpacking. We set out for the Greenstone Ridge Trail, a challenging 40 miles long, with sweeping vistas of forest and sparkling water. Around one lake we found several places where moose had browsed, and once we came upon the remains of a moose, killed and stripped to the bone by wolves.

One evening, near Lake Richie, as we lay in our sleeping bags watching our breath in the cold air, we heard a long, piercing howl. I listened carefully. Was it a wolf or a loon? Again the howl rose in the distance, far across the misty lake. It was not a loon. It was a lone wolf creating his own chorus. Another howl, then silence engulfed us. Moments later, the breaking of branches and a heavy snort directly behind camp told us that a moose had been feeding under cover of darkness. It too must have heard the voice of its mortal enemy.

Hiking for days on end with a 40-pound load can quickly become a trip into one's self, testing lungs and legs and the will to make it over the next rise. Talk dies down; one seeks, as Thoreau did, to live simply, deliberately—if only for a week. But days evaporate quickly in the wilds. Too soon it was time to leave.

As our floatplane climbed out of a bay, I watched its tiny shadow sweep from bog mat, tamarack, and white cedar to an old burn where birch and aspen swayed above the fallen trunks of white pine. The marks of man, a few mine tailings and the park headquarters on Mott Island, seemed somehow to blend with the great striations left by a glacier. The island wilderness that had seemed so large while we were hiking now appeared small and strangely vulnerable. I thought of those who had once ripped copper ore, swung axes, and hauled fishing nets, of those who now seek the meaning of a world where human footprints link with the tracks of moose and wolf. In the ecology of earth each thing creates its own meaning by what it does, which here, for man, must surely mean preserving the wilderness.

Ozark interlude: Venturesome hikers pause beneath Big Bluff's stony brow to view the Buffalo River as it winds—350 feet below—through hardwood-clad hills of northwestern Arkansas. The Goat Trail, here narrowed to a cliff-hanging catwalk, cuts straight across the bluff's shale and limestone face.

One of several spectacular rock walls carved by the river, the cliff rises more than 500 feet above the valley floor and lies in a primitive area under study for Wilderness Act preservation. The Buffalo, protected as the country's first National River, flows through shaded glens and fern-draped hollows splashed with waterfalls. Unexplored caves and Indian encampments dating as far back as 10,000 years add adventure to places where mystery yet whispers in the dells.

WALTER MEAYERS EDWARDS, NATIONAL GEOGRAPHIC STAFF

BOUNDARY WATERS: CANOEING IN A MAZE

Seymour L. Fishbein

Canoes racked above our heads, we ferried the first six miles of wilderness. Our launch cut briskly through waltzing wavelets, making bigger waves for brigades of canoeists plying Moose Lake. The paddlers, keeping their cool, smiled us by. An August sun sequined the waters, and stands of young aspen and birch crowded the lakeside bluffs, flaunting their deep summer green.

Most canoes were headed north. Some would cross into Canada's Quetico Provincial Park a few miles away; others would track the border, in the footsteps of the legendary explorers and voyageurs who pioneered the first pathways into America's heartland. There, as Sigurd Olson has written, every lake, rapids, and portage has its story to tell. But the border route draws crowds, and motorboats are permitted all along the way. We turned eastward, bound deeper into the arrowhead of Minnesota, on a nine-day loop through the heart of our one-of-a-kind national forest wilderness, the Boundary Waters Canoe Area. We felt a little foolish about motoring the first leg in canoe country, but it saved us half a day.

The excursion ended at the portage to Splash Lake; ahead lay a 200-yard carry for our packs and two 17-foot-long, 60-pound canoes. The porters: my wife Louise, our sons James, 15, and Jerry, 12, photographer Bob Madden, and myself. Ideally a portage is a one-way trip, and in nearby Ely we had ordered an "ultra-light" outfit to help make it so. In fact the outfit was a kind of hybrid. We had light aluminum canoes (15 pounds less than the standardweight 17-footer), along with bulky, durable cookpots. Much of our food came freeze-dried, but the bacon came in old-fashioned slabs. The gear included tents and backpacks of nylon—all light, bright, comfortable. But three of the bags were capacious canvas Duluth Packs, of a design dating back to

Early birds—bustling mergansers and a languid angler—greet a new day in the Boundary Waters Canoe Area. Man is no recent intruder here. Indian and voyageur coursed the trails. Iron ore and vast pineries lured miner and logger; motors invaded—by land, sea, and air. Designation of the Boundary Waters wilderness on a third of the Superior National Forest slowed the tide. Here, fly-in campers are barred, motorboats curbed. Deep in the maze, man and his canoe may rediscover the beauty and the challenge of the wild north woods.

ROBERT W. MADDEN,
NATIONAL GEOGRAPHIC PHOTOGRAPHER

Civilization behind them, laden flotillas fan out across Moose Lake, 20 miles east of Ely, Minnesota. Most popular entry point of the wilderness, Moose funnels travelers on watery trails west, east, or north to the voyageurs' highway and the Quetico country beyond the international border (map, page 189). Easy riders, like the author's party, make a quicker getaway by motor launch.

More than 160,000 visit the Boundary Waters each year. To channel the flow, protect water purity and plant life, rangers restrict party size and limit campers' stays at crowded lakes. A "ban the can" rule allows only burnable food and beverage containers. But hundreds of campsites are beyond help; too fragile to take the wear and tear, they have been permanently closed.

fur trade days and still prized hereabouts for durability and easy fit in a canoe. Loaded, our canvas packs weighed up to 45 pounds—not much in a land that remembers voyageurs trotting along under 180-pound loads of beaver pelt.

At Splash I donned a Duluth Pack and bulled a canoe overhead. The canoe teetered, the low-slung bag dragged, and its leather straps punished my shoulders. With every pace admiration for the voyageurs grew in proportion to my distaste for the pack. Clearly we were undermuscled and overloaded; until the weight of food dropped by half, every portage would be a far-from-ideal double trip.

Three beige-brown young mallards sunning on a log at Splash paid us the ultimate compliment as we bustled around the boats a few feet from them and prepared to push off. The ducklings kept right on sunbathing. A few minutes' paddling took us across tiny Splash; the link to the next one, Ensign Lake, appeared open—a level rapids, not too swift but running against us. Stroking hard, we tried to nose into it straight on. We missed. The flow flipped the bows around and flung us back. After a few more tries, we got wise; we banked the canoes, got out and pulled them through. The French had a word for it: *décharge*. Awkward, but better than a portage.

We tried various combinations at the paddles before the division of labor sorted out, and Ensign, a four-mile pull, offered a good shakedown. On a big, choppy lake, flat-water canoeing can test a paddler. Otherwise, it's a grind, with a minimum of expertise involved. The bow man simply paddles and scans ahead for boulders or sunken logs that can flip a boat; the stern man steers, and paddles with a J-stroke—a little outward twist of the paddle at the end of each pull—to hold the desired course.

ROBERT W. MADDEN, NATIONAL GEOGRAPHIC PHOTOGRAPHER

Even so, harmonious canoe teams are as rare as happily married bridge partners.

Three centuries ago Père Le Jeune briefed westering missionaries on canoe etiquette: "It is wise not to ask too many questions nor should you yield to the itch for making comments. . . . Stick to your place in the canoe. . . . Once you are set down as a trouble maker . . . you will not easily get rid of such a reputation."

Excellent. But the abrasions persist. To make the best of it, take the stern seat whenever you can. The bow man can only speculate on the energy output behind him, but if his paddle slows up, you've got him. Approaching an awkward landing, it's the bow man who gets wet feet beaching the canoe. And should you tickle a boulder in mid-lake, the stern man can live one-up for days. As we settled into cruising order, I took a stern paddle in one canoe, with James up front and Louise as referee and relief paddle. Jerry was Bob's whipping boy in the other.

Along the trails our burdened bodies, seeking surcease, welcome distractions. Spotting a moving shadow, we're happy to halt, happier to discover a mink scuttling through the shrubs, people-watching; in summer, out of prime, his mink coat looks dowdy. A fresh hoofprint spurs a vain search of a swale for the moose that must have just passed by. Animal scats generate a full-scale family conference. Deer? Bear? Beaver, concludes James, our ranking scatologist by virtue of having logged the most time cleaning hamster and gerbil cages.

The portage between Gibson and Cattyman lakes stole a good part of our first afternoon. Who can hasten by a bosky waterfall to splash in, lakeside rock walls to jump from, a sun-warmed clearing to bask in?

Small wonder, then, that on the first day we undershot our goal by some four miles, nearly half the distance we'd planned to cover. On Jordan Lake we flopped into a campsite on a lovely spit of land. Sunbeams filtered through the forest on one side; the lake rippled gently out for about half a mile on the other. A fireplace, a corporal's guard of jack pines for cover, pine-needle carpets for tent sites—we were well set. And, courtesy of the previous tenants, we found a supply of firewood neatly stacked—a Boundary Waters custom, encouraged in the brochures.

To be a non-paddler and a woman is double jeopardy. Afloat, squeezed amid the packs, she must be map reader, warden of the drinking cup, dispenser of nibbles, and a foil for the darts that fly between bow and stern. Ashore? Fresh from non-paddling, who can quickly dig out the freeze-dried menu, cook it, and decide when the mess resembles food? And who scrapes charred pots while hypocrites pollute the twilight with such venomous one-liners as "Heck, why bother, they'll only get black again"? Guess who. Every little breeze, as the song goes, seems to whisper Louise.

We had dinner music. White-throated sparrows sang unseen, the pensive melodies seeming to waft from some distance. In the Northeast the Yankee ear hears the song as "Poor Sam Peabody Peabody Peabody"; here it's more like "Pure Sweet Canada Canada Canada." I listened closely, trying to distinguish, then gave it up. And just listened. Later, a little night music—loon yodeling and wailing and giggling; *tremolo, con brio*. The eerie calls complemented the restless watches, when the ground seemed to get bumpier and the sleeping sack smaller and smaller.

The dark-hooded divers seem as much a fixture in this wilderness as the pines. But like most of us, they're only summer visitors. They come here to nest—always at water's edge, for loons, with their swimmers' feet set far back, are all but helpless on land. With autumn's chill, they're off to ice-free coastal waters.

Morning sun and breeze swept the broad lake clear of fog, the mind clear of night's hobgoblins. As the cookfire roared up, the dawn patrol winged by—a brace of

Trail marker signifies that the lake ahead is off-limits to motors. Rod measure, echoing surveying days, may buoy portagers' morale: "109 rods" somehow looks easier than its equivalent—600 yards. Poking through a fallen pine, though, strains morale and muscles. Nature downed this giant; in bygone days feuding traders sometimes felled trees to foul competitors' portage paths. On long hauls voyageurs made rest stops—called posés—every third of a mile or so. Today, at trailside rigs, travelers stand canoes against high horizontal logs and walk out from under to take a breather. When paddle power fails against a rapids (far right), paddlers disembark and lend a hand.

mergansers locked in tight echelon, low on the water, twisting with the shoreline; hot pilots. The scrambled powdered eggs went well with the jelly and low-calorie crackers (our lightweight option in place of bread). But the slab bacon slithered under the knife, producing thick, ragged slices. The result: slightly charred bubble gum. We policed the site—really combed it—packed up, and pushed off. In seconds a sanitation squad arrived to mock our efforts. A trio of gray, or Canada, jays, moving in that bold deliberate way of theirs—flapping a little, hopping a little—descended on the site and somehow discovered a feast of leftovers.

We were soon in big, island-studded Ima Lake, but not soon out of it. A crosswind apparently pushed us far off course. At the east end of Ima we found no sign of a trail —no brown ribbon cutting through the forest green, no break in the rock ridges, no Forest Service sign. We rechecked the canoe-country map and our big topographic maps. No help. We cruised the shoreline. And Bob and I communicated by voice and visual signals. One called out a suggested course; the other shook his head. And vice versa. Since we were both stern men—I mean men in the stern, of course—and thus endowed with independent command, we split up for a while. At last several canoes hove into view, not wobbling futilely, but beating smartly across. We intercepted them near a mass of rock that we'd paddled by at least four times.

"Hi, any idea where the portage is?" "Right here"—the rock jumble that looked to

"Mazy and wandering" waters— in Washington Irving's words— vary from a tranquil old beaver flowage at Elton Lake to the racing Kawishiwi River (below) and worse: boiling rapids that have killed many a canoeman. Avoid white water, officials warn; only fools run rapids, goes an old Indian saying; no one ever drowned on a portage, veterans caution. But wise words grow faint before the Lorelei that lurks in every swift stretch.

In the days of birchbark canoes, the forest supplied the means to mend a tear—thread of spruce root, gum of boiled pine pitch. For aluminum, duct tape—used for heating systems and photographic gear— makes a quick fix on a canoe ripped at a campsite landing.

ROBERT W. MADDEN, NATIONAL GEOGRAPHIC PHOTOGRAPHER

us like part of a ridge. You pick your way over some boulders and—presto!—there's the trail. "We wouldn't have found it in a million years," said Bob.

By mid-afternoon we'd about had it with wide-open lakes, Ima, Thomas, Fraser—hour upon hour of paddling, uncertainty about landfalls, the scenery a hazy, distant blur. Gerund was a delightful contrast, small, shadowed; sunrays angled into the clear water, tinted it amber, lollipop lime . . . like wrinkled cellophane.

Details along the shore stood out: a whir of olive and yellow darting back and forth, up, down, sideways—a flycatcher catching. A grove of tall cedars drifted by, trunks bare near the bases as though they'd been pruned. They had been. A forester in Ely had tipped us to look for that. In winter, deer walk the frozen lakeshores, browsing on cedar limbs within reach. "High-lining," it's called.

We slept that night at Strup Lake, some of us too soundly. Louise and James awoke with talk of hearing a wolf call. I was skeptical, but they insisted; they had boned up on wolf recordings back home. And there are eastern timber wolves here, subjects of much study and dispute. For even on this federal preserve the wolf has endured a protected status so full of loopholes it would take a Philadelphia lawyer to tell him where he can safely tread. He has had full protection on national forest *land*. But not all the forest land is federally owned; and Minnesota, which has traditionally regarded the wolf as a varmint, controls the lakes and streams—including those of the Boundary Waters, where nearly one out of every five acres is water. On the open, frozen lakes, the wolf does some of his most successful deer hunting.

Some conservationists see hope in a plan that reclassifies the wolf from varmint to game animal, makes the Boundary Waters and adjacent areas an inviolate sanctuary, and permits rigidly controlled hunting elsewhere. Not good enough, insist others who demand a total ban on killing wolves until the survival of this critically endangered species is assured.

Up from Strup the trail winds to Kekekabic Lake, 512 hilly yards booby-trapped with breakfasting mosquitoes. On the breezy waters no one thinks of bug repellent. Now in the woods, hands gripping the gunwales overhead, you are defenseless. The hill is not high, only hard, harder downhill as the 17-foot helmet seesaws with every step. As we stagger to trail's end, we meet a family in two canoes heading uphill. I try to warn them. Those six blond heads—I should have known better. "Oh,

ROBERT W. MADDEN, NATIONAL GEOGRAPHIC PHOTOGRAPHER (ALSO OVERLEAF)

Overleaf: Parting gift of the glaciers, the wilderness unveils its 24-carat charms as night retreats at pine-fringed Jordan Lake. Relentless ice sheets uprooted forests, crushed and scoured the Canadian Shield rocks, including Ely greenstone nearly three billion years old. When the ice receded, glacial melt and flowing water filled the scars. The Boundary Waters boasts 1,060 lakes more than ten acres in size.

Bridge of boats and one of timber parry obstacles—a bog at Malberg Lake, a cataract near Agamok. Rocks, logs, and fancy footwork plug the gaps in the jury-rigged span.

Lunch break often coincides with map seminar. The small canoe-country chart traces trails and pinpoints campsites. Topographic sheets, larger in scale, detail lake contours and landforms. With a compass they solve most problems of novice navigators. Luck and passing strangers do the rest.

we know all about it," Mother breaks in. "We're from around here. There's worse up ahead for you. There's a half-mile carry to Mueller Lake. Then there's a swampy one where our youngest sank in up to his waist and we had to toss stones ahead of us for footing. Gabimichigami is awful windy, and Insula is jammed; not a campsite to be found there. But it's all so beautiful."

Kekekabic—related to the Ojibwa word for "sparrow hawk"—is a big, high-banked piece of water, busy and loud with loons and strung-out canoe parties. Deep, too; 180 feet, the topo made it. Big lake trout dwell in those depths, but hooking lakers takes time and skill, and we are short of both.

Much else of interest lies in some deep lake bottoms for those who cherish the wilderness as more than a pleasuring ground. Scientists are fascinated by the diversity of the great natural ecosystem of water and woodland, how it evolved, and how it changes. From tree-ring counts, aerial surveys, logging and fire records, ecologists have mapped a history of the living forest, concluding that fire plays a role in the natural cycle of life. But these woodlands have short life spans; the Boundary Waters patriarchs, majestic red pines on an island in Sea Gull Lake, date from about 1595. In undisturbed lake muds, preserving the layered sediments that have drifted down year by year since the end of the Ice Age, lie clues to the more distant past. Microscopic pollen grains reveal the progression of plant life—tundra-like grasses and sage, spruce and birch, and jack, red, and white pines. Bits of charcoal bedded in the layers reveal that fire has helped cycle and shape the mosaic of the north woods for at least 10,000 years.

Crossing four miles of Kekekabic took us a couple of *pipes*. This was how the voyageurs measured a lake, not in miles, but in rest stops, when they pulled in their paddles and lit their pipes. For our "pipes" we drank, nibbled, and drifted.

At 4 p.m., our agreed quitting time, we parked at an islet in Ogishkemuncie Lake which our outfitter had starred for fishing. In short order James had a fair-size walleye, Jerry reeled in about a pound of northern pike, and I landed a 2½-pound walleye. By now Jerry and I had the fever, and slid a canoe down the rocky slope to go out for more. As I moved aft, he yelled, "Dad, it's filling with water!"

Sure enough, near the bow Ogishkemuncie was gurgling up through the bottom.

Open house: tiny bedrooms, smoky kitchen, all outdoors for a living room. Upturned canoes make good closet space when rains come, not so good if bears come. For bearproof housing, islands are best. Fuel is free, usually plentiful; where dead logs are scarce, canoeists cruise the lake for drifts of "beaver peelings." Blueberries abound around some sites in midsummer. More common, less appetizing, is tripe-de-roche—rock tripe— *a flaky lichen, edible when boiled; voyageurs could stomach it only as a last resort.*

Campfire and coffee curb evening chill; then it's early to bed, early to rise, and back to the paddles.

ROBERT W. MADDEN, NATIONAL GEOGRAPHIC PHOTOGRAPHER

219

We beached the canoe and stared in dismay at a small, jagged cut—caused, I would guess, by a jutting piece of stone. Back home I've bumped and bruised my aluminum canoe for years, but never pierced it. Perhaps the lighter metal on this one made the difference. At any rate, I hadn't given a thought to repair material.

So the trip we'd planned was over. Two of us could paddle back for help—a four- or five-day round trip. Or we could intercept the Kekekabic Trail nearby and hike back, some 23 miles over unfamiliar terrain. Either way, a stymie.

Bob Madden had a better idea. From his pack he pulled a roll of duct tape that photographers use for attaching lights, mending camera bags, any number of things. "I wonder if this'll hold," he said. With a stone we pounded the rip flat, spread tape over it inside and out, and—gently—slid the canoe into the lake....Not a drop seeped in. Wheeoooh. . . .On with the fish fry!

A drizzly night and half a day later, the half-mile slog to Mueller and the swamps of Agamok behind us, we threshed across broad Gabimichigami Lake—our farthest east. Again we settled on an island, a big one this time, and posh. A little cove harbored the boats, a path led up around a huge red pine to a high granite ledge. On it stood a picnic table—the first we'd seen. Behind the campsite another path wound upward through a wild garden of fireweed, ground-hugging bunch dogwood, raspberry, and shrub hazel to a clearing crowned by a privy—another first for us. We had stumbled onto a wilderness Hilton; here we'd luxuriate for a day and a half.

Time, actually, was the great luxury, and we made the most of it. We plunged off our campsite ledge, felt the shock of Gabimichigami's chill depths, and quickly scampered out to convalesce on our sloping rock solarium. Later I dipped a thermometer; I still can't believe 68° F. can feel that cold.

We discovered trails around and across the island, crossed beds of feather moss silent to the tread, and piles of dead wood that crunched under every footfall. We lingered in a grove of scraggly, blistered balsams dying of spruce budworm. I touched a blister and fragrant fluid squirted out; in laboratories it's known as Canada balsam, used for cementing specimens to microscope slides.

Field trip to a wilderness art show turns into a guessing game. On stained, broken rock at Fishdance Lake faded paintings seem to portray a sun, a large mammal, canoeists, a tepee. Some, like the symbol below (at left), defy description. Queried by an art scholar, one modern Ojibwa laughingly said it looked like a rocking chair. Hundreds of such pictographs adorn rock walls of the lake country, at heights indicating the painters sat or stood in canoes. The pigment is mainly red ocher, an iron oxide, applied perhaps by fingers or brushes of willow fiber. But no one knows the artists' identity, when they painted, or why.

Opposite: In a cold cascade the pause that refreshes is usually brief. The Boundary Waters look and taste pure. But quality may vary; rangers advise purification pills or boiling for drinking water.

ROBERT W. MADDEN, NATIONAL GEOGRAPHIC PHOTOGRAPHER

221

In a dark copse we played hide and seek with a spruce grouse, the five of us beating around the bushes as he flitted among them. But he wouldn't be spooked. The species is famed for tolerating humans nearby. We got a long, close look.

The lake lies at the core of 230,000 acres of virgin landscape, the largest pristine tract in the Boundary Waters. In the controversies of the 1960's, which burdened the canoe wilderness with compromise, this treasure was preserved. But vast areas of the Boundary Waters' southern perimeter were left open to logging. Conservationists have fought the policy tirelessly, the more so since the perimeter zone includes some 150,000 virgin acres. With time, disturbed terrain may return to wilderness, but in the forest, as elsewhere, virginity is irreplaceable.

To some, the unyielding opposition to wilderness woodcutting smacks of druidism, mindless dendrolatry. Yet the cause gains ground. A federal judge in Minnesota found such activities as logging "anathema to all wilderness values." And partisans of the forest keep pressing for the ultimate triumph of wilderness values.

Bob, James, and I spent part of our free day on a pilgrimage to neighboring Howard Lake. Here in 1969 came a crew representing owners of mineral rights to prospect for copper-nickel ores. After a few brushes with the Forest Service, the crew left. But the threat remained and the Izaak Walton League went to federal court. Three years later the court ruled that mining would "destroy and negate the wilderness." If this landmark decision prevails, it could provide a new legal safeguard here and possibly for other wildernesses now open to mineral exploitation.

All was serene round Howard's shore. We lunched on sausage and crackers, sprawling the while on a blanket of moss that shrouded the rotting timbers of a prospector's cabin built a century ago. The cuisine was so-so; the setting, delicious.

Returning from Howard, we slammed into one of those famous Gabimichigami winds; it creamed the wave tops and had all three of us windmilling paddles furiously. We tacked often to keep the combers head on, taking a soaking spray with every ker-plunk; but riding the swells broadside would have risked a swamping. Near camp we swung around hard and roller-coastered downwind into our cove.

It blustered on into evening, jerking up tent pegs, turning mashed potatoes and gravy into cold gunk. Through it all a trio of loons bobbed blithely on the scalloped waters. Occasionally the little one hitched a ride on the back of an elder. Their tremolo calls added wild harmony to the soughing in the woods.

Homeward from Gabimichigami it was all downhill. We were west of the Laurentian Divide, whence the waters flow eastward toward Lake Superior, westward and north toward Hudson Bay. Bound west, we ran with the flow, at times with the wind as well. Then the canoes skimmed swiftly over the waters, the paddling rhythmic and easy, the mood lighthearted.

Kivaniva Lake gave us an enchanted evening—Jerry and Bob rippling the surface of polished ebony as they traced the vee-wake of a beaver, James and I adrift in silence and darkness, and Louise at lakeside, lit by ember glow, hand-feeding our overstock of night crawlers to a pair of painted turtles. Fishdance Lake was an embarrassment; Louise caught all the fish. And Insula gave us a nightmare as we blundered through its jumble of islands.

We were back in the motorboat lakes. We could see them and we could smell them. In another day we were out of the wilderness. Through some 60 miles of it, our canoes had carried us; for more than 6 miles over 47 portages we had carried them. We saw only a little of this vast wild land, a brief encounter. Yet knowing it intimately matters less than knowing it's there—and keeping it wild.

Fish danced at Fishdance Lake for Louise Fishbein—a mess of pan-size bluegills. Most Boundary Waters canoeists cast for the powerful walleye, largest of our perches, and the slender northern pike—though some find small northerns too bony to eat. Wise anglers rig wire leaders to cope with the pike's razor teeth.

Should fisherman's luck fail, the unfailing lure of the north country remains, casting its timeless spell. "I have been 24 years a canoeman, and 41 years in service," mused a voyageur in his sunset days more than a century ago. *"... Were I young again, I should spend my life the same way over. There is no life so happy as a voyageur's life."*

RUDI SCHONBECK

Duckweed blankets the water, maples reach for the sun in New Jersey's Great Swamp Wilderness, a pocket paradise in suburbia that nearly became a jetport.

NOT FAR FROM THE MADDING CROWD

Michael Frome

The spray of the falls tickled my arms and misted my face. I was a boy, and I was alone with a grove of virgin hemlocks and hardwoods in a rocky little gorge worlds away from home. Wolves and bears hadn't roamed there for many years, but I knew where I could spot a few of them—just a short hike to the south of my ravine in a habitat called the Bronx Zoo.

The northern rim of New York City was the unlikeliest of places to find a bit of wilderness like the Bronx River Gorge. But as a city boy I learned to make the most of nature wherever it might be found, whether in large dimensions or small. By subway, streetcar, and sidewalk I sought out the green places that here and there broke the monotony of concrete canyons.

Mention the East and most people think of chronic urban sprawl, overpopulated and overpolluted, its wilderness all but wiped out, its cities and suburbs pressing hard against every empty lot, every cornfield, every patch of woods. Sadly, the image is all too close to truth. Yet, as I found with my boyhood retreats, there is far more wilderness in the East than many people suspect, and of far more diversity: luxuriant swamps and salt marshes teeming with life; forests that have managed without our "management" to survive fires, insects, and hurricanes; fragments of the original seacoast of rock or sand, the tidal rendezvous of creatures of land and ocean; weathered mountains, patriarchs like the Adirondacks and the Smokies whose rocks are among the oldest on earth. In such surroundings—a shady trail, a mountain overlook, a stretch of unspoiled seashore—the uptight mind can find release.

On one February day I unwound on a walk-and-wade tour through a pocket-size wilderness of surprising diversity smack in the lap of the most populous megalopolis in the United States. The Great Swamp near Morristown, New Jersey, nestles in the basin of an ancient lake barely 25 miles west of Manhattan. Its life zones reach from marshes—where rails and herons stilt about—through meadows and dry woodlands to high ridges and, in remote spots, towering virgin beech and white oak.

The Great Swamp is never dull. Marsh-marigolds brighten the bogs in April; blue flags take over in May; showy mountain laurels and pink azaleas spangle the ridges as summer begins. In spring and autumn flocks of migrating waterfowl drop to the wetlands for rest and food. There is an enormous variety of plant life, an abundance of animals, and 204 kinds of birds. I watched in vain for the elusive fox, the scurrying

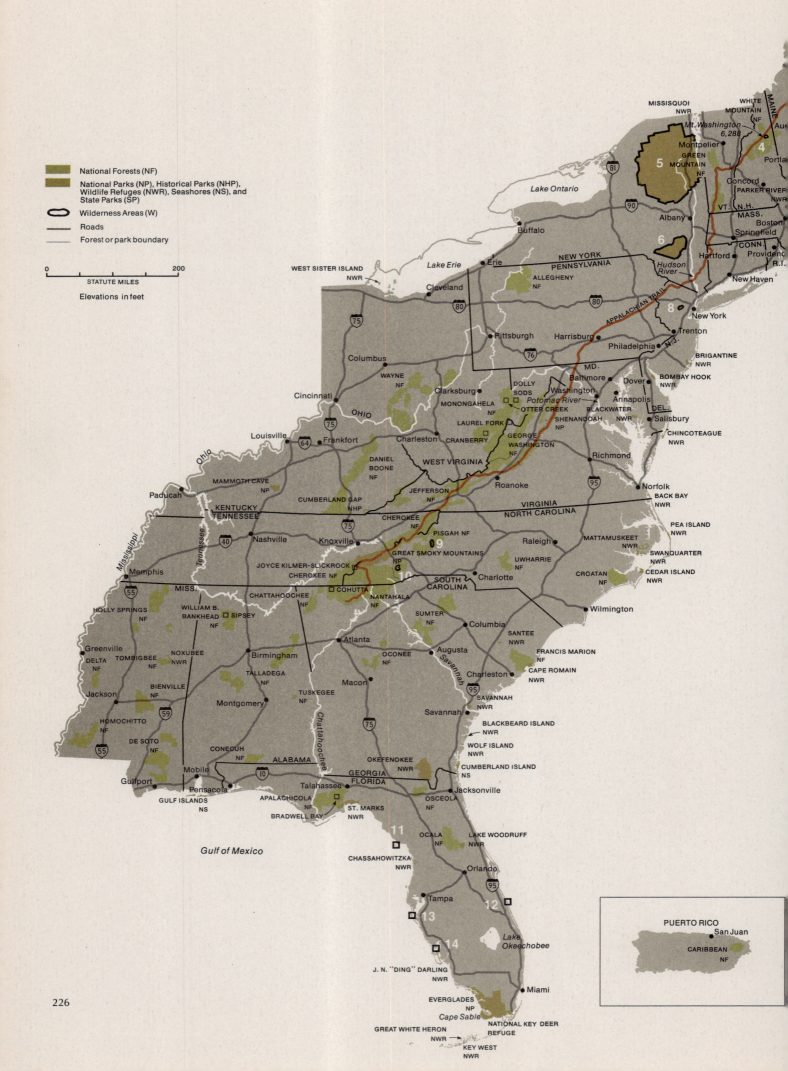

National Forests (NF)

National Parks (NP), Historical Parks (NHP), Wildlife Refuges (NWR), Seashores (NS), and State Parks (SP)

Wilderness Areas (W)

Roads

Forest or park boundary

0   200
STATUTE MILES

Elevations in feet

WEST SISTER ISLAND NWR

Lake Ontario

Lake Erie

Buffalo

Cleveland

Erie

NEW YORK
PENNSYLVANIA

ALLEGHENY NF

Hudson River

Albany

Montpelier

GREEN MOUNTAIN NF

5

Mt. Washington 6,288

WHITE MOUNTAIN

4

VT. N.H.

MASS.

Concord

PARKER RIVER NWR

Boston
Springfield

CONN.

Hartford

Providenc

R.I.

New Haven

6

8

New York

Trenton

Philadelphia

N.J.

BRIGANTINE NWR

MD.

BOMBAY HOOK NWR

DEL.

Pittsburgh

Harrisburg

Columbus

WAYNE NF

Clarksburg

DOLLY SODS

MONONGAHELA NF

OTTER CREEK

LAUREL FORK

CRANBERRY

Washington

Potomac River

Baltimore

Annapolis

Dover

SHENANDOAH NP

BLACKWATER NWR

Salisbury

CHINCOTEAGUE NWR

Cincinnati

OHIO

Louisville

Frankfort

Charleston

GEORGE WASHINGTON NF

Richmond

DANIEL BOONE NF

WEST VIRGINIA

JEFFERSON NF

Roanoke

VIRGINIA
NORTH CAROLINA

Norfolk

BACK BAY NWR

MAMMOTH CAVE NP

CUMBERLAND GAP NHP

Paducah

KENTUCKY
TENNESSEE

CHEROKEE NF

Nashville

Knoxville

PISGAH NF

Raleigh

PEA ISLAND NWR

MATTAMUSKEET NWR

SWANQUARTER NWR

CEDAR ISLAND NWR

9

GREAT SMOKY MOUNTAINS NP

Memphis

JOYCE KILMER-SLICKROCK

CHEROKEE NF

10

Charlotte

SOUTH CAROLINA

UWHARRIE NF

CROATAN NF

Wilmington

MISS.

CHATTAHOOCHEE

COHUTTA

NANTAHALA NF

SUMTER NF

Columbia

HOLLY SPRINGS NF

WILLIAM B. BANKHEAD NF

SIPSEY

Atlanta

OCONEE NF

Augusta

Charleston

SANTEE NWR

FRANCIS MARION NF

CAPE ROMAIN NWR

Greenville

DELTA NF

TOMBIGBEE NF

NOXUBEE NWR

Birmingham

TALLADEGA NF

Macon

Savannah

SAVANNAH NWR

BLACKBEARD ISLAND NWR

Jackson

BIENVILLE NF

TUSKEGEE NF

Montgomery

WOLF ISLAND NWR

HOMOCHITTO NF

CONECUH NF

ALABAMA

Chattahoochee

GEORGIA
FLORIDA

OKEFENOKEE NWR

CUMBERLAND ISLAND NS

DE SOTO NF

Mobile

Talahassee

Jacksonville

Gulfport

Pensacola

GULF ISLANDS NS

APALACHICOLA

BRADWELL BAY

ST. MARKS NWR

OSCEOLA NF

11

OCALA NF

LAKE WOODRUFF NWR

Gulf of Mexico

CHASSAHOWITZKA NWR

Orlando

Tampa

12

13

Lake Okeechobee

14

J. N. "DING" DARLING NWR

Miami

EVERGLADES NP

Cape Sable

NATIONAL KEY DEER REFUGE

GREAT WHITE HERON NWR

KEY WEST NWR

MISSISQUOI NWR

MAINE

Au

Portla

81

90

80

76

75

64

55

40

95

59

10

75

95

PUERTO RICO

San Juan

CARIBBEAN NF

atahdin
7

3

Bangor

THE EAST

Numbered sites are established Wilderness Areas; unnumbered entries are units considered for wilderness designation. A figure after the name indicates wilderness acreage only, not total acreage of the park or refuge. Pages cited offer fuller description; page 337 lists contacts for obtaining further details on particular areas.

MAINE

1 Allagash Wilderness Waterway. 22,840. See page 230.

2 Baxter State Park. 201,018. See page 231.

3 Moosehorn NWR W. 2,782. Scenic solitude of rocky hills; woods, bogs, lakes, and streams. Woodcock habitat. Abundant wildlife. Fine hiking, fishing. Additional 4,598 acres proposed for wilderness.

NEW HAMPSHIRE

White Mountain NF wilderness proposals: Kilkenny, 24,000; Wild River, 20,000; Dry River-Rocky Branch, 34,000; Carr Mt., 10,000; Caribou-Speckled Mt. (Maine), 12,000. Generally high rugged country; many streams. Good trails.

4 Great Gulf W. 5,552. See page 232.

VERMONT

Missisquoi NWR. Woodlands, river delta marshes. Waterfowl, muskrats, otters, beaver. Refuge restricts public use.

NEW YORK

5 Adirondack State Park W. 997,960. See pages 229 and 242.

6 Catskill State Park W. 91,000. Dense forest, barren peaks, numerous waterfalls. Excellent hiking and climbing.

MASSACHUSETTS

Parker River NWR. Sand dunes, salt marsh. Six miles of ocean beach. Migratory waterfowl.

7 Monomoy NWR W. 2,420. Windswept coastal barrier beach; dunes, marshes. Large and varied shorebird population. Popular for nature study, hiking, fishing, photography.

NEW JERSEY

8 Great Swamp NWR W. 3,660. See page 225.

Brigantine NWR. 4,250. Barrier beach, salt marsh, dunes. Nesting and wintering area for waterfowl, shorebirds. Additional 12,500 acres proposed for wilderness designation by conservationists.

DELAWARE

Bombay Hook NWR. Salt marsh on Delaware Bay. Shorebirds, waterfowl, muskrats.

OHIO

West Sister Island NWR. 85. Wooded island. Herons, egrets. Refuge restricts public use.

KENTUCKY

Mammoth Cave NP. Forested hills cover magnificent limestone caverns. Surface and underground trails.

Cumberland Gap Nat. Historical Park. Also in Virginia and Tennessee. 6,375. Rugged crest area of Cumberland Mt., to 3,500 feet. Precipitous trails challenge experienced hikers.

WEST VIRGINIA

Dolly Sods. 10,215. High, rocky plateau, sphagnum bogs. Flora comparable to Canadian tundra. Many trails unmarked.

Otter Creek Wilderness. 20,000. Scenic highlands. Trails parallel pure streams; many waterfalls. Abounds in bears, turkeys.

Cranberry Wilderness. 36,300. See page 243.

MARYLAND

Blackwater NWR. Wetlands and woodlands. Migratory waterfowl. Excellent interpretive program.

VIRGINIA

Shenandoah NP. 73,280. Scenic Blue Ridge Mountains, one of the world's oldest ranges. Highest peak 4,049-ft. Hawksbill. Trails include 94 miles of Appalachian Trail.

Laurel Fork Wilderness. 11,656. Feeds Potomac River headwaters. Gentle wooded slopes, to 4,100 feet. Beaver, bear, deer, trout.

Chincoteague NWR. Beach, dunes, marshes on Assateague Island. 275 bird species. Wild ponies.

Back Bay NWR. Bay islands and Atlantic barrier beach. Winter home for migratory waterfowl and shorebirds.

TENNESSEE

Great Smoky Mountains NP. Also in North Carolina. See pages 228 and 267.

NORTH CAROLINA

9 Linville Gorge W. 7,575. Deep, rocky 12-mile river gorge. Rugged but rewarding trails. Many rare plant species.

Joyce Kilmer-Slickrock Wilderness. 32,500. Sheltered mountain cove, old Cherokee hunting ground. Extensive trail system.

10 Shining Rock W. 13,350. Gentle mountain slopes, named for gleaming white quartz outcroppings. Many waterfalls. Cone-shaped Cold Mt. 6,030 feet. Easy trails. Good fishing.

Pea Island NWR. Outer Banks island. Greater snow geese.

Mattamuskeet NWR. Woodlands and marsh border 15-mile-long lake. Canada geese, whistling swans. Excellent fishing.

Swanquarter NWR. Hardwood swamp and piney woods on Pamlico Sound. Swans, ducks.

Cedar Island NWR. Barrier island in Pamlico Sound. Migratory waterfowl.

SOUTH CAROLINA

Santee NWR. Reservoirs and croplands. Waterfowl, otters, raccoons. Good fishing.

Cape Romain NWR. 28,000. See page 255.

Savannah NWR. Reclaimed rice fields between river and coast. Migratory waterfowl. Fishing.

GEORGIA

Cohutta Wilderness 53,860. Rugged mountains, to 4,149 feet, interlaced with deep gorges, cascades. Good trails, fishing.

Blackbeard Island NWR. 3,000. Winter habitat for migratory waterfowl. Salt marsh, savanna, virgin forest, miles of beach. Hiking, fishing, beachcombing.

Wolf Island NWR. 4,218. Coastal island beach, marsh. Migratory waterfowl, shorebirds. Sea turtles. Refuge restricts public use.

Cumberland Island NS. Pristine ocean beaches, teeming estuaries, subtropical forests. Alligators, wild pigs, deer, rattlesnakes.

Okefenokee NWR. 343,850. See pages 228 and 250.

ALABAMA

Sipsey Wilderness. 12,000. See page 249.

MISSISSIPPI

Noxubee NWR. Wooded uplands and reservoirs. Waterfowl, deer.

FLORIDA

Gulf Islands NS. Barrier islands stretching 150 miles. Migratory waterfowl. Miles of sandy beaches. Alligators.

Bradwell Bay. 24,512. Hardwood and titi swamp, low pine ridges. Alligators, bears, possibly Florida panthers.

St. Marks NWR. 17,740. Salt marsh, swamplands, and forest. More than 300 bird species. Alligators, deer, bobcats. Good hiking, fishing.

11 Cedar Keys NWR W. 375. Four islands. Nesting area for osprey, ibis, herons, cormorants. Refuge restricts public use.

Lake Woodruff NWR. Low marsh and hardwood swamp around lake. Waterfowl, alligators, deer.

Chassahowitzka NWR. 16,900. Saltwater bays, swamplands, rivers and springs. Migratory waterfowl; manatees. Good fishing and bird watching.

12 Pelican Island NWR W. 6. Mangrove-covered river islands. Rookery for brown pelicans, ibis, egrets. Nation's first wildlife refuge, established in 1903. Restricted public use.

13 Passage Key NWR W. 36. Barren sandy island, constantly re-shaped by storms. Feeding ground for terns, gulls, pelicans. Refuge restricts public use.

14 Island Bay NWR W. 20. Mangroves predominate in these feeding grounds and rookeries for gulls, terns, shorebirds. Refuge restricts public use.

J.N. "Ding" Darling NWR. On subtropical Sanibel Island. Shorebirds, waterfowl, sea turtles, otters. Popular for shell collecting, fishing.

Everglades NP. See page 251.

Florida Keys. 4,740. Proposed wilderness includes parts of Great White Heron NWR, National Key Deer Refuge, and Key West NWR. Subtropical islands, rookeries for brown pelicans, osprey, bald eagles. Key deer, many snakes. Refuges restrict public use.

An amended Wilderness Act, according to the Forest Service, would qualify additional areas in the east for preservation. Some, long endorsed by citizen groups under the existing wilderness law, are described above. The rest are listed below.

Alexander Springs, 10,000, Ocala NF, Fla.; Beaver Creek, 5,500, Daniel Boone NF, Ky.; Presidential Range, 40,000, White Mountain NF, N.H.; Pocosin, 1,100, Croatan NF, N.C.; Craggy Mountain, 1,100, Pisgah NF, N.C.; Clear Fork, 19,000, Wayne NF, Ohio; Wambaw Swamp, 1,500, Francis Marion NF, S.C.; Ellicott's Rock, 3,600, Sumter NF, S.C.; Big Frog, 3,000, and Gee Creek, 1,100, Cherokee NF, Tenn.; Bristol Cliffs, 4,900, and Lye Brook, 9,100, Green Mountain NF, Vt.; Ramsey Draft, 6,700, George Washington NF, Va.; James River Face, 8,800, Mill Creek, 4,000, Mountain Lake, 8,400, and Peters Mountain, 5,000, Jefferson NF, Va.; El Cacique, 8,500, Caribbean NF, Puerto Rico.

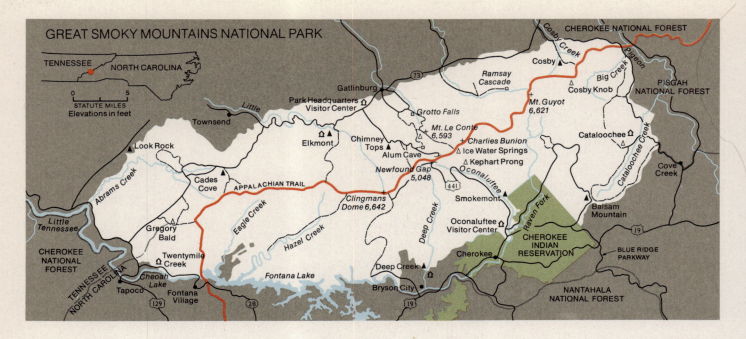

GREAT SMOKY MOUNTAINS NATIONAL PARK

TENNESSEE   NORTH CAROLINA

0   STATUTE MILES   5
Elevations in feet

CHEROKEE NATIONAL FOREST

Cosby Creek
Cosby
Cosby Knob
Big Creek
PISGAH NATIONAL FOREST
Ramsay Cascade
Gatlinburg
73
Park Headquarters Visitor Center
Grotto Falls
Mt. Guyot 6,621
Pigeon
Cataloochee
Little
Townsend
Elkmont
Chimney Tops
Mt. Le Conte 6,593
Alum Cave
Charlies Bunion
Ice Water Springs
Kephart Prong
Cataloochee Creek
Cove Creek
Look Rock
Cades Cove
APPALACHIAN TRAIL
Newfound Gap 5,048
Oconaluftee
Smokemont
Balsam Mountain
19
Abrams Creek
Eagle Creek
Hazel Creek
441
Clingmans Dome 6,642
Deep Creek
Raven Fork
Gregory Bald
Oconaluftee Visitor Center
CHEROKEE INDIAN RESERVATION
BLUE RIDGE PARKWAY
Little Tennessee
CHEROKEE NATIONAL FOREST
Twentymile Creek
Fontana Lake
Deep Creek
Cherokee
Cheoah Lake
Bryson City
Tapoco
Fontana Village
129
28
19
NANTAHALA NATIONAL FOREST
TENNESSEE NORTH CAROLINA

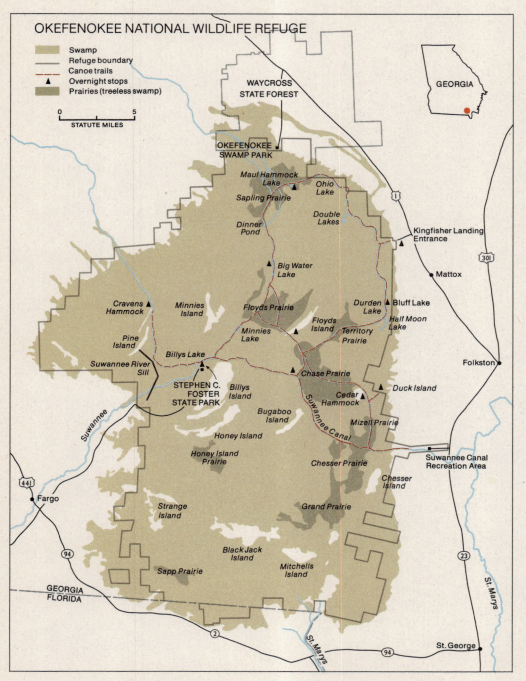

OKEFENOKEE NATIONAL WILDLIFE REFUGE

Swamp
Refuge boundary
Canoe trails
▲ Overnight stops
Prairies (treeless swamp)

0   STATUTE MILES   5

GEORGIA

WAYCROSS STATE FOREST

OKEFENOKEE SWAMP PARK

Maul Hammock Lake
Ohio Lake
Sapling Prairie
Double Lakes
Dinner Pond
1
Kingfisher Landing Entrance
301
Big Water Lake
Mattox
Floyds Prairie
Durden Lake
Bluff Lake
Cravens Hammock
Minnies Island
Floyds Island
Half Moon Lake
Pine Island
Minnies Lake
Territory Prairie
Suwannee River Sill
Billys Lake
Chase Prairie
Folkston
STEPHEN C. FOSTER STATE PARK
Billys Island
Cedar Hammock
Duck Island
Suwannee
Bugaboo Island
Suwannee Canal
Mizell Prairie
Honey Island
Suwannee Canal Recreation Area
Honey Island Prairie
Chesser Prairie
Chesser Island
441
Fargo
Strange Island
Grand Prairie
94
Black Jack Island
Sapp Prairie
Mitchells Island
23
St. Marys
GEORGIA FLORIDA
St. Marys
2
94
St. George

GREAT SMOKY MOUNTAINS

Wild island in a civilized sea, Great Smoky Mountains National Park rears haze-draped summits above North Carolina and Tennessee. Down its valleys run streams famed for brook and rainbow trout; up its slopes wind 700 miles of trails, some for man and horse, many for man alone—and one motor nature trail.

Along the roofline winds the Appalachian Trail, its 70-mile Smokies segment studded with shelters a day's hike apart. Permits for overnighters ease crowding at favorite spots, but day hikers still clog popular trails—a few so footworn they had to be paved. Backpackers on lesser-used trails often have primitive sites to themselves. Tenters and trailerites may find the park's seven campgrounds full.

Record-size trees and some 1,300 kinds of plants thrive in abundant rainfall. Sharp eyes may glimpse bobcat, wild boar, or the 20-inch Hellbender salamander. Shy in the backcountry, bears may turn to panhandling at campgrounds and by roads.

The idea which shaped the Wilderness Society grew on a Smokies trail in the 1930's. The park, first to be studied under the Wilderness Act, embraces a half million acres. Major parts would be set aside for wilderness designation under current proposals.

OKEFENOKEE SWAMP

Indians venturing into this watery wilderness found floating islets of peat that shook underfoot; they called the swamp "Trembling Earth." Pioneers rounded their word to Okefenokee. The swamp remains much as it was when Indian and pioneer hunted and fished on its lakes and islands, threading bewildering channels amid black gum and cypress. It covers about 680 square miles of wilderness land—585 of them set aside as a national wildlife refuge.

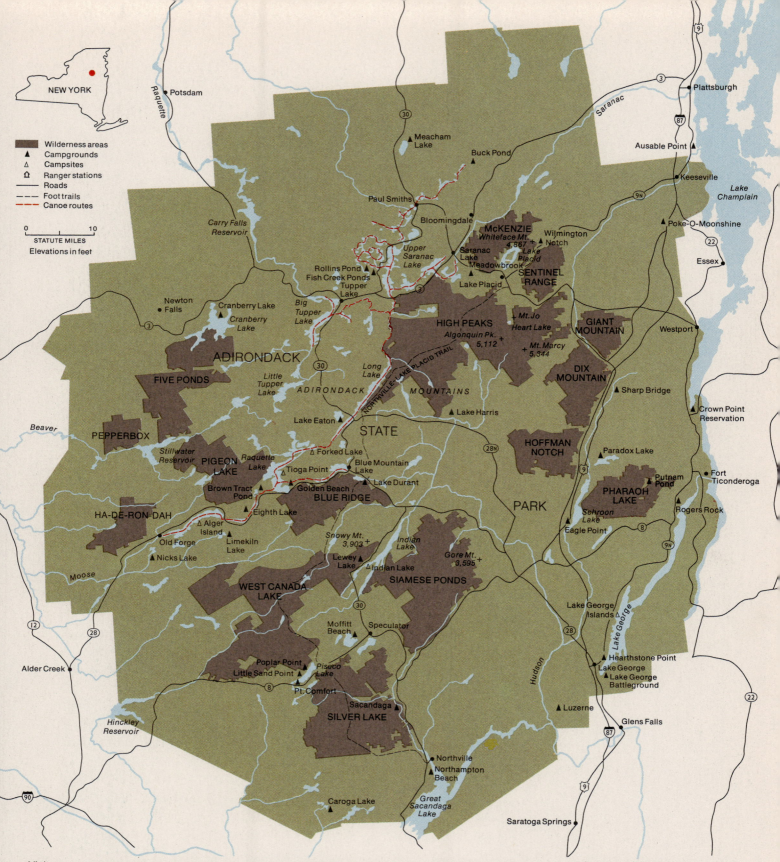

Visitors sample the swamp's allure in the exhibit centers at three entrances: Suwannee Canal, Stephen Foster, and Swamp Park. Observation towers, boardwalks, and boat tours offer a closer look. At Suwannee and Foster boats can be rented. An exception to normal wilderness rules allows motors up to ten horsepower— but paddle a canoe to hear best the calls of birds, the frog chorale, the alligator's bellow.

Colored markers guide paddlers along trails laid out for trips of two to six days; on some motorboat tours guides are required. By refuge rule, sunset clears the waterways. Day trippers leave the swamp, overnighters hole up in tents or cottages at Stephen Foster State Park; canoe campers set up at designated island clearings, shelters, or 14-by-20-foot platforms along the trails.

THE ADIRONDACKS

Wild lands, resorts, recreation areas, private tracts, and 87 towns make a patchwork of the 6-million-acre Adirondack State Park in New York. Shaped in 1885 by a farsighted act putting aside lands to be "forever kept as wild forest," this unique park offers some of the best backcountry in the East. Fifteen areas are managed as wilderness.

More than 5,000 miles of streams vein the peaks and forests, linking lakes and ponds in a boater's paradise. A favorite canoe route takes adventurers from Old Forge to Paul Smiths and beyond in a week or so; side trips stretch the jaunt to more than 125 miles. Some waters allow motors, others are solely for motorless craft, including the famed guideboats that blend canoe and skiff.

At water's edge and along 1,000 miles of footpaths in the forest preserve string shelters called "open camps." Users get them on a "first come" basis. Wilderness trails serve man and horse in summer, skier and snowshoer in winter; snowmobiles find a niche in over a million acres classed as "wild forest" lands.

Slender hope for the future, an American chestnut sapling ventures from a stump whose roots still cling to life. Sometimes towering 100 feet, the versatile chestnut— source of lumber, pulpwood, tannin, and nuts—dominated eastern forests until this century, when an Asian fungus all but wiped it out. Science still hopes to find or produce a resistant strain. Nature may restore herself without aid; from the roots of yesterday's fallen giants may sprout a few saplings that retain their juvenile immunity and return their kind to forests strewn with barkless trunks.

DRAWINGS BY GEORGE FOUNDS

mink, the water-loving muskrat—but I was lucky to spot a belted kingfisher, always a solitary traveler, fishing in a quiet pool. Pitted bark on maple trees showed where sapsuckers had drilled for insects and sap. It was almost dusk when a young deer stopped on the trail ahead, exchanged curious stares with me, then bounded away.

And this was almost a jetport! For generations eastern swamplands have been drained, filled, flooded, logged, and burned without restraint. But in 1957 the North American Wildlife Foundation began buying land in the Great Swamp for a wildlife sanctuary. Three years later the powerful Port of New York Authority fingered the Swamp as an airport site—and thousands of contributors in all parts of the country amassed $1,500,000 to save it. Some 3,000 acres became a national wildlife refuge. Subsequently other acres were added, bringing the total to 4,600. Then in 1966 the Port Authority tried again. The Swamp's best chance for survival lay in the Wilderness Act. For wildlife refuges are created by a commission; the Secretary of the Interior can permit invasions where he sees fit. But Congress alone designates Wilderness Areas, and Congress alone can reverse the decision.

Almost a thousand people thronged a hearing in Morristown to espouse wilderness status for the Swamp. Some talked about it as a natural basin for water supply and flood control. Spokesmen for nearby colleges defended it as a living laboratory. A corporation official stressed the need to balance economic development with green areas and wildlife preserves. "Our own wilderness is gone," said a Staten Islander. "We need the Great Swamp and to know it is there." Almost all regarded the proposal of some 2,500 acres as inadequate; they insisted on about a thousand acres more. And in due course Congress granted it.

To the Great Swamp victory, the words of Henry David Thoreau seem singularly fitting. "This curious world," he said, ". . . is more wonderful than convenient; more beautiful than it is useful; it is more to be admired and enjoyed than used."

The heart of Thoreau's wilderness is the north woods of Maine. On Moosehead Lake he started a classic adventure down the Allagash River in a slender canoe of birch bark sewn with roots of the black spruce. The foot of Telos Lake is now the popular approach; from there it takes about two weeks to paddle 92 miles down the north-flowing Allagash, poling over rocky waters for as many as nine miles at a stretch, easing across broad lakes, portaging around waterfalls to a splashy rendezvous with the St. John. The entire course is about three-fifths lakes and two-fifths river, each section with its own mood and personality. In one stretch the river roars and cascades; in another it rests in dark murmuring pools.

I had paddled in Thoreau's wake in the early 1960's during the battle over the Allagash, considered the finest of all canoe streams in a state famed for them. Hopes ran high for saving the river and its wooded borders as a wilderness. But the Allagash cuts straight through millions of acres of prime timber country: Why should its timber not be harvested with all the rest?

Seeking understanding, I traveled with Morris Wing, who managed a million acres for a paper company—and managed a canoe as if he'd been born in one. It was a joy to watch his delicate touch ease us around a rock. And he showed me much more.

One evening we were fishing as a bronze sun sank beyond Umsaskis Lake. Across the lake in a slack-water cove called a "bogan," a moose raised dripping antlers, then submerged them again to browse on water lily roots. Entranced by the setting, I thought of Thoreau's description: "It is all mossy and moosey. In some of those dense fir and spruce woods there is hardly room for the smoke to go up." I couldn't resist breaking the silence to comment on the utter tranquillity there.

"Don't forget," Morris replied. "I feel as proud of the wild land as anyone." He was typical of a breed of Maine men, close to the land, interested in pulpwood and timber, but also in wildlife and solitude.

Just then we came to an old dam and logging camp, ghostly relics of lusty river drives. Those early loggers were wasteful. They disturbed the river with a canal that floated logs to the mills of Bangor. They lacked incentives and technology for managing resources about them. Later, Morris showed me a modern logging operation where a third of the taller trees were marked for felling, the rest guarded for future growth. In this "selective logging" a forest always remains. Wildlife habitat is usually not much disturbed, and may even be improved for some species.

The Allagash has not been a virgin wilderness for generations. The land has been cut over several times, railroad tracks have been laid, dams erected and roads built, but as a well-managed commercial woodland its essential character has not changed. In 1966 the people of Maine voted funds to earmark 200,000 acres around the Allagash to be logged only under strict control of the state. Paper companies sold the 20,000 acres bordering the stream to the state, then donated 700 more, including Allagash Falls, the scenic highlight of the trip. In 1970 this inner corridor became the first state-administered waterway to be added to the National Wild and Scenic Rivers System.

In the rest of New England one cannot miss the relentless pressures for summer homes on lakeshores and riverfronts, for ski developments on mountain slopes and winter resorts in valleys below, for industrial sites and residential areas. They are reshaping the pastoral beauty of this tight little corner of the United States. Yet beyond them the north woods still looks much as it did in Thoreau's day.

Years after my canoe trek I returned to the Allagash with Tom Deans of the Appalachian Mountain Club for a perspective Thoreau never knew. Beneath the wings of our light plane stretched millions of acres of forest, flecked with hundreds of gleaming lakes, a great natural frontier almost without towns and roads. As cities grow, the north woods becomes a more and more valuable treasure to Maine and the nation. But its future is a question, as nearly all of it is privately owned. Logging roads have been expanded—and behind the bulldozers come the automobiles. "Where hundreds used the Allagash before," said Tom, "now there are thousands." Powerboats lay a stuttering wake. Airplanes land on lakes that once took days to reach by canoe and trail. It's tough to get away from noise, especially at Umsaskis, where diesels roar on the logging road long into the night.

We banked off from the Allagash and headed southeast to Mount Katahdin, towering above the lakes and forests of Baxter State Park. Maine has 10 mountains rising more than 4,000 feet, a hundred over 3,000, but none more impressive than 5,267-foot Mount Katahdin. That granite peak and its wild environs belong to Maine, thanks to one man's efforts. "Man is born to die," wrote the late Governor Percival P. Baxter. "His works are short-lived. Buildings crumble, monuments decay, wealth vanishes. But Katahdin in all its glory forever shall remain the mountain of the people of Maine." With his own funds he acquired 200,000 acres, including Katahdin, and gave it to the

Home in the wild: a shelter of logs, a fireplace of stones by trailside. Dozens dot wild areas in the East, most of them variants of the Adirondack "open camp"—itself a permanent version of pole and bark lean-tos erected by Adirondack guides for their hunting parties in the 1800's. Fire in front cooks hikers' food, warms the shelter, and shoos bugs away with its smoke.

Wilderness managers must decide the shelters' fate: here, perhaps, razing one to enhance the natural scene, there building one to lessen visitors' impact on the land.

state. A grateful legislature renamed the mountain's summit Baxter Peak, and in accord with his wishes has kept Baxter State Park's roadless interior unspoiled, laced only by foot trails and visited only by hikers.

To get the land, Governor Baxter had to allow one paper company to retain cutting rights on two tracts. But in March, 1973, the state bought out the company's rights— and saved 16,000 acres from the chain saw's bite.

As we circled the mountain, vistas changed—now a huge rampart wall, now a series of volcanic cones. And scores of hikers streamed toward the summit, seeking the northern terminus of the Appalachian Trail.

"What we need is another Percy Baxter—or another Katahdin," said Tom. "The park is overrun by far more visitors than it can support and still be 'forever wild.' Fortunately the state is starting to regulate use; it must, to save the resource."

Flying may be the best way to take in a forest of millions of acres. But the only way to get to know the postage-stamp Great Gulf Wilderness, a 5,552-acre preserve tucked in the curve of New Hampshire's Mount Washington, is to hike over the mountain and sleep on it a night or two. Minus airplane, Tom and I arrived at the Pinkham Notch Camp of the AMC—more than a hut, less than a hotel, peopled invariably with climbers and hikers. Rain cascaded; Pinkham was as chaotic as an airport with all flights grounded. But the talk buzzed of tramping and mountaineering. Those who insist we need more motorways in parks and forests because Americans are too lazy to walk need only visit this lively center.

The AMC is the oldest mountain club in the country. When it was organized in 1876, there was no White Mountain National Forest encompassing these peaks as it does now. Few of the peaks carried names; a mere handful of trails existed. Today the AMC operates nine huts, each a day's hike from the next. It maintains hundreds of miles of trails, builds shelters, offers training, guidebooks, maps. It cooperates with the Forest Service in rescue work; if you're ever lost or hurt in the White Mountains, chances are such a crew will be the one to get you out.

Next day the weather cleared and Tom and I set off up Mount Washington, bound for the Great Gulf on its northeastern flank. In my book, (Continued on page 241)

Portfolio Notes

OPPOSITE: *A brook near Buck Pond courses the black and white of winter in the Adirondacks. New York's six-million-acre state park offers a habitat for every type of visitor in posh resorts, campgrounds, and unmarred wild lands.*
ELIOT PORTER

PAGES 234-235: *Icy beards combed by winds of winter, stone giants of Algonquin Peak in the Adirondacks dwarf adventurers on a climb toward a listless sun. Some 100 peaks garrison the range. Only Mount Marcy looks down on 5,112-foot Algonquin, chilly classroom for these students of winter mountaineering.*
SAM ABELL

PAGES 236-237: *An Adirondack autumn dabs a woodscape upside-down on the wrinkled canvas of Bigsby Pond. Anglers, canoeists, and hikers with dry throats find thousands of crystal lakes and streams in this patchwork of public and private lands. Trees were nearly the realm's undoing. Pines made masts for the king's navy in the 1700's; a century later*

the lure of lumber had left vast stretches desolate. Now protected, forests again paint portraits on the ponds.
RUDI SCHONBECK

PAGES 238-239: *A warming sun ignites flowery fireworks in Dolly Sods, a West Virginia fastness named for a family that once farmed its "sods"—meadows. Now laurels thrive there and on old logging swaths where fires and erosion left the soil too shallow for trees. In uplands, winds have "flagged" the spruces, drying western sides and nipping buds with airborne ice crystals.*
ARNOUT HYDE, JR.

PAGE 240: *Fisherman's idyll: the veil of Hills Creek Falls, the twang of line as a trout comes to net. Dolly Sods, Otter Creek, and Cranberry Backcountry were first proposed for Wilderness Act protection by citizens, among them anglers who find here some of West Virginia's finest sport.*
ARNOUT HYDE, JR.

this mountain mass rates among the world's most unusual peaks. Here on the ridge of the Presidential Range you can meet weather as severe as any on this continent south of Alaska and the Yukon. To climb Washington—at 6,288 feet the highest peak in the Northeast—during winter is a daunting challenge. Two days out of three are unsuited to ascent. Winds often top 100 miles an hour; indeed, the highest surface wind ever recorded, 231 miles an hour, blasted across Mount Washington in 1934. Temperatures have hit 46° below zero F. Winds and cold here can create a chilling effect equal to that of Antarctica. People have died, even in summer, when storms of incredible violence arrive unannounced. Rocks become ice-coated, blinding fogs roll in, winds of brutal force exhaust the strongest tramper.

As we hiked the barren, rocky fields at the summit, a stiff summer wind was blowing: 40 miles an hour and picking up. We ducked into Summit House, terminus of both the cog railway that climbs the western slope and the auto road that snakes up from the east. "I got to know fog, ice, snow, and wind as I never dreamed they might exist," said an acquaintance who spent a winter in the summit's observatory. "If anyone wants to see and feel the forces of nature unleashed, here is the place."

The wind was still building as we left. The Gulfside Trail led over rocks tumbled and broken by frost, scarred by time—typical of rocky trails that challenge hikers in the White Mountains. Beneath us on both sides were sculptured basins and deep valleys with semicircular headwalls, handiwork of glaciers that once reached high on the Presidential Range. For a while we walked in fog. My eyes strained to see ahead. And I understood why the trail is marked by large cairns, closely spaced, each topped by a yellow-painted stone.

Who says the alpine barrens are barren? As the fog began to thin we walked through balsam and spruce barely three feet tall, hardy conifers clinging to rocky soil, withstanding long winters and flailing winds. Beneath the trees, tiny bluets appeared in unexpected places. The white petals of arctic diapensia hugged the ground, and oxalis robed the shaded banks. I saw wild raspberry, bunchberry, cloudberry, Labrador tea with its cream-white blossoms—many plants I had seen on the tundra in Iceland, struggling against whistling winds that can dehydrate them faster than they can absorb water from the soil.

Soon the day brightened, though the wind kept its sting. We sat on the ridge to rest, looking down into the Great Gulf, a deep, bowl-like ravine with bean-shaped Spaulding Lake beckoning below. The Gulf isn't very big; we could look across it easily to a clear-cut scar beyond. But as we headed down into it on the Sphinx Trail, we felt insulated from the world. We dropped a thousand feet through head-high thickets of birch and mountain ash to pick up the Great Gulf Trail, our way still beset with a demanding jumble of boulders now following the West Branch of the Peabody River. Add water to terrain like this, and you get cascades; they seemed to be everywhere beside the route, and I couldn't resist stopping along the mossy stretches between them for a drink, thirsty or not.

In late afternoon we reached one of the Great Gulf shelters in a forest of maples, birches, and evergreens. It is a popular destination, especially for climbers from Dolly Copp, largest campground in the White Mountain National Forest and five miles away by the Great Gulf Trail. Some other hikers had beat us to it, so we pitched our tents nearby. Around the shelter the ground was bare of plant life, a sign of heavy overuse and a silent reminder that 30,000 people visit the Gulf each year, many of them coming to this very spot to camp or rest. But in this shallow soil and temperamental climate it takes far less than that to tip nature's delicate balance.

"For a while," said Tom, "we considered building another hut on the high trail to take the pressure off the others. But each hut begets crowds and pollution; it cuts down our options to close down an area that's overused."

Next morning as we headed out we looked back into the diminutive wilderness. Above the forest rose the rocky crest of the Presidentials, within a day's drive of sixty million people. The AMC and others have fought for Wilderness Act preservation for eight other areas in the White Mountain National Forest. We need them. For certainly every ridge, crag, and wooded ravine will become increasingly valuable in the flood tide of supercivilization around them.

Mount Jo is as little as its name, a kid brother to the many giants that surround it. But it's steep. Student climbers scale it for practice. With my friend Garfield Jones of the Adirondack Mountain Club, I scaled it one summer morning for the view, a far circle of roller-coaster horizon comprising New York's Adirondack State Park, bigger even than some states.

Before us stood the lords of the High Peaks Region: Mount Marcy, New York's highest at 5,344 feet—*Tahawus,* or Cloud Splitter, the Indians called it—shrouded in mist though the valleys were bright. Algonquin, the second highest, much closer to us. Haystack, the third, with its long, rocky crestline. The Gothics, with bare rock flanks. Roads encircle this region, but within their embrace 219,000 acres remain unspoiled, the largest wilderness unit in the park.

"You ought to see these high peaks in winter," Garfield mused. "A stand of trees becomes a snow-covered flat. Waterfalls become walls of ice. We walk over frozen lakes on snowshoes and maybe build a fire to melt snow for drinking water." The thought stirred my summer thirst. I hoisted my canteen. And drank in the liquid jewel of Heart Lake, cupped in the trees below.

One of the first real efforts to safeguard wilderness by law began here nearly a century before the Wilderness Act of 1964 when New York State established the forest preserve in and around the Adirondack Mountains. Today Adirondack Park, including the preserve, encompasses some six million acres—more than Yellowstone, Yosemite, Grand Canyon, Glacier, and Olympic National Parks lumped together.

From our grandstand perch, the park seemed an unbroken expanse of forests and lakes and mountains. But on a map it breaks up in a crazy quilt of public and private tracts. Only 40 percent of the lands within the park boundary are owned by New York—and even these are constantly under pressure for development. Over the years, New York's voters have had to cope with scores of attempts to weaken the constitutional amendment designed to keep these lands "forever wild."

The greatest danger comes in the private domain. Subdivisions, ski resorts, and summer homes have burgeoned in recent years, and with them tourism, litter, pollution. Old controls over development no longer were enough. In 1970 a study commission recommended new restrictions on the use of private lands; designation of unspoiled state-owned tracts as wilderness; establishment of a wild, scenic, and recreational rivers system; propagation of rare species such as marten, lynx, loon, and raven; and reintroduction of locally extirpated species, which may well include the wolf along with the moose. No federal program has gone this far, nor relied this much on the direction of private citizens.

Today almost a million acres are safely tucked into a wilderness system modeled after the national program. But it is being over-loved. I could see telltale erosion everywhere. It may seem drastic to close certain peaks and campsites for a few years to let them recover, but it may become necessary. For the present, mountain clubs everywhere encourage careful use. What they plead for is obvious. The landscape should be as sacrosanct as the home environment. If the hiker treats it as such, he helps preserve the wild country for those who follow.

And preservation is what it's all about. Listen: "Civilization . . . has no business among these mountains, these rivers and lakes, these gigantic boulders, these tangled valleys and dark mountain gorges. . . . I would consecrate [them] to the Vagabond Spirit, and make them a place wherein a man could turn savage and rest, for a fortnight or a month, from the toils and cares of life." Journalist and outdoorsman Samuel H. Hammond penned that eloquent plea for the Adirondacks in 1857.

"Wild, Wonderful, West Virginia," sing travel folders to an appreciative audience of tourists in the surrounding eastern and midwestern cities. That any fragments of nature should endure in West Virginia owes little to the design of man. Early in the century the loggers left thousands of naked, fire-wracked acres. Miners burrowed after deep coal—a destructive process at best, but nothing to compare with modern strip mining, which can shear great layers of earth and rock off a mountainside and dump tons of mud and debris into a stream.

The folders are right; there *is* wild country in West Virginia. And it is all the more wonderful for having escaped destruction by its very remoteness—or for having recovered through nature's power of self-restoration, a power she readily displays in the moist and fertile East when we leave the land alone.

For four decades the land had been left alone in the Cranberry Backcountry, a tract of some 53,000 acres in the Monongahela National Forest. After intensive timbering, the railroads were dismantled, the roads were gated, the logging camps were razed. Around the rotting old stumps the seeds poked down tentative roots; seedlings grew into lithe saplings, saplings into spreading trees. Black bears multiplied; there are more of them there now than anywhere else in the state. Hikers and bicyclists proliferated, too, and found here a thriving wilderness with life in its soil and hatchery-born trout in its streams.

Then loggers were allowed to come back, for timber was mature. Bulldozer and chain saw began the cycle anew, scarring half the Backcountry before an outcry arose to save the rest. Protect it under the Wilderness Act, the people said; time and nature had made "the imprint of man's work substantially unnoticeable," as the Act requires. Citizens in other eastern and midwestern states were saying the same about tracts there. The Forest Service took the position that the Cranberry Backcountry and similar sites have not retained their "primeval character," as the Act also requires. Amend the Act, the Service finally suggested; allow once-disturbed areas in the East and Midwest to qualify—but keep the more rigorous standards in the West. Many conservationists disagree; they feel the Act would be weakened by amendment or by establishment of a parallel "Wild Areas East" system. More and more areas in forgotten corners of the national forests are being explored, studied, proposed. And each thus added to the Wilderness System is a permanent tribute to nature's urge to replace a plundered forest with another just as green.

With two young trailmates I spent a summer weekend in the Cranberry Wilderness—the name citizens' groups

Automation finds a habitat in the wilds of West Sister Island, an 85-acre refuge in Lake Erie proposed for the Wilderness System. On the island's only beach stands a crumbling lighthouse whose keepers tended its beam in days of sail. Since 1937 an automatic light atop the old tower has warned mariners away. The Coast Guard maintains the light— but herons and egrets rule the roosts in the hackberry trees, commuting nine miles to the mainland several times a day for food for hatchlings in more than a thousand nests.
DRAWING BY GEORGE FOUNDS

gave to the unscarred half of the Backcountry plus an adjacent 10,000 acres. We started where the Middle Fork and Little Fork join the Williams River, a white-water stream that skirts the steep-sided ridges and high knobs of the Backcountry as it hurries westward. We waded the river, headed up a path along the Little Fork, and four miles later turned east on a ridgecrest trail. There were no views to lead the eye into infinity, but rather a kind of intimate inspiration in watching the forest change from hardwoods to stands of spruce and hemlock as we hiked along.

After lunch we dropped off the ridge trail and went cross-country—bushwhacking, some call it. Exhausting, I called it as we followed a stream down steep slopes covered with dog hobble and dripping rhododendron, an almost impenetrable jungle with only an occasional patch of sunlight on the red partridgeberries. We picked up a bear path, secure in the knowledge that bears here are very shy. They don't raid campsites, but they love to chew up signs that mark the major trails; sometimes you have to work a splintery jigsaw puzzle to read where to go.

Finally we broke out on a grassy path, an old railroad grade along beautiful Hell for Certain Branch ("Hell fer Sartin," a mountain man would say). Summer is the season for black midges and we were properly devoured. We tried swimming in the swift water, but it was frigid even in mid-July. Bug repellent was our only salvation.

Three days in the Backcountry vanished all too quickly. Eight open-front shelters dot the tract, but none along our route, so we slept out each night. Once we camped in the lee of an overhanging cliff near a cold, swift creek. After supper we huddled around the fire against the chill of fog, listening to the nocturnal concert of whip-poor-wills and screech owls, their calls riding the night winds that toyed with the hemlocks and sycamores.

We had seen lilies, violets, lady's-slippers, massive ferns, and an amazing variety of fungi and mosses—and, of course, the onion-like ramp, springtime delicacy of the southern hills, pungent and garlicky, tender when yanked up before the leaves fully expand. People enjoy their flavor in soups and salads; the brave risk them raw.

Thundershowers here can begin on any sunny afternoon with a low rumble on a distant ridge; soon the hiker is enveloped in a dark canopy of fast-flying clouds. Thunder echoes and re-echoes. Suddenly rain falls in a sheeting and crackling as deafening peals shake the mountains. Then the torrent subsides. Wisps of fog rise from the valleys while low-hanging clouds roll through the gaps. The sun is strong again, the world more green and glorious.

In three days we had seen just a fragment of the Backcountry, and nothing at all of two smaller areas identified by citizens as prime wilderness regions in the Monongahela Forest. Next time, perhaps, we'll wander the Otter Creek Wilderness, 20,000 acres that have escaped the ax for fifty years or more (Continued on page 249)

Portfolio Notes

OPPOSITE: *In the pixie parasols of* Marasmius siccus *mushrooms, life springs from dead wood along the Sipsey Fork in Alabama. Big as buttons, they sprinkle color through this unspoiled corner of Bankhead National Forest. Venerable trees tower above them—including a mammoth tulip poplar 22 feet in circumference.*
MIKE HOPIAK

PAGES 246-247: *Scented beauty with a heart of gold, the white water lily steals the show at a grand opening in Okefenokee Swamp.*

Spanish moss beards an audience of cypresses. Visitors paddle the refuge, serenaded by the song of the Carolina wren, the hoot of the horned owl, the cry of the bobcat, the bellow of the alligator.
FARRELL GREHAN

PAGE 248: *White ibises turn black against a westering sun as they reach for toeholds on mangroves of Cape Sable in the Everglades. Teeming rookeries dwindle as civilization taps the park's water sources, helping dry up pools where the long-legged waders feed.*
PATRICIA CAULFIELD

despite good access on all sides. The Otter Creek Trail bisects the wilderness from end to end, never more than a few feet from the edge of a stream — and waterfalls and swimming holes that make the trail a hiker's delight.

Or maybe we'll accept the challenge of Dolly Sods, a remote wilderness plateau on the crest of Allegheny Mountain. Deep, wooded canyons carve it. Heath barrens resembling northern tundra cover tablelands. Sphagnum bogs abound. On the barrens azalea and blueberry vie with carpets of mosses and ground pines; stunted spruces dot the rocks. In the bogs grow cranberries, orchids, and the tiny, insectivorous sundew plant. From late May to killing frost, wild flowers provide splashes of color that change virtually from week to week. In late summer, local people camp out while picking enough blueberries to put up for the winter. Mid-September bird migrations attract ornithologists, professional and amateur, to Bear Rocks to watch hawks and other birds. And in every season the rugged, windswept fastness beckons the hiker to tree and tundra in the midst of southern Appalachia.

Sooner or later, one begins to wonder: Are there *any* virgin wildernesses in the eastern national forests, any nooks and crannies that stand today as they stood when the pioneers pushed west? Yes, a precious few. One survives in a rather unlikely place, the William B. Bankhead National Forest in Alabama — a state in which millions of acres of hardwoods have been "phased out" to make room for tree farms of pulpwood pines. But in the small and nearly inaccessible box canyon of the Bee Branch, the great trees have never felt the sting of steel.

I visited the area a few years ago with people from the Forest Service and a group called the Alabama Conservancy. For years the Service had protected 1,112 acres of the Bee Branch wilds as a scenic area. But the Conservancy, after careful study, proposed a 12,000-acre Sipsey Wilderness, with the canyon at its heart.

We approached the Bee Branch of the Sipsey River on a road that passed a large clear-cut, stark as a battlefield, a peculiar foreground to a wilderness. But soon we were hiking down into the deep gorges between bluffs of fissured sandstone, the rim-rock cliffs tinted in grays and yellows, with waterfalls tumbling over gigantic boulders to the valley floor. Only a remnant of the original forest survives in the 30-mile chain of gorges, but it is impressive nonetheless. Cool summer temperatures, deep shade, and constant moisture provide a refuge for eastern hemlock, sweet birch, and other plants normally found farther north.

Before 1816 Chickasaw and Cherokee Indians roamed the forest; so did the mountain lion, bear, and beaver. Some of the animals still remain. And in the Sipsey River and its tributaries survive fish species lost elsewhere from pollution, silting, damming, and ditching. Two kinds of colorful little darters are found only here. Gone are the once-familiar raven and ruffed grouse. But the vales still ring with songs of the northern whip-poor-will and southern chuck-will's-widow. And because birds are so mobile, the Sipsey ecology may affect populations thousands of miles away that depend on food and cover here during migration or overwintering.

A soft, warm spray splashed us as we hiked past a ledge, and we ducked under it into a "rockhouse" to watch the water catch the sunlight as it fell to a mossy pool. Expectantly, I turned over a rock — and was rewarded with the sight of a zig-zag salamander, its dorsal stripe contrasting with dark and light spots on its belly. A little luck, and it might have been one of the lungless salamanders. A rock-turner in Appalachia is seldom disappointed.

Many salamanders are native to the Appalachians, found in their own corners of streams and mossy floors of the mountain forests and nowhere else. Of what use are they, I asked myself as we headed back. To man, perhaps no obvious use at all. But as exemplars of environmental adaptation and survival, they serve us well.

Of what practical use is a swamp? There was no dearth of answers for the wild Georgia swampland known as Okefenokee. Half a century ago, logging railroads on spindly pilings were thrusting into its jungles. Ideas were hatching to slash a highway through, even a barge canal. Fortunately, a better idea won out: to see that the treasures of the swamp, unique in all the world, were safeguarded for all time.

In 1937 the Okefenokee became a national wildlife refuge, putting a final end to the logging, the threats of highways and drainage ditches, and the uncontrolled attacks on alligators and other animals. It was then still quite remote, but it is much less so now. A busy airport lies 40 miles away, and two major highways converge almost at the eastern edge. Yet investigators found that 343,850 acres out of its 368,950 qualify under the Wilderness Act.

On each visit to this primitive, mysterious world, I realize how little I know about it, and how little it has really been studied. Last time I entered from Okefenokee Swamp Park, an interpretative area run by a non-profit group just outside the northern boundary. There you can rent boats to get you deep into the swamp and guides to get you back out. I jest, of course. Boat tours are offered at all three park entrances. Self-guiding canoe trails wind for the paddler.

"It's not a true swamp, you know," guide John Hickox explained as we passed forests of cypress, black gum, and bay, with a rich understory of aquatic shrubs and vines. "A true swamp is a low basin which acts as a drain for the surrounding area. But Okefenokee is mostly higher than its backcountry; it's a watershed." Only a few feeder streams come in from the north. The water is dark-stained from the swamp vegetation, but pure enough to drink. It doesn't look as if it is moving, but it is—slowly, continuously emptying into the St. Marys River on the southeast and Stephen Foster's Suwannee River on the west.

Balanced today on extinction's brink, the Florida sandhill crane once strutted wetlands from south Georgia and Florida to the Texas border. Now a few thousand haunt their remaining breeding grounds in south Florida and the Okefenokee; a handful may still breed in Mississippi. North America's sandhill crane is one of the oldest living species of birds, changed but little from fossils 9,000,000 years old. If man's encroachment obliterates still more of this bird's domain, it could become a rarity even in refuges—or a creature that endured the ages and ended here.

We rode in a small outboard—up to ten horsepower is permitted—but we could just as well have poled a narrow skiff as did the pioneers who ventured in after a military force pushed the Seminoles out in the 1830's. The old-timers gave logical names to plants that make Okefenokee a place of loveliness —the never-wet, floating heart, poor man's soap, and he-huckleberry. They saw the alligator's eyes shine red in the dark and called him "Old Fire Eyes."

Now and then we spotted an alligator, looking for all the world like a floating log. The Okefenokee holds one of the largest remaining concentrations of alligators. Once they were found in coastal swamps and rivers from northern North Carolina to the southern tip of Texas. But from the early 1800's until 1940 at least ten million were killed for hides—large adults first and then the smaller ones, one population and then another. Finally, laws are going after the hide market. But alligators are still slaughtered by the thousands—most of them illegally—and are an endangered species over much of their range.

"I shudder to think of what Okefenokee would be like without the gator," Johnny said. "But this is no small business run by swamp folks. The big-time poachers just can't resist the high prices offered by the hide merchants. If there were no markets or international syndicates, poaching would end tomorrow."

There is nothing monotonous about the Okefenokee. The swamp forests interweave with expanses of marsh and water called "prairies," created during droughts by extremely hot fires that burned the surface layers of peat so low that woody

250

vegetation could not grow back. Prairies in the eastern section provide a major year-round habitat of the sandhill crane. Scattered through the swamp are 60 lakes large enough to be named, and islands of trees and shrubs called "houses" for the great numbers of creatures that make homes on them.

We followed markers about a mile apart and soon found our shelter for the night, an Adirondack affair on a high and dry platform. We shut down our outboard, and instantly the noises of nature took over. You may not go as fast by canoe, but your ears are free to tune in on the world. As shadows of night covered the swamp, we heard the eerie hoot of barred owls, the grunting of bullfrogs, the varied piping of countless smaller frogs—an elemental chorus rolling out of the misty marsh. I lay awake for hours, hoping in vain to hear a bull alligator calling for a mate—a bellowing roar in the breeding season that carries for miles.

Next day we headed out of the wild swamp, crossing Big Water Lake, Minnies Lake, and Billys Lake, three of the most popular fishing spots in southern Georgia. On this weekend morning, traffic on the waterways already was substantial. It looked like fun for all, but I was glad to be going. We hadn't seen a soul the day before—and that's the way I like to think of the Okefenokee.

At the southernmost corner of the eastern mainland, beneath white clouds in a blue Florida sky, waits a rare natural marvel: the Everglades, a wonderful land of limitless horizons, an eternity of tall grass and shining water, an infinity of life-forms in miniature, all interrelated worlds. Our third largest national park protects close to a million and a half acres, most of it wilderness of a kind found nowhere else in the United States. It ranges from low islands or keys in Florida Bay to tangled mangrove swamps (forests, if you wish), monotonously flat saw-grass prairies, thick pinewoods, and tropical hammocks of broad-leaved trees and shrubs. A thousand kinds of plants find a home in the Everglades.

And birds! Visitors in winter and spring can still watch a symphony of flight, even though present populations are only a memory of the million and a half wading birds that nested here 30 years ago. In its original condition, south Florida offered one of the greatest wildlife spectacles on earth.

One day ranger Jason Houck and I explored the 'Glades by canoe, the only practical way to take an intimate look. We paddled the Hells Bay Trail, one of four canoe trails linking a chain of shelters. As soon as we pushed off, we were swallowed by mangrove forest, with the watery trail—sometimes no wider than the canoe—tunneling through the tangled thickets. Mangroves 50 to 75 feet high stood on stilty roots arching out and down like the legs of giant crabs. The tree tolerates salt water and thus grows where most other plants cannot.

White floats marked the trail, but still we managed to lose it now and then. Waters darkened by tannic acid from the mangroves mirrored the jungle in striking clarity. A heron fishing at water's edge broke the silence with a squawk. At thicket openings we caught sight of egrets and ibises on the mud flats, the dark back of a limpkin barely visible among mangrove roots, a brown pelican in the top of a small tree, blue-winged teal scooping food from the shallows.

Another day, another boat, another ranger, another trail. This time we took the 100-mile Wilderness Waterway that begins at Everglades City, in the northwest end of the park, and winds through waters both fresh and salt. We wove among 10,000 tiny islands, one of the largest mangrove forests in the world. Seeds of the

The Florida panther looks toward a future even more precarious than that of the crane. Thousands of the pale brown "painters" roamed the Deep South a century ago. Settlers decimated deer herds on which the cougar preyed, but brought with them easier game: pigs, chickens, even colts. Hunter became hunted as dogs treed the hated cats so men could shoot them down. Now less than 25 pad through the Everglades, the subspecies' final toehold on survival. Smaller than western kin, it may span seven feet from nose to tail's dark tip.

DRAWINGS BY GEORGE FOUNDS

mangrove often trail long roots by the time they drop from the tree. These fasten to the bottom, catch sand and seaweed in their netlike structure. As the roots spread, islands form. At mouths of streams the trapped silt builds mud flats that eventually rise above the reach of tides; then the tree that created the land dies, for its roots need the wash of salt water at least at high tide each day.

Offshore from us, a school of porpoises performed gymnastics. A score of white egrets flapped their wings as if in greeting. Here a bald eagle, there an osprey perched in a nest atop a tall dead mangrove at the water's edge. The eagle is rare in the East, but the park harbors a stable population of between 150 and 200 of the birds, with an average of 40 young hatched each year.

It takes seven days to cover the park's Wilderness Waterway by canoe. But it took us only one day in our powered patrol boat. I wondered later about the place of power: Is it possible, really, to justify a man's presence in wilderness unless he gets into it under his own steam? Traveling by machine makes a man part of the machinery, rather than part of nature; he detracts more than he contributes.

The Everglades owes its fertility to a mild, subtropical climate and the gentle contours of the land, nowhere more than ten feet above sea level—here the Gulf of Mexico. But it also depends on the flow of fresh water—shallow, sunlit, rich in nutrient, and mixed with salt water in the estuaries. For thousands of years the Everglades was essentially a river laden with microscopic life and flowing slowly southward. Micro-organisms by the trillions fed the fish, which in turn fed the birds. During the dry months of late winter and spring, marsh snails, frogs, and fish would concentrate in the deep sloughs and "gator holes." Then summer would bring the rains anew, the waters would gradually rise, and aquatic life disperse to repopulate glades and swamps. All life in the park is attuned to this rhythmic water cycle—even in the brackish estuaries, the areas of highest biological productivity, nurseries for the smaller denizens in the food chain that supports the larger game fish of the deeps.

In 1947 the Army Corps of Engineers began in Florida the biggest earth-moving project since the Panama Canal: construction of levees, canals, earth dams, and spillways for flood control and "other purposes." The natural flow of fresh water to the Everglades is now controlled by man, inadequately at best. The summer-wet, winter-dry cycle has been disrupted. The water table is much lower, allowing salt water to intrude inland. The environment still seems at peace with itself, but the picture is deceptive. The life systems have been seriously damaged; the wilderness is but a fragile copy of its former self.

And that is a tragedy. We can always build a new dam, but we can never reconstruct an Everglades. We save it as nature built it, or we can lose it.

We have already lost some of the choicest wild areas in the East. Yet it is not too late, even within urban sprawls, to preserve many areas that remain, where people can experience the grace and beauty of nature undisturbed. The Wilderness Act holds great promise for preservation of relatively large tracts; now perhaps we need to go beyond it to find smaller sites and save them while we can.

"We can't all be great explorers, like Peary and Powell, nor great naturalists, like Thoreau and Humboldt," wrote Benton MacKaye, father of the Appalachian Trail. "But anyone who prizes the sights and sounds of nature in action, whether robins at the window or muskrat in the stream, or bog born of ages, such a one is, within his measure, an explorer and naturalist. And his job is cut out for him: to make of his region, as seen from its highest hill, a place for taking expeditions."

More monster than mermaid, a Florida manatee thrusts its bristly snout above the clear waters of the Everglades, sucking in a great gulp of air that can keep it submerged for as long as 13 minutes. A face only a lonesome sailor could love gave substance to myths of fin-tailed maidens in days of Columbus. Hunters seeking its meat, oil, and hide helped push the paddle-tailed mammal toward extinction until Florida law ended the slaughter. Powerboats still take a toll, slashing the sluggish browsers with keel or propeller before they can undulate out of the way.

Once found from Texas to the Carolinas, the harmless sea cow holds its own in some areas of Florida. But as boating, silting, and pollution continue, it may be forced to a final stand in the wild heart of the Everglades.
PATRICIA CAULFIELD

SANCTUARY AT CAPE ROMAIN

Tom Allen

The island, so still and lifeless only moments before, exploded with a barrage of birds as soon as we anchored our boats. We slogged through a marsh under a blizzard of screaming terns and flapping, squawking pelicans. Ashore, near a cluster of pelican nests, Burkett Neely, manager of the Cape Romain National Wildlife Refuge, assembled his birdbanders for last-minute instructions.

"Don't waste time," he said, glancing up at the late-morning sun. "The chicks will cook if we keep the parents off the nests too long. And we have to watch the tide or we'll hang up the boats." The volunteers on the team—my wife Scottie, our teenagers Connie and Roger, and I—needed special orders: "Watch your step." In rookeries covering barely an acre on this low-lying island were 1,000 pelican nests and 5,000 dips in the sand that cradled the eggs or chicks of royal terns.

We had come to Marsh Island, about four miles off the South Carolina coast, to put leg bands on 100 pelicans and tag their wings with the bright orange streamers that would identify them at a distance as Cape Romain birds. We would sweep the island, banding and tagging a few birds in an area, then moving on to another spot so that only a few irate parents would be off their nests at a time.

Sounds simple enough, I thought as I walked over to pick up a young bird about the size of a kitten. "We want big ones," Burkett said, "ones that are just about to fly." He pointed to a scowling pelican with wings as long as my arms.

I chased it, leaned over to grab it by the beak, and watched my sunglasses slip off my nose and into its pouch. We both gaped in surprise. Then my sunglasses reappeared, followed by the bane of pelican banders: the contents of the bird's considerable, and upset, stomach.

To catch a pelican you must clamp your hand on the bird's beak at the precise moment it snaps shut (hopefully not on your hand). Then, holding the beak closed

TOM ALLEN, NATIONAL GEOGRAPHIC STAFF. OPPOSITE: GENE GIBBS. FAR RIGHT: RONALD A. HELSTROM

with one hand, you scoop up the bird with the other, clutch the pelican against your chest, and bear your squirming burden to the banders.

In about 90 minutes we banded 103 pelicans. In years to come, with luck, some would be traced to their yet unknown wintering grounds. Aided by such information, scientists may find ways to save the eastern brown pelican, an endangered sub-species which has vanished from places where once it flourished.

We were on Marsh Island, an outpost of the island-dotted refuge, to help, not sight-see. Visitors are not allowed on the islands while birds are nesting. Like the other refuges proposed for, or part of, the wilderness system, Cape Romain exists to serve wildlife. People can enjoy refuges—but not at hazard to the protected creatures.

The list of all that live in the sanctuary of Cape Romain echoes Genesis on the fifth day: "Let the waters bring forth abundantly the moving creature . . . and fowl that may fly above the earth. . . ." For this is a refuge that harbors the life of sea and sky. Its marshes, stirred by the tides, launch food chains extending as far as 50 miles offshore. Sea turtles hatch in the warm sands of its outlying islands. Alligators prowl its ponds. Porpoises frolic in its great bay, which sustains shrimp, clams, oysters— and what they eat and what eats them. Over sea, over beaches, or in the dense forest of its largest island, Bulls Island, fly more than 250 species of birds, some in the tens of thousands, some represented by a cherished few.

Along the Atlantic Coast, marshes are disappearing and cities sprawl to the shore. Cape Romain's headquarters at Moores Landing, 20 miles northeast of Charleston, is within an hour's drive of 400,000 people. But the refuge's marshy coast stretches for

Treading a Marsh Island rookery dotted with the eggs of royal terns, wildlife researchers seek a rarer bird: the brown pelican. A few, flapping amid the terns, rise from one of two known sites in South Carolina where this declining species still nests. Helpless young (opposite) rely on parents for meals of regurgitated fish and protection against the broiling sun.

Biologists, probing a pelican die-off that began in the 1960's, compared new-laid eggs with those in museums. Modern shells were much thinner; brooding parents often crushed them. The lethal new ingredient: DDT, whose residues impair eggshell formation. The birds eat fish which ingest DDT washed into the sea from farms. State bird of Louisiana, the pelican has vanished there; even imports in refuges died off.

The Bulls Island wildlife walk, bowered by festooned branches, beckons visitors to a rendezvous with animals. Along the two-mile trail cautious hikers can see—or perhaps only hear—dwellers of marsh and seashore, pond and subtropical woodland.

Monarch of the forest is the live oak; some here were saplings in Columbus's time. Shaggy strands of Spanish moss are not parasitic. An epiphyte, misnamed

a moss, the plant draws food from the air.

A garden spider, spinning a snare across the path, won't wait long for a meal; so many insects live on Bulls Island it became a proving ground for GI bug repellent. A bumblebee forages in the flower of a prickly pear, the East's only widespread cactus. A ribbon snake poises for prey, preferably a frog. A black fox squirrel, largest North American species, shares the path.

25 uncluttered miles. One day, returning from Marsh Island, we spotted a 21-foot cruiser grounded in tall cordgrass. The three men aboard had been stranded more than 24 hours. We threw them our lunches, then called the Coast Guard.

On Bulls Island I could look upon a seaward shore as wild as it was on the day in 1670 when English settlers anchored here and beheld their New World. The island is named after one of them, Stephen Bull. He saw, as I did, a beach strewn with seashells and dotted with strutting shorebirds. The beach slopes to a sandy rise tufted with rippling sea oats and other grasses. Beyond a thicket of wax myrtle stands a row of dwarfed live oaks, bent and cropped by the wind.

Bank, bush, and tree form the rampart of this barrier island created by the sea — a corduroy of ancient dunes and hollows that evolved into tree-covered ridges and sloughs. As the sea alternately built and battered from one side, a tidal marsh reached out from land, bearing soil and seeds, lacing the island with creeks and ponds. In time came a forest of palmetto and magnolia, loblolly pine and gnarled live oak draped in Spanish moss. Today the island is about two miles across at its widest point, a splinter of land delicately balanced between marsh and sea.

Each morning a boat from Moores Landing threads a four-mile maze through the marsh and carries visitors to Bulls Island. The boat takes them back in the afternoon, for they cannot camp here. This is the heart of Burkett Neely's realm. Elsewhere in the refuge he and his staff stand off and let nature prevail. But Bulls Island has been kept out of the area covered by the Wilderness Act. To preserve this sanctuary where men and wildlife meet, man must intervene.

With Scottie, Roger, and Connie, I explored the island, hiked its trails, combed its beach for shells—and fed its mosquitoes, gnats, and ticks. We marched along one stretch slapping each other's backs. I—or Scottie, depending upon how you look at it—hold the record: 25 mosquitoes squashed on my back with one wifely swat. We beat the ticks that day, 36 (tweezered off clothing) to 1 (burrowed into Roger's leg). But even ticks are forgotten when you can stand at the edge of a pond and see nine alligators glide by. Or peer into a forest so thickly spun with vines and bristling with trees that you rarely spy the life you hear: the drumming of woodpeckers, the soft gobble of wild turkeys, the rustling of shy deer.

On patrol with Burkett I began to learn about the backstage managing of this wild world. An orange paint splotch on a pine tree marked the center of a browse study area 24 feet in diameter. Within such circles refuge workers each spring inventory all plants and observe how the deer feed on them. By noting how much of the less favored plant foods is eaten and by measuring the "browse line" to see how high the animals have stretched to find a meal, Burkett can gauge the deer's desperation. "Like kids, they eat their favorite foods first—and save the spinach for last," he told me. "We know the deer population has been building to the starvation point. We

The lofty osprey, falling to
pollution elsewhere, and the
alligator, target of hide poachers,
find sanctuary at Cape Romain.
The ospreys' treetop cradles
a hidden pair of young.
The alligator, an endangered
species, thrives here. Some grow
to 13 or 14 feet, their size
warily estimated by this rule:
Each inch from eye to nose
equals a foot in body length.
    The raccoon, which can earn
a living by snatching prey from
food-rich waters, enjoys easier
fare here by stealing the eggs
of wild turkeys and sea turtles.
Refuge workers capture thieves
and exile them to mainland
forests, where they may face
a peril unknown at Romain:
the guns of hunters.

have to crop them.'' The refuge allows bow-and-arrow hunters to do the job before the animals succumb to starvation and the ravages of malnutrition.

We stopped by a pond clogged with cattails. Man's chemicals will kill them, man's fire will burn off the stalks. Controlled salinity will encourage the growth of more desirable plants for a waterfowl habitat. Such tinkering with the ecology helps provide room and board for as many as 80,000 migrating ducks each fall. And the ducks have lured a predator some thought extinct on the East Coast: the peregrine falcon. Two, possibly three, of these duck hawks have wintered at the refuge. The ponds also support 700 to 1,000 alligators—so many that Romain has set up a program to trap some and ship them to other refuges with gator shortages.

Driving along a Bulls Island trail in a jeep, we flushed a pair of wood ducks. "Mr. and Mrs.," Burkett said. "They're courting." They would probably nest in one of the wooden boxes perched on poles around the ponds. Shields thwart raccoons that shinny up to steal eggs. Raccoons, which somehow reached the island long ago, are notorious egg thieves. I saw one in the middle of a trail boldly feasting on the freshly laid eggs of a cooter turtle. Along the beach, the raccoons' taste runs to the eggs of a much bigger—and much rarer—turtle, the Atlantic loggerhead.

The loggerhead is mammoth. Some weigh as much as 500 pounds; Cape Romain's are considered big at 300 pounds, with a shell 36 inches across. Yet loggerheads need little from man's land—only a hole in the sand of a warm, undisturbed beach. The female, after mating in the island-shielded waters of the refuge, crawls ashore, digs a hole with her flippers, lays about 125 eggs, covers them, and returns to the water. Some two months later the hatchlings emerge from eggs and sand to scuttle off to sea. Those that survive to adulthood begin the cycle anew, the females seeking the strand of shore that nestled them.

But as man has claimed the coasts along the Gulf of Mexico and the Atlantic, the loggerhead has lost nearly all its nesting sites. Among the few places left are the 20 miles of seaward beaches on the islands of Cape Romain. From May through July and into August refuge workers patrol these shores looking for the sign of the turtle: tracks, or "crawls," from the tide line to the dry upper beach.

RONALD A. HELSTROM

A place they can call their own

Mirroring waters of a Bulls Island pond double the beauty that bird watchers behold. Here, as in more than 330 other refuges covering 30 million acres in 49 states, the mission is also double: preservation of the animals and enhancement of man's vision of his world. At Cape Romain we can look upon species that plume hunters nearly wiped out: common egrets and the smaller snowy egrets. Like a shadow, a Louisiana heron appears amid them.

Another heron promenades with its dappled image. A quintet of coots plies deeper water, away from the wader's domain. A green heron and a catbird, tail up in tense response to an intruder, perch in the tracery of branches. Day visitors can huddle in a blind to observe or photograph wildlife; 105 bird species have been spotted on the island in a single day.

With management programs based here, Bulls Island is outside the 28,000 refuge acres envisioned as part of the wilderness system. About 100 refuges, with 25 million acres, have been accorded or are being studied for Wilderness Act protection. Lacking such legislative safeguards, refuges in the past have been invaded by mining operations, oil rigs, and bulldozers making new habitats for the human species.

I joined the turtle trackers on the refuge's outermost reach, Cape Island. We were looking for crawls made the night before. The females come ashore in the darkness, their number increasing with the waxing of the moon and simultaneous swelling of the tide. By local lore, nights of the full moon in June and July—the "turtle moons"— witness a surge of crawls.

Burkett crouched near a fresh nest, the rumpled sand not yet smoothed by the wind. "Here's a strange one," he said, reading the tracks. "It looks to me like the turtle came up the sand, started to dig, and discovered she had reached an old nest— a week or so old, I'd say—when she broke a couple of eggs. Then she refilled the hole, crawled a few feet, dug this new nest, and laid her eggs. They can lay at least twice, maybe three times, a season."

Near certain nests we drove in poles topped with streamers and tagged with the probable date the eggs were laid. In a couple of weeks the eggs would be dug up and transplanted to refuges in North Carolina and Virginia. Scientists hope the new generation will return to the adopted shores, re-establishing lost nesting beaches.

Several times we followed raccoon tracks to the churned sand that marked a raided nest. At one we found the signs of other marauders. Stamped upon the raccoons' tracery were the footprints of human egg thieves. Twice pillaged, the nest seemed empty. But deep in the urn-shaped hole Burkett found a few eggs. He handed me one. It felt rubbery and warm, for there still was life within it. We reburied the eggs and smoothed the sand, planting seeds in a refuge that is a garden of life.

Out of the sea comes a vessel of life, an Atlantic loggerhead turtle. Streaming tears that protect her eyes from sand, crawling beyond the tide line on a Cape Romain shore, she finds a site, usually where her life began. Facing inland, she digs a hole with her rear flippers and lays some 125 eggs. After covering her nest, she returns to a realm she leaves only for this rite.

Opened by a storm, a nest is ravaged by a sand crab (right). Refuge manager Burkett Neely gently unearths another clutch; these eggs will hatch in northern refuges and perhaps revive old turtle beaches.

In 60-odd days hatchlings emerge, drawn by night's cool cover. These go seaward in light, sent forth by watchful man.

FOOTLOOSE IN THE SMOKIES

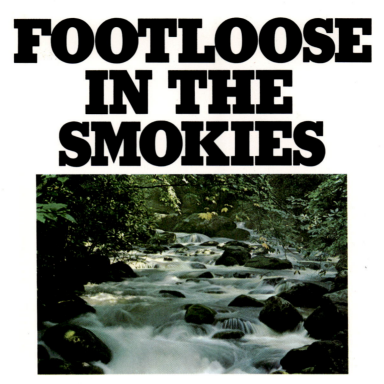

David F. Robinson

It sounded like the *oink-oink-oink* of a pig. I sat up, sleeping-bagged from face to foot, and stared out of the rustic log shelter at a woodland nocturne in black and gray. Moore Spring burbled from pool to pool, and our campfire had dozed off to a dull red ember and a languid dream of smoke. A half moon like a sleepy eye stared down for a moment, then winked out under a cloudy counterpane. We had just hit the sack, and David and Scott, my teen-aged sons, were already snoring. Surely they hadn't oinked, I told myself. But what had?

I could think of only one answer: a bear. A hungry one. One that smelled food in the backpacks we had hung from the rafters. And this old shelter, all by itself in the wilderness, was one of the few in Great Smoky Mountains National Park without a stout bear screen across its open front.

"Yell at 'em," a ranger had advised. "Bang pans," counseled one hiker. "Peg rocks," offered another. All agreed on step two: "Run." But where do you run if a bear comes in the front of the shelter and that's the only way out?

For me, it was a long night of snapping twigs, rustling leaves, ominous shadows, and snoring boys. But no more oinks. And nary a bear.

Dawn poured cold light on my face, and I sat up to watch it fill in the colors outside. Across the shelter's tiny clearing a shadow moved, took shape, and became a deer. Another shadow metamorphosed into a second doe. The two minced to the spring and dropped their muzzles into the molten glass, big ears semaphoring, big eyes watching as I shook life into the boys. Can a deer oink? I wondered.

Three sleepy appetites awoke to the aromas of breakfast. Freeze-dried eggs and sausages had helped keep our packs light for the eight-mile roundabout climb to Gregory Bald and on to the shelter; now with a little water they fueled our return to the summit. A blue sky atoned for yesterday's clouds; we'd have a view today.

One foot in North Carolina, one in Tennessee, a backpacker leads his laden companions across sunstruck Gregory Bald on the crest of adventure in Great Smoky Mountains National Park. Thrust up 230 million years ago, worn down by weather, shaped by bouldered streams, the Smokies still rear 22 summits above 6,000 feet. Though settlers cleared valleys called "coves" and loggers bared many slopes, virgin forest blankets a third of the park—and young trees mature on much of the rest.
MARTIN ROGERS

We checked for litter, doused our fire, and hit the trail. Minutes later we left the trees behind and strode onto Gregory Bald. All around us spread our reward: the wind running its fingers through the summit's grassy scalp; flame azaleas challenging rhododendrons to a blossoming bout; a serrated horizon so sharp and clear you could cut your finger on it. From this western outpost of the park we could see only part of its 800-square-mile immensity, and sense only distantly the wildness of remote valleys and storm-lashed summits too rugged for the early settler. But not for the latter-day logger; his railroads snaked ever deeper into the virgin stands, his saw and ax rang a knell for many a giant tree until the clamor was stilled in 1934 with creation of the park, a third of it still in virgin forest.

Slowly, slowly, the scars heal; hikers tramp the grassy rail beds, and young trees rally round old veterans the sawyers bypassed. And beyond the paved park roads, behind the jam-packed campgrounds, just past the rusting potbellied stove where the last lumber camp stood, the wilderness that once owned the East now lives in stately retirement in this heavily visited national park.

We found the park in a rare mood that day. Its peaks and hollows had flung to the wind the bluish veil they nearly always wear, a veil woven of moisture and plant oils that the Indians likened to smoke. Our every sense reached out and gathered it all in—birdsong and flower scent, the glint of distant lakes, the melony taste of the bulbous white galls that clung to the azaleas, the cushion underfoot that bade us shuck our packs and sprawl.

"Let's live here," Scott said to the sky. He's been saying that for most of his 13 years. The three of us have camped since our respective infancies in everything from a rolling palace to a pup tent in the snow, and we usually fall in love with each new spot we visit. This was our second day in the Smokies, nature's stone wall between Tennessee and North Carolina—and already we wanted to stay forever.

We wouldn't be the first; some folks had indeed spent their whole lives in the valley called Cades Cove, where our climb to Gregory had begun. We found out about one of them on the summit when we heard a voice behind us ask, "Is this bald named for a kin of yours?" and another voice answer, "Russell Gregory was my great-grandfather." In a flash I was on my feet and asking questions.

"He tended his neighbors' cattle up here all summer," answered Burl Gregory, a retired Tennessean of six or seven decades. "Then he'd take 'em down to a lot where the owners would cut out their animals and pay him so much a head."

"This would make a good grazing spot," I said.

"Better one in his day. Bushes are taking over now. Pretty soon the trees'll be. Seedlings don't take hold very well in the grass, but they do in the bare patches—like that one there—where the sod's been rooted up by the pigs."

"Did you say pigs?"

"Wild ones. Don't see 'em much, but they're here. Used to be a game preserve south of here, and some of their Russian boars got loose. Mixed with local hogs. Park people try to stop 'em from spreading, but they don't have much luck."

"Three, four hundred pounds and meaner'n hell," volunteered another day-hiker. "All tusk and no brain. Y'all meet one, better start lookin' for a tree to climb."

The Mystery of the Midnight Oink had been solved. Had we known all this last night, we'd have slept in a tree.

Today two-legged animals invaded the bald, most of them via the five-mile Gregory Ridge Trail—and all of them to admire the flame azaleas, better in late June on Gregory than anywhere else. Naturalist William Bartram called the blossoms "fiery" in 1776; to the 20th century I hasten to point out that they are not the color of

Overleaf: Sculptured summits of the Smokies and the distant Cheoah Mountains look down on an evanescent sea as clouds cling like spindrift to Mount Le Conte. Untouched by glaciers, these peaks gave refuge to northern flora that still flourishes in a highland climate like the north's. About 160 tree species grow here, several to record size.

Climbing in early summer is an odyssey back into spring. A chestnut-sided warbler near Charlies Bunion trills for a mate (above) as cousins in the valleys brood eggs. Clover lures an American painted lady butterfly in the foothills while buds still swell higher up. The black-bellied salamander goggles for gnats by a stream whose headwaters cradle his still-dormant kin. And in the lowlands, toadstools set about recycling a log, watered by a sun-sprinkled rill with the chill of snow in its veins.

a pilot light or welding torch or cigarette lighter flame. They are the color of a campfire in the woods after a bone-wearying hike to the top of the world.

We stashed our packs under a bush and jaunted a mile to Parson Bald, feeling light as moonwalkers without those 35 pounds aboard. A Canada warbler modeled his gray-and-yellow finery along the trail; towhees and a hummingbird took seats in front-row bushes to watch us animals eat lunch atop the bald. Scientists wonder what tonsured these mountaintops—wind, fire, maybe a hot dry spell. But the Indians knew: A bald marks the spot where lightning struck a monster.

"Time's a-wastin'," I said through my trail lunch—an energizing hash of raisins, peanuts, and chocolate bits. In this park, wilderness comes in several big areas and a variety of styles, and we wanted to sample it all. Popular spots, like Gregory at its blooming best or Abrams Falls on a sultry Sunday, become more like fairgrounds than backwoods. But others, as wild and inaccessible as when Cherokee hunters ghosted among the massive trunks, challenge the hardy hiker.

"What happened to the trail?" David wondered as he led us back to Gregory. "Looks like it's been rototilled." Then he stepped in a definitive clue; horses had been through since we left. Horseback travel is allowed on perhaps half the park's 700 miles of trails, but most people come in on their own two feet.

We shouldered our packs with a ritual groan; they still felt like anvils. Scott toed the dirt where a boar had snouted up the sod. "What do they root for?" he said.

"The home team," I answered. Sorry—but in the wilds even the jokes go primitive. "Okay, okay," I added above the groans, "they root for grubs and such."

One chill gray morning, as we started up the Alum Cave Trail, I announced: "Today we're going to hike a thousand miles." Actually we'd be doing five, but by climbing 2,800 feet up Mount Le Conte we'd find woods like Canada's.

"In that case," David predicted, "we'll be in Canada inside of three hours."

"No you won't," growled a thunderhead. Moments later it doused us faster than we could scramble into our ponchos. Rain-slicked roots turned the trail into one long banana peel, but it was all very educational. We learned not to look up; the poncho's hood catches the rain and waters your back with it when you look down again. And don't sneeze with the hood up; the acoustics in there can make your ears ring.

Finally an emerging sun bade us unwrap again. The trail brought us to a log spanning Alum Cave Creek, and we stepped aboard and teetered across—into a hell. Trailside rhododendrons locked arms so tightly not even a bear could push through. No wonder the mountaineers called these thickets hells; no wonder the moonshiners hid their stills in them. But to us, Huggins Hell seemed an Eden. Blossoms spangled the bushes, fallen petals dabbed the trail with pink and white. And beside us, the creek stumbled down its stony staircase, cold and clear.

There is no cave at Alum Cave. It's all a bluff—a towering, overhanging bluff with a scattering of shrubs on its rim. We lunched in its echoing hollow, our vista a rumpled robe of velvet forest, and tried to imagine Confederate soldiers who came up here, in legend if not in fact, to mine alum for gunpowder.

David's freshened pace led us past fragrant evergreens and knotted hells, along don't-look-down ledges with steel cable handholds, into a fairyland of stunted conifers—ah, Canada—and out onto Cliff Top. Somewhere up here a 12-berth shelter waited for us, but thanks to the park's permit system we felt no rush to claim a bunk. Besides, who could leave such a view?

"Hey, I can see Gatlinburg," David said. Down there, we knew, tourists in bright plumage were tithing to snack stand and souvenir shop as cars inched past in 90-degree heat. I watched it shimmer awhile, then smiled and put on my sweater.

After a rest we ambled off to find the shelter. We found it—full of Boy Scouts. Other hikers stood outside; more soon arrived. We whispered in little knots, eyed each other, fidgeted, pondered. Finally the "outs" exchanged credentials, then casually asked the "ins" for a look at theirs. Sure enough: 12 bunks, 24 permits.

Most of the "outs" trudged away, perhaps to find room in the rustic cabins of Le Conte Lodge nearby. But the boys and I were equipped for a night in the open, so we broke out tarp and ground sheets and began setting up.

"A bear! A bear!" Scott shouted. I turned to see a family of picnickers from the lodge scoot off their blanket as a shaggy brute shuffled up. I sidled in, camera to my eye and caution to the winds. He'll be busy eating, I thought.

Wrong. He'll be busy defending his meal. He warned me just once with a growl. But I took one step too many; with a booming snort he exploded from the blanket and charged. I spun so fast my camera stayed where it was; it clung by a strap and banged my back as I set a record for the 40-yard rout. With dented dignity I watched from a sensible distance as the victor dispatched the spoils, gulping foil and plastic with the pickles and bread, crunching open a Thermos, slurping down its cargo of black coffee, and ambling off with a rumbling belch.

The sun that evening dropped into its crib like a petulant child, flinging cloud shreds all over the sky and yelling in loud reds and purples until night's black blanket muffled the tantrum. Next morning it rose up after we did, but soon was poking brassy fingers in our eyes as we struck out for Mount Kephart.

"That damned boulevard," a tired hiker once cussed the brush-choked ridge linking Le Conte and Kephart, and it's been the Boulevard ever since. But in two hours the trail along it merged us onto a superhighway: the Appalachian Trail that

Mini-mountaineers scramble up a lichened ledge beside Abrams Falls, an easy 2½-mile hike from idyllic Cades Cove. Thundering waters soon join the Little Tennessee River where a Cherokee village stood. Old Abram reigned as its chief 200 years ago. Settlers dubbed his squaw Kate; her name may echo in Cades Cove, where Abrams Creek wends toward the falls.

Indians seldom hunted in the Smokies; lowlands offered more game and easier going. But hundreds hid in the wilds when soldiers in 1838 drove the tribe from lands of its ancestors. Some 16,000 trudged at bayonet-point down the Trail of Tears; a fourth died on that winter march to Oklahoma. Descendants live today on a reservation bordering the park. Names on the land honor such forebears as Sequoyah, who completed the first Indian alphabet in 1821.
MARTIN ROGERS

275

runs like a shiver down the Smokies' spine and feels more feet—and, alas, hoofs—than almost any other trail in the park. We were booked into New Ice Water Spring, one of the shelters beside the AT. No snafu this time; we found it empty.

While the boys snoozed, I broke out the stove and transformed a packet of freeze-dried pillow stuffings into a lunch of potatoes and pork au gratin. Then I turned to the two prone forms behind me and bellowed a lusty "Sooo-eee!"

"What was *that?*" Scott said.

"A hog call. Farmers do that to bring the pigs in. Sooo-eee! Pig-pig-pig—"

"Hi there," waved a hiker who strolled up at just that perfect moment. He and his two companions still don't know what turned a man and two boys into laughing hyenas. We swapped some of our freeze-dried ice cream—a little chalky, but a reasonable facsimile of the real stuff when you chew it—for some of their crackers and cheese. To taste buds dulled by lightweight fare, the fresh goodies were a treat—and doubly so since they came up on someone else's back.

In 1929, a downpour stripped the soil from a peak just east of Kephart. Hikers came to survey the damage, among them a man complaining of a bunion. They were stunned when they saw their peak, now a ragged jut of rock falling sheer to the valley like a great ship's prow. "That," said one, "sticks out like Charlie's bunion."

The boys and I perched on Charlies Bunion and gazed out at towering green billows in a motionless sea. Mount Le Conte was scraping the bottom off a low-slung cloud, and in the troughs a haze was beginning to collect. Somewhere in the valley a raven croaked. An upstart breeze dared me to light a match; it took me four to get the stove going and forever to boil the water for supper. Full of stew and scenery, we trudged the mile back up to the shelter with twilight at our heels.

Lifeblood of the wilderness, water in pool and cataract invites the dusty hiker in. Son-splashed father shivers in Grotto Falls (opposite); swimmers find a warmer pool by Abrams Falls.

From peaks receiving an average 80 inches of rain a year pours a crystal bounty that carves out valleys, waters luxuriant forests, gives goosebumps to hikers who brave the frigid flood. For generations it turned mountaineers' mill wheels; a few still creak as rangers tell visitors of bygone ways. In some 600 miles of streams naturalists count more than 70 species of fish—and sportsmen try for favorites like brook and rainbow trout. Some sections bar adult anglers; there kids may fish for anything—and with almost anything. One lad claimed a trout on a hookful of bubble gum.

MARTIN ROGERS

Down Kephart's slope I could see headlights winking on a distant segment of the highway that bisects the park. I wiped out civilization with a turn of my head, and watched the orange moon sift through a Fraser fir. A single star discovered me, and soon the whole universe was crowding close for a look. The heavens stayed outside as I closed the bear-screen door and bedded down.

Summertime commitments called the boys home. But I was determined to plumb these Smokies for a wilderness without people, without shelters, maybe without trails. Slack muscles were tighter now; I felt ready for a challenge. John Greer offered one: Raven Fork on the Carolina side. He'd hiked the Smokies trails since childhood; now, as a forestry student, he hiked them to gather bear droppings for analysis at the University of Tennessee. If John says wild, it's wild.

Some 95 primitive campsites dot the Smokies, most of them just clearings with water. But what clearings! Haw Gap, near Spence Field, the largest grass bald in the park . . . Upper Ramsay Prong, reached by clambering a mile above the breathtaking Ramsay Cascades, with only a stream for a trail . . . Mount Sterling, with a beanstalk fire tower you can climb to enjoy the heart-stopping views. Campgrounds overflow, shelters fill, but there's rarely a crowd at these remote islands in the forest. Ours for tonight would be at Big Pool up Raven Fork. "Facilities: none," warned a park listing. Not even a trail, just something called a manway. Perfect.

John set a panting pace—I panted, he paced—up and over Hyatt Ridge to the kind of stream that steals a man's soul. Spouting between boulders, sheeting over ledges, pooling in dark wells, oozing through green mosses, bubbling, glinting, rushing, resting, rushing on again it went, purring as it licked my hand and filled my cup and rinsed the dust out of my mind. In a quiet eddy it held a school of trout for me to admire, and rocks for me to turn in search of skittering salamanders and the jellied geometries of their eggs. It called down a kingfisher and a spring azure butterfly; it brought me petals from a laurel and promised me more upstream.

So I followed John as his practiced eye found the trail, once maintained, now all but erased by the hungry forest. Nettles stung our bare legs as we filed along. When hells choked the manway, we bulled through like fullbacks or crashed our way around and—sometimes—found the path again on the other side. And when the river stole it, we took to the slippery rocks, backpacks weighted low for balance as we picked our way carefully upstream. We didn't break any speed limits—a mile an hour, if that—but show me a highway half as beautiful, and with no other traffic all day. And show me a motel to rival the simple clearing at Big Pool, true to its name with a great crystal bowl gathering three freshets and pouring them out again in the stream that had led us there.

Next day we struggled homeward up Breakneck Ridge. One leg protested, bruised from a fall on a mossy rock; a few weeks ago I'd have pampered it. But in those weeks I'd hiked some 130 miles; I'd felt that anvil on my back become a part of me. I'd tramped 16 miles up and down Le Conte in a day and felt it less than the first day's 8. I'd caught a glimpse of what the settlers found, and what the mountaineers struggled to tame—and what the nation now struggles to plunder or to save. I wasn't the same tenderfoot who wondered what oinked in the night.

My litter was in my pack. My footprints would soon be rained away. I hadn't changed these old Smokies. Nor had anyone else very much; here and there a cabin or a still slowly rots away as the forest reclaims her own. Even these may be gone when David and Scott puff up to Ice Water Spring and tell their kids about Grand-dad's hog-calling. By cracky, maybe I'll puff up and tell 'em myself.

ENTHEOS

Margerie Glacier, rasping at the flanks of the Fairweather Range, winds toward Glacier Bay in the panhandle of southeastern Alaska.

ALASKA

THE LAST GREAT WILDERNESS

John P. Milton

Our small plane, minutes out of the old mining town of McCarthy, skimmed low over a river snaking down from the hills, then climbed in circles, reaching for altitude and a flight among the Alaskan peaks. To the north the Wrangell Mountains hid behind a solid bank of clouds. To the east Mounts Logan and St. Elias heaved their white tops thousands of feet into the early morning light.

At 10,000 feet pilot Jim Edwards leveled off, headed south into the looming Chugach massif, picked up the soft curve of the Tana Glacier, and followed that icy trail that has been thousands of years in the making. Suddenly, the fluid bend of the glacier spread out into a white panorama of staggering extent—the Bagley Icefield. Hundreds of square miles of glistening plateau stretched away in all directions, broken only by the occasional thrust of a jagged point of rock. The sea of ice rested cold and quiet under a spotless azure sky.

I felt dwarfed, a speck drifting in an infinity of blue and white.

Here was a land of superlatives, Alaska on its grandest scale. As I squinted against the blinding sunlight reflecting from ice and crusted snow, I found it difficult to believe that man could ever make a lasting mark on such boundless wilderness. Yet even as we absorbed its majesty, debate swirled around this and other wilderness in Alaska, debate that would surely lead to winning for all of us the preservation of such natural wonders as the Great Kobuk Sand Dunes, the vast waterfowl breeding ground known as Yukon Flats, and the mountainous Gates of the Arctic, an area more than four times the size of Yellowstone National Park.

My interest in Alaska goes back many years. I had first come north to work as a salmon fisherman along the southeast coast. Five times I returned to explore, to study the ecological fabric of the arctic, to help fight for environmental conservation. Now I had come back for a long look at Alaska's wilderness as a whole, to see it, as a recent tourist said, "before it was too late."

Alaska's size—586,400 square miles, twice as big as Texas—had impressed me on previous visits, but this time weeks of travel left me in simple awe of our 49th state's immensity. More than anywhere else I have ever been the sky seemed larger, the land more open. Beyond each far horizon lay secrets waiting to be uncovered. Each day I lived on the edge of discovery.

The land presents a rugged but strangely delicate and fragile face. Two large mountain masses arc across the state, the Brooks Range above the Arctic Circle and the Alaska Range below, the latter curving south of Fairbanks to merge with the

Aleutian chain, whose long volcanic tail cleaves into the Bering Sea. Between the two mountain ranges, tributaries feed the mighty Yukon River as it winds some 1,200 miles through the heart of Alaska. It's a varied land, stretching from icy Arctic coasts and rolling tundra highlands to lush lowland valleys; a wilderness web of mountains, water, and weather, each strand integral to the broad scheme and each a unique microcosm. Here is our last great preserve of the caribou, grizzly, and wolf, the haven for millions of migratory waterfowl, the showcase for the highest mountains and largest rivers of ice on the North American continent.

No other place in the United States has more changeable moods, more shifting patterns of sun and cloud, light and darkness, heat and chill, rain and snow than Alaska. The weather is a continuing study in contrasts. A clear summer day on the tundra can be as benign as a spring day in Kansas. Then in the space of an hour the fog drifts in from the Arctic Ocean and wraps the earth in a dull grayness that dims the soul for a week. From May to August the sun, swinging in a great circle above the horizon, banishes night. When darkness finally comes, it stays all winter. But even the long Alaskan night brings contrasts: the shimmering blaze of the northern lights, the waxing and waning of the moon, the sparkling pinpoints of infinite stars.

The isolation, severe winters, and expanse of this wild arctic region all played a role in staying the hand of man. The earliest human migrants came during the Ice Age when the Bering Land Bridge connected the area with Siberia. Nomads established a precarious but harmonious relationship with the land, shifting with animal migrations. Because their numbers were few, their impact on the fabric of life was minor. Even today the three aboriginal groups—Aleuts, Eskimos, and Indians—total only some 60,000 in Alaska, according to the Bureau of Indian Affairs. Some of their old culture persists, but many natives are rapidly converting to the ways of the white man, a process begun when Russia founded the first settlement on Kodiak Island in the late 18th century. Later Western involvement at first was minimal. When Secretary of State William H. Seward purchased the territory in the 1860's, many Americans termed it "Seward's Folly." But when oil was discovered under the North Slope of the Brooks Range at Prudhoe Bay in 1968, Alaska became an ecologically embattled land. Energy-conscious America prepared an invasion that even this giant of the north found difficult to withstand.

In contrast to the Lower Forty-Eight, at least 90 percent of Alaska is still primitive, even pristine, in character, making it our last great wilderness. Ironically, Alaska has only six official Wilderness Areas compared to twenty in California. Of Alaska's 375 million acres, 368 million are public lands belonging to all Americans, not just to the third of a million people who live there.

What does the future hold for these public lands? Rapid exploitation of natural resources? Preservation of delicate ecological systems? A balanced compromise? On a crowded and increasingly technological planet, will we be able to keep Alaskan wilderness as America's spiritual safety valve?

The charter of statehood gave Alaska the right to claim 103 million acres of public land. Under the Alaska Native Claims Settlement Act, signed into law by President Richard M. Nixon in 1971, the native people will obtain 40 million acres. As authorized by other provisions of the act, the Secretary of the Interior has set aside a total of 79 million acres as "national interest" lands (map, page 294). After review, and with the approval of Congress, these will be preserved as national parks and monuments, forests, wildlife refuges, and wild and scenic rivers. In addition, vast acreages may be held under federal ownership as "public interest" lands—for such uses as mining, timbering, recreation, and flood control. On my travels over the state I encountered scientists and Interior Department experts enthusiastically surveying the matchless trove of national interest lands. Many of them include prime wilderness that, it is hoped, will eventually be considered for inclusion in the National Wilderness Preservation System.

The Secretary of the Interior also set aside two utility corridors for the controversial North Slope oil and gas pipelines. Conservationists' outcries against the ecological danger of these pipelines almost drowned out the broader issue involved — the distribution of Alaska's public lands. The conflict came into sharp focus when the state and federal governments selected some of the same lands. Native groups joined in, claiming that the acreage from which they were to make their choices was not adequate. The great land rush was on. During my stay in the Wrangells, it seemed that the struggle for Alaska's future was being played out in microcosm in McCarthy, a tiny community cupped by the tawny moraines at the foot of Kennicott Glacier on the southern slopes of the mountains.

Early in the 1900's rich veins of copper ore were found at Bonanza Peak above the glacier. The mining towns of Kennicott and McCarthy sprang up, then withered when the mines played out in the 1930's. I found Kennicott deserted, the only sound the chill voice of mountain winds. But a dozen people lived in and around McCarthy, so I made the semi-ghost town a base of operations for this part of my tour. I bedded down inside the sagging timbers of the abandoned general store and cooked my meals on a potbelly stove in the shoemaker's shop. Outside, the main street hid under a carpet of purple fireweed, and green willows and alders invaded the yards of gray, forlorn buildings as though wilderness sought to reclaim its own. It was there in McCarthy that I discovered what it means to be a pioneer in 20th-century Alaska and learned a good deal about the sharp conflict of values confronting the community.

The only easy access to McCarthy is by plane, so Jim Edwards, who has lived there for 18 years and works for a local air service, flies in staples. In part the people live off the land, hunting, fishing, and raising vegetables in gardens primed by long days of summer sunlight that produce crops in record time. A sometimes harsh way to live, but the majority prefer it to the pace of crowded cities, prizing their independence and peaceful existence.

Beneath the town's serenity, however, a storm brewed. A primitive road, generally following an old railroad grade, had been bulldozed partway to McCarthy from Chitina, 50 miles to the west. I watched a trailer camp take shape along the road, and I saw some visitors come into town. With this trickle of tourism, the residents grew uneasy. They feared the flood to follow, particularly if the state pursued its plan for an expensive new all-weather road. The idea was to open the core of the Wrangells country to more tourists, recreation, and renewed mining.

Loy and Curtis Green, brothers who have made McCarthy their home for years, seemed to express the prevailing sentiments of the townsfolk. The Greens' small log

Beautiful Dall sheep thread lofty barrens with amazing grace and agility. Cloven hoofs grip like pincers; heel pads prevent backsliding. Keen eyes scan for predators, and curling horns arm rams for the butting of rutting season. The white mountain sheep adorn Mount McKinley's ridges, delighting visitors. Proposed parks in the Brooks Range and the Wrangells would safeguard other populations.
DRAWING BY GEORGE FOUNDS

cabin, with one room, loft, and kitchen, sits just out of town close below the looming Kennicott Glacier, surrounded by streams pulsing from the melting ice and enclosed by a dense growth of forest. Inside the cabin, volumes on philosophy and Alaskan natural history fill the bookshelves.

Loy, an artist, has covered the walls with surrealistic, powerful paintings of Alaska. "Winter is the most beautiful season here," he said. "The sky flames with the aurora borealis and the clear light of stars and the moon. At 40° below, the land is gripped in silence. For me, the stillness and solitude are McCarthy's greatest assets."

Curtis plays the flute. As I approached the cabin on my first visit, his music filled the forest, mingling with the singing of the streams. He too is a painter, but one who paints his rhythms on the wind, composing poems that linger in melody. Like his brother, Curtis is a quiet and gentle man.

"Most of us oppose the road," he said. "Nearly all our country has seen wilderness —and the independent life it offers—converted to the demands of consumer civilization. Now we watch the last vestiges of a free frontier life dying in places like the Wrangells. Somewhere the country has to halt its assault on wilderness—and the road into McCarthy is a good place to begin."

Others in the community felt differently, however, and welcomed the chance to strike it rich from increased tourism and real estate values. To me they embodied the old American spirit dedicated to taming the frontier, perhaps believing there is little profit to be made from solitude and the spiritual value of the wilds. Since my visit the state has decided that, instead of a new road, it would patch up and maintain the old rail route. Most people around McCarthy accept the compromise, hopeful that it will keep the disturbance to the land and their way of life to a minimum.

The Wrangells and Canada's St. Elias Mountains form the greatest mountain kingdom in North America. In selecting lands for preservation under the Native Claims Act, the Department of the Interior chose more than ten million acres in the Wrangells. Combined with Canada's Kluane National Park, this region could become the continent's most striking international park, extending from the Copper River eastward 200 miles to Yakutat Bay and the rain-drenched coastal lowlands.

Southeast of the Bagley Icefield, the walls of Mount (Continued on page 293)

Portfolio Notes

OPPOSITE: *Cloud-plumed Mount Bona keeps a wintry vigil from its 16,421-foot vantage in the Wrangells-St.Elias complex near the Canadian border. Amid these heights glaciers spawn: Snows compact, and rivers of ice begin the slow grind down the valleys.*
AUSTIN POST, U. S. GEOLOGICAL SURVEY

PAGES 286-287: *Watery woodlands, peppered by wind-driven sediments, take on a Death Valley look above the Arctic Circle. The Great Kobuk Sand Dunes push westward about an inch a year, gnawing at a forest of spruce, forcing Kavet Creek to cut a sidestepping course as it flows toward the distant Kobuk River. Beyond rise the Baird and Schwatka Mountains, weather-worn outriders of the western Brooks Range.*
JOHN P. MILTON

PAGES 288-289: *Summer's brief thaw jewels the dimpled, grimy face of Bagley Icefield, a 600-square-mile waste rimmed by the Chugach Mountains. "Soaring over the*

glittering and seemingly endless ice fields with the azure blue of countless little pools and lakes," wrote Sigurd Olson, "one has the impression of looking at the frozen surface of a different planet."
JOHN P. MILTON

PAGES 290-291: *Nourished by seven glaciers, the braided Chitina weaves westward to join the Copper. Channel-clogging silt forces the river to find new paths through a valley rich in wilderness contrasts. To the south, scarcely a trace of man exists; northward, where the snowy Wrangells loom, boom-and-bust copper mining scarred the land, and talk of new development stirs fears for the future of the healing wilds.*
ALISON EHRLICH

PAGE 292: *Sunset gilds a golden habitat— Seward Peninsula's marshy coast and the Chukchi Sea. Plankton-filled seawater enriches food webs that include polar bears, whales, and waterfowl by the millions.*
JOHN P. MILTON

St. Elias drop more than three miles almost straight down to the sea; toward the Gulf of Alaska lie massive glaciers like the Bering and Malaspina. These spectaculars are only part of the appeal of the Wrangell-St. Elias region. Recreation, solitude, and superb fishing beckon in the tributaries of the Copper River.

To really get away from it all, a backpacker could venture the 45-mile-long Bremner River Valley, an area so remote that few men have set foot there. Someday hikers and fishermen may be lured south to this forgotten wild land from the Tebay Lakes country, rich in rainbow trout and already a favored fly-in rendezvous. But it will challenge the most adventurous wilderness traveler to find a way into the Bremner fastness. Walled by mountains rising to more than 7,000 feet, the valley is virtually inaccessible except by helicopter. Flying a thousand feet above it one day, I watched the Bremner tumble and plunge through precipitous gorges, cutting its way to the Copper through forested tablelands. In some places the thickets of alder and willow looked too dense for a man to force his way across them.

One way to approach the valley is by boat on the Copper, from the towns of Chitina or Cordova. But at the mouth of the Bremner the boat would have to be left behind, for cascades make the river all but unnavigable. A determined explorer might also get close by searching out and landing at an old mining airstrip on Golconda Creek high in the hills back of the Bremner headwaters. Whoever battles his way into this valley will know that, except for a few sourdoughs who may have poked around the edges for gold, he breaks trail in one of the wildest pockets in the United States.

North of the Bremner and the Tebay Lakes, another Eden for anglers spreads out along the Chitina Valley, where rainbows and other game fish leap from lakes embraced by patches of forest. Leading into the valley from the north is the Nizina River, gateway to the crest of the Wrangells. And into the Nizina flows the Chitistone, coursing through a beautiful canyon whose towering limestone cliffs match the grandeur of Yosemite's granite walls. The rugged Goat Trail—which dates back to Indian days and is a possible addition to the National Scenic Trails System—climbs the canyon, offering a view of the great Mount Bona massif.

The Chitina and the Wrangells grew on me in a quieter way, however. Here is a land of subtle, shifting moods: the distant whiteness of clouds merging with high icefields; the brown of moist river mud dimpled by fresh wolf tracks; the cobblestones of a poplar-lined creekbed and the air suddenly filled with a blizzard of fleecy seeds; the Dall sheep clustering in a nearby range of hills; moose lumbering down the trail each evening to feed in the willow flats.

Below the town of Chitina, the Copper River gnaws through Wood Canyon. If a proposed hydroelectric power project is built there, water will back up behind a massive dam and drown the Chitina Valley to a point near McCarthy.

North of the Wrangells country the Taylor Highway winds toward the Yukon, passing through or near a string of towns with intriguing names: Chicken, Jack Wade, Poker Creek, Bonanza Bar. The road ends at the trading post town of Eagle, population about 35. Near here the Yukon River surges out of Canada. For 180 miles it carves a sinuous course through rolling terrain, receiving major streams like the Fortymile and the Charley, both candidates for protection as wild rivers. The Interior Department has set aside more than a million acres around the upper Yukon, an area that stretches nearly all the way to the town of Circle.

At the turn of the century, steamers plied the river with supplies for the Canadian Klondike and the American goldfields, churning down to Fort Yukon and the Hudson Bay Post there. If the talked-about revival of steamer service between Fort Yukon and

ALASKA

Numbered sites are established Wilderness Areas; unnumbered entries are units officially considered for wilderness. A figure after the name is wilderness acreage only, not total acreage of the national park, wildlife refuge, or forest. Pages cited offer fuller description; page 337 lists contacts for obtaining details on particular areas. Lettered sites are lands selected by the U. S. Interior Department for consideration as parks, forests, or refuges under the Alaska Native Claims Settlement Act; figures given may be approximations and are subject to change. These selections include some seven million acres in extensions to the existing areas of Arctic NW Range, Mt. McKinley NP, and Katmai NM.

Arctic NW Range. See page 311.

Chamisso NWR. 455. Seabird colonies; horned puffin abundant.

Mt. McKinley NP. Glacier-carved land of forest, tundra. Bears.

1 Bering Sea NWR W. 41,113. Polar bear trails visible. Breeding area for waterfowl.

Nunivak NWR. Tundra-covered musk ox sanctuary. Walruses, seals, reindeer, birds.

Hazen Bay NWR. Tundra island. Nesting area for waterfowl.

Clarence Rhode NW Range. Largest water-bird refuge in U. S.

Cape Newenham NWR. Nesting area for birds. Migration stopover.

2 Bogoslof NWR W. 390. Volcanic islands. Seabirds nest on cliffs. Northern sea lions breed here.

Izembek NW Range. 301,451. Vast nearby eelgrass beds sustain black brant. Alaska brown bear, caribou.

Simeonof NWR. 25,140. Established to preserve sea otter.

Semidi NWR. 256,000. Seven remote islands, reefs. Pelagic bird colonies. Sea lions.

Kodiak NWR. Mountains, lakes, tundra. Salmon spawning area. Trout. Kodiak brown bear.

Katmai NM. 2,553,100. Fishing. Campgrounds. Wolves, bears.

3 Tuxedni NWR W. 6,402. Two islands. Seabird colonies.

Kenai N Moose Range. 1,093,200. Forested lowlands, mountains. Dall sheep. Canoe trail system.

Nellie Juan, Chugach NF. 704,000. Forested lowlands, glaciered peaks.

Russell Fiord, Tongass NF. 227,000. Rare glacier bear. "Galloping" movement of Hubbard Glacier.

Glacier Bay NM. 2,210,600. Spectacular show as advancing glaciers "calve" icebergs.

Tracy Arm Fords Terror, Tongass NF. 902,000. Tide meadows, ice fields.

Petersburg Creek, Tongass NF. 24,000. Typical of island ecosystem in southeast Alaska.

4 St. Lazaria NWR W. 65. Volcanic island. Seabird nesting area.

Granite Fiords, Tongass NF. 590,000. Glacier-carved region.

5 Hazy Islands NWR W. 42. Seabirds breed here. Sea lions.

6 Forrester Island NWR W. 2,630. Nesting site of burrow-using birds.

King Salmon Capes, Tongass NF. 120,000. Representative of island group facing ocean.

Aleutian Islands NWR. 1,395,400. Treeless islands rich in wildlife; seabirds, sea otters. Unimak Island under consideration as separate wilderness unit.

A Chukchi. 88,800. Potential refuge combining Capes Lisburne and Thompson. Seabird colonies.

B Cape Krusenstern. Possible NM. Early-Eskimo archeological sites.

C Noatak. 8,000,000. Park or refuge designation possible.

D Gates of the Arctic. 9,388,100. Prime parkland. Overlaps national forest proposal.

E Yukon Flats. 11,086,000. Great waterfowl producing area. Overlaps proposed national forest and items L and M.

F Koyukuk. 8,372,000. Four waterfowl nesting areas proposed as refuge; also, in part, as national forest.

G Great Kobuk Sand Dunes. 1,454,400. Wind-blown mounds moving west.

H Selawik. 2,300,000. Waterfowl breeding area in alluvial plain.

I Shishmaref. 1,518,000. Waterfowl habitat. Migration way point.

J Fairway Rock. 60. Addition to Bering Sea NWR. Nesting seabirds.

K Imuruk. 2,150,900 park; 529,000 refuge. Tundra coastal ecosystem. Lava flows. Archeology. Wide variety of wildlife. Overlaps item I.

L Upper Yukon. 1,233,660. Gold rush country. Canoeing. Caribou, peregrine falcon.

M Fortymile. 6,640,000. Potential NF. Backpacking, canoeing.

N Kuskokwim. 3,000,000. Potential national forest.

O Yukon Delta. 5,704,000. Tundra paradise for nesting waterfowl and other migrant birds.

P Togiak/Hagemeister. 2,783,120. With Cape Newenham, Togiak forms ecosystem from sea to watershed.

Q Shumagin Islands. 12,000. To be included with Simeonof NWR.

R Aniakchak Crater. 740,200. 30-sq.-mile crater. Potential national monument.

S Iliamna area. 4,163,000. Alaska's largest lake; ideal for wildlife, recreation. Overlaps item T and national forest proposal.

T Lake Clark Pass. 3,725,620. Glaciers, two dormant volcanoes. Studied as national park and national forest.

U Barren Islands. 10,000. Treeless, rocky. Seabirds, sea lions.

V Kenai Fiords, "Norway of Alaska." 160,000. Parkland, or refuge and extension to Kenai NMR.

W Wrangell-St. Elias. 10,613,540. See page 284. Park envisioned. Copper River, Tetlin areas studied as refuge. Wrangell Mountains NF also proposed.

Gulf of Alaska

ALEUTIAN ISLANDS NATIONAL WILDLIFE REFUGE

Rat Islands

Andreanof Islands

Islands of the Four Mountains

Umnak Island

Dawson, Canada, ever materializes, hunters, fishermen, photographers, and boaters seeking the interior may ride in paddle-wheelers reminiscent of gold rush days.

Glaciers played little part in molding the land here. Frost heave, water erosion, silt deposits, and wind shaped its contours. The hills retreat from the river in rounded crests like gentle frozen waves. Streams trace long fingers of silver back into the rolling landscape. The waters teem with whitefish, grayling, and salmon. For canoeists, hundreds of miles of waterways offer a variety of boating experiences—quiet drifting through scenic, bluff-bound valleys, paddling through marshy, meandering sloughs, riding the swift currents of upland creeks.

Here caribou calve and winter in the alpine tundra, forests, meadows, and bogs. Moose forage in the lowlands and Dall sheep crop the highlands. Together with small mammals and insects that burrow into the soft spongy ground, they provide food for bear, wolf, wolverine, and lynx. This varied wildlife, however, is but a shadow of the large-mammal population that dwelt here during the Pleistocene Epoch—large-horned bison, elk, horse, woolly mammoth, mastodon, camel, saber-toothed tiger. Shielded by mountains from the ice sheets that blanketed so much of the Northern Hemisphere, the tundra-clad highlands sustained a delicately balanced ecosystem. Around 6000 B.C., as the ice receded and man the hunter probably became more deadly, this incredible collection of life disappeared. Will today's survivors vanish before the onslaught of man the builder?

Farther down the river lies Yukon Flats, another rich wildlife haven. A 150-mile-long basin of 10,800 square miles centered on Fort Yukon, the Flats serves as a breeding ground for more than two million migratory birds, including a third of North America's canvasback ducks. Under my low-flying plane the lakes and ponds, streams and lagoons wove a tapestry of gleaming threads and jewels against dark, brooding spruce forest and amber muskeg.

A proposal by the Fish and Wildlife Service to protect Yukon Flats as a national wildlife refuge may once and for all rescue the area from the threat of a dam downriver at Rampart Canyon. As proposed by the Army Corps of Engineers in the mid-1960's, the Rampart Project would produce nearly five million kilowatts of power, helping, many Alaskans believed, to promote settlement, development, and prosperity. But ecologists were appalled at the cost to the environment: The reservoir, which would take about twenty years to fill and cover an area larger than Lake Erie, not only would wipe out Yukon Flats but also devour the lower Porcupine River all the way to the Canadian border.

Waters from the impoundment would inundate the homes and villages of about a thousand Athabascan Indians and destroy their fish and game. Even below the dam people and wildlife would suffer, for animal habitats in and along the river draw nourishment from the Yukon's seasonal flooding.

Seven hundred miles southwest of Rampart Canyon, the Yukon spreads out into the gentle fan of its delta. Over the millenniums, the Yukon and the adjacent Kuskokwim River have deposited immense quantities of silt in the Bering Sea, building a low, level land of stream- and lake-laced tundra. Half the continent's black brant and nearly all its emperor and cackling geese nest in this 26,600-square-mile area that surpasses even Yukon Flats in overall bird populations. During the fall migration, nearly three million ducks congregate here and head south. Walrus, beluga whales, and seals ranging the coastal waters supplement the fish and terrestrial wildlife that support native Alaskans scattered in villages along the waterways. The Fish and Wildlife Service is hoping to add nearly six million acres to the Clarence Rhode Wildlife Range here, thus preserving much of the Yukon delta.

The role that Alaskan, and especially Yukon, waterfowl play in other parts of the Northern Hemisphere is sometimes overlooked. From as far away as South China and the Caribbean, millions of birds migrate thousands of miles to nest in Alaska. There they replenish their numbers in unspoiled lands and unpolluted waters, enacting a ritual born during the Pleistocene when glaciers melted and formed flood plains that to this day nurture the birds. Each fall, waterfowl funnel down flyways, some five million spilling over the Lower Forty-Eight to be enjoyed by Americans everywhere. Lesser scaups from Yukon Flats and the delta alone visit 40 states, and canvasbacks winter in 25. If these wild flocks are to survive with their life cycles unbroken, their nesting grounds must be preserved.

Far, lonely horizons and wilderness at once forbidding and breathtaking— that's the challenge of the Brooks Range. A stormy sea of craggy peaks and unexplored valleys stretching from Canada to the west coast of Alaska, it guards the North Slope, a vast tundra cut by rivers that drain into the Beaufort Sea. I have visited the Brooks Range often and sometimes felt I was beginning to understand the land's allure. But this is no ordinary country and I am always surprised by its unpredictable character. I have walked the sparse slopes for months and seen almost no sign of animal life, then watched amazed as the ground came alive with a blanket of migrating caribou. For days I have explored unnamed passes under clear skies and balmy temperatures, then suddenly found myself pinned down by a blizzard riding the tail of a summer storm sweeping in from the Arctic Ocean.

I got to know the Brooks Range most intimately in 1967 when two companions and I lugged 90-pound packs from the lower Sheenjek River on the southern slope, up over the mountains, and down across the North Slope to Barter Island. We lived off the land and dried food, and reveled in the solitude. For five weeks our 300-mile journey took us to the tops of ridges and the bottoms of gorges untrod by white men. We slogged through foot-sucking muskeg, endured clouds of mosquitoes, slid down steep talus slopes, ignored pulled muscles, and anxiously pondered doubtful routes across the North Slope's trackless tundra during sudden fogs. At times the land's limitless sweep tricked our eyes with mirages. Far-off objects on which I had taken sightings would suddenly disappear. Distance also distorted scale, and I remembered the story Arctic explorer Vilhjalmur Stefansson told about spotting what he thought was a grizzly sitting on a hill outside its den a long way off. The hungry Stefansson stalked his quarry for an hour, but when he finally got to the hill he found only marmot tracks around a small mound on which the "grizzly" had been sitting.

It is the very vastness of this Arctic prairie that needs protection if two of North America's great caribou herds are to be preserved. As with the millions of bison that once ranged our plains, caribou require large tracts of open, undisturbed land in order to thrive. Wildfire that destroys their lichen food has always been a menace, but now new dangers threaten them. Oil and mining development disrupts their calving grounds and migration routes. Low-flying aircraft panic them. And though the overall toll may not be severe, indiscriminate hunting claims some of the strongest and finest specimens.

The Arctic herd of 240,000 ranges from wintering grounds on the forested southern slopes of the central Brooks Range to summer calving areas on the North Slope. The international Porcupine herd of

Crafty, belligerent, incredibly strong, the wolverine earns a billing as—pound for pound and claw for claw—the world's most ferocious animal. It stands a mere 17 inches tall and weighs less than 60 pounds, but can drive mountain lions or wolves from kills or bring down a moose. Powerful jaws can crush large bones; paws able to wrestle aside logs ten times the animal's weight grow coarse hairs in winter to serve as snowshoes. As do others in the weasel family, it spreads a skunk-like stench with musk from anal glands.

Once this cold-land denizen roamed into forests from Maine to Washington; now its chief home is the taiga and tundra of Alaska and Canada. It lives most of the year as a solitary wanderer and ranges widely to feed a voracious appetite. One of our rarest mammals, it is keenly dependent on wilderness preservation to keep its toehold on survival.

DRAWING BY GEORGE FOUNDS

With hands-in-mittens forepaws a sea otter clutches her pup; with rear feet like a diver's flippers she swims amid the kelp along Aleutian shores where abundant sea urchins and other creatures of the shallows feed her kind. Chowtime finds her pup among strands of kelp while mother clutches her catch — and often a stone as an anvil for cracking shellfish.

Dense, velvety fur an inch deep traps air to keep the mammal afloat and shield it from cold. But not from near-disaster: Hunters seeking the prized pelts gunned the otter to near extinction by the late 19th century. Now otters multiply on California's coast, new colonies have been established elsewhere on Pacific shores, and the species thrives in the Aleutian National Wildlife Refuge, whose islands are under study for wilderness protection.

DRAWING BY GEORGE FOUNDS

100,000 winters along the Porcupine River in Alaska and Canada, and in spring also calves on the North Slope, mainly within the 8.9-million-acre Arctic National Wildlife Range. To improve the ecological integrity of the range, which extends north to the Beaufort Sea and stretches from the Canning River on the west to the Canadian border, additions totalling just under 2.5 million acres have been proposed; one lies west, the other south of the range. If the Canadian government follows through on plans to create a major new protected area contiguous to the United States, the value of the Wildlife Range and its extensions would be enhanced as part of a vast bi-national preserve where wild creatures could continue their age-old ways undisturbed.

Even with the extensions, however, the Wildlife Range and the Porcupine herd face a direct threat from pipelines. One pipeline corridor would wrap around the range's southwestern border, then cut east — right across the path of caribou cows migrating to calving grounds. Of even greater significance to the delicate environment of the North Slope, the Brooks Range, and the Gulf of Alaska is the Trans-Alaska pipeline route, which would run 789 miles south from Prudhoe Bay to Valdez.

The source of the pipeline controversy lies 9,000 feet beneath the North Slope in an immense reserve of oil amounting to some 10 billion barrels, in addition to natural gas. Oil isn't new to the North Slope. Eskimos for centuries used chunks of frozen oil seep as fuel. When the U. S. Geological Survey found oil near Barrow in 1906, the government held it for potential military use, later setting aside an area nearly the size of Virginia as Naval Petroleum Reserve No. 4.

Though the government, spurred by World War II fuel needs, explored in Pet 4 during the 1940's, development was insignificant — unlike the amount of junked hardware and the thousands upon thousands of oil drums that littered the region.

Then came the 1968 strike on the Arctic coast at Prudhoe Bay.

In his attempts to wrest this oil from the Arctic, man and his technology triggered a bizarre series of conflicts related to both the severity and the fragility of the North. The fragility is born from life's struggle to survive under some of the most hostile conditions on the planet short of the Poles themselves. The thin carpet of earth that sustains life is underlain with permafrost, a perennially frozen subsurface of rock, gravel, and soil mixed with ice in varying amounts, and in some places 2,000 feet deep. The little rain that falls on the Arctic desert of the North Slope lies atop the permafrost and, along with surface thawing, keeps the matlike, sedgy tundra soggy in summer. Winter, with temperatures plunging to 50 below, turns it into white armor. The plants and animals that have adapted to the rigors of this frozen, often lightless terrain are relatively few. And they are essential to each other in the Arctic's exquisitely wrought web of life.

When the "black gold" boom swept across the Arctic, oil companies began bidding for leases, the state bulldozed a winter road over the Brooks Range at Anaktuvuk Pass and on across the tundra, and diesel trucks rumbled north with equipment. Drilling rigs, like artificial flowers tapping the nourishment of fossil energy below, sprouted from the land. Spring revealed a grim reality, however: In some places the exposed permafrost along the roadway thawed into an impassable quagmire. It is a gigantic scar on the land that may take centuries to heal.

Building the Trans-Alaska pipeline—whether below or above ground—became the central controversy. Could the four-foot-wide pipe safely cross the tundra, mountains, some 350 streams, and a highly active earthquake zone without suffering stresses that would break the line? The oil industry, pouring time, money, and its best engineering efforts into tests, announced that it was sure the pipeline could be built "without severe damage to the land, the people, or the wildlife. Environmental disturbances will be avoided wherever possible, held to a minimum where unavoidable." And any damage would be repaired "to the fullest practicable extent."

Many ecologists were not reassured. The pipe would carry two million barrels of crude oil a day at temperatures of about 145° F. If buried, sections of the pipe might turn ice-rich permafrost into unstable mush. A break could devastate large areas of tundra, pollute rivers, and create death traps for fish, waterfowl, and marine mammals in coastal waters. The threat of oil spills from supertankers moving from the pipeline terminal at Valdez down the Alaskan and Canadian coasts was especially ominous. A major accident could cripple marine fisheries, pollute coastal recreation areas, and throw the marine environment out of balance.

Finally, the pipeline would seriously impair the quality of solitude that, for me, is the major wilderness asset of the Brooks Range and the North Slope beyond the mountains. The flatness of the tundra emphasizes even minor signs of civilization; on a recent return visit to the North Slope, to what I thought was an isolated spot, I was startled to see oil rigs about fifteen miles away. Those few distant towers completely and instantly destroyed the "feel" of wilderness.

It was ironic that the winter road, built by Alaska at a cost of more than $700,000, should slice hundreds of miles across an area that Bob Marshall, perhaps the greatest explorer of the Brooks Range, once recommended "should be zoned as a region where the federal government will contribute no funds for road building and permit no leases for industrial development." He argued that "Alaska is unique among all recreational areas belonging to the United States. . . . In the name of a balanced use of American resources, let's keep northern Alaska largely a wilderness!" Many concerned Americans—and I am one of them—agree with Marshall. Others see things differently, of course. For them, the state's vital interest lies in the development of natural resources waiting, untapped, in the wilderness. They maintain that the $900 million the oil companies paid the state in 1969 for Prudhoe Bay leases, plus royalties from future oil production, would go a long way toward easing Alaska's unemployment problems and lack of capital. As talk of a national "energy crisis" intensifies, so does pressure to deliver the oil. Major conservation groups have come to feel that if pipelines must be built there may be less potential hazard in a single corridor for both oil and gas lines that run overland through Canada, than in a separate Trans-Alaska oil line with its risk of spills at sea.

The mountains "constituted a series of sensational needlelike peaks extending for six or eight miles in a horseshoe around the gushing creek which rose in the glacier." So wrote Bob Marshall about his 1931 visit to the central Brooks Range with famed Alaskan frontier trapper Ernie Johnson. "The Eskimos called this range Arrigetch which means 'fingers of the hand extended,' and admirably expresses the appearance of these mountains." Marshall was a skilled and enthusiastic climber, but he noted that "Since neither Ernie nor I belonged to the human-fly category, we did not try to climb the Arrigetch peaks." Yet in the intervening years, these granite pinnacles have lured more and more mountaineers to their challenging heights—some smooth monoliths rise 3,000 feet above their bases.

The Arrigetch country lies in the western portion of the Interior Department's Gates of the Arctic tract, more than nine million acres of wilderness long dreamed of as a national park and ideal for timeless, unrestrained travel—a mosaic of superb mountain land, glacial lakes, and braided rivers.

It was on the eastern side of the study area that Marshall, on his first trip to Alaska in 1929, spotted two mountains flanking the North Fork of the Koyukuk River. "I bestowed the name of Gates of the Arctic on them," he wrote, "christening the east portal Boreal Mountain and the west portal Frigid Crags." Heading for a camp in the valley between them, Marshall judged Boreal to rise "straight up for almost 6,000 feet. . . . it seemed impossible to climb."

Visitors to the central Brooks Range today fly in by light plane to highland lakes for fishing, or to gravel bars along major rivers such as the Alatna, John, and the North Fork of the Koyukuk for float trips, an increasingly popular activity.

My first exposure to this region began in spring not far from the small Eskimo community at Anaktuvuk Pass north of the Gates. Earlier I had been investigating the environmental impact of the new discoveries of North Slope oil with a group of ecologists. Now my work was done and I had flown into the village alone to immerse myself in the joyful beauty this country holds.

When I wasn't roaming the treeless valleys and smooth mountain slopes, I stayed with an Eskimo family in a small wooden hut. It was a serene period in my life, a time when I felt the truth of an old Eskimo song:

My fears,   One great thing,
Those small ones   The only thing:
That I thought so big,   To live to see in huts and
For all the vital things   on journeys
I had to get and to reach.   The great day that dawns,
And yet, there is only   And the light that fills the world.

For months the land had lain silent and cold under skies continually dark, the North Slope foothills lifeless except for a prowling Arctic fox or the rare emergence of a lemming from its burrow beneath the snow.

I had arrived as the sun reappeared over the Arctic Ocean, illuminating high peaks on the southern horizon. Sunsets six hours long flamed reddish toward the Pole. Day by day the sun rose higher and higher, finally casting a golden glow over all the land. Then spring rushed in with an explosive burst of life. Cold prairies warmed and bloomed in a profusion of color—and mosquitoes.   (Continued on page 305)

Portfolio Notes

302

Geese and ducks arrived in joyous flocks that broke the spell of silence. Wildlife once more roamed the tundra. Even the lakes and rivers heralded spring's thaw, cracking and booming as the ice broke up.

Life's prime season in the Arctic is short but intense. Summer's clouds of mosquitoes and caribou are quickly replaced by the reds, purples, and yellows of tundra plants, which shortly wither with the fall. Before the colorful display is finished, the first blizzard sweeps in, drawing the land once more back to the dark skies, white earth, and numbing gales of winter.

To Eskimos, Noatak is said to mean "deep inside," and the river is well named, for it twists for 400 miles far into the heart of the Brooks Range. It rises in the glaciers of 8,510-foot Mount Igikpak, or Big Mountain, in the western reaches of the Gates of the Arctic country, but for most of its way the river cuts through an eight-million-acre proposed wilderness reserve extending to Kotzebue Sound. Setting aside the Noatak, in addition to the Gates of the Arctic, helps bring Bob Marshall's dream for northern Alaska a step closer to reality.

On my first visit to the Noatak during the summer of 1972, I spent a day following the river from source to delta by air. We had swept close under the huge hanging glaciers of Igikpak, then swooped down to the silver Noatak. Suddenly the mountains receded, revealing a vast basin.

"What a wilderness river," I wrote in my journal. "No sign of man. Bands of caribou cluster on windy hilltops, waiting for breezes to blow away the mosquitoes. We slip over a round brown spot ambling along a river flat. We swing back. It's a large grizzly, now standing manlike and surprised, forepaws dangling."

For more than an hour we followed the meandering river. Then mountains again pressed in closely, and the water grew angry. We twisted through the Grand Canyon of the Noatak, its precipices reaching out as if to snare our wingtips, then skimmed above a wide, forested plain splattered with shimmering lakes. Nearing the coast we passed the Eskimo village of Noatak, clinging to a river bluff. South of the village, on Cape Krusenstern, lay the remains of several prehistoric cultures, visible to us only as ridges of sand parallel to the water. The sites can be counted like tree rings: 114 distinct beach ridges, the earliest, farthest inland, dating back at least 5,000 years. In this trove archeologists found stone tools and lamps; arrow, spear, and harpoon heads of flint; pottery; and ruins of ancient whale hunters' lodges.

I noted in my journal at the time: "The Eskimo's long tenure in the lower Noatak gives eloquent testimony to his ability to survive in harmony with the land." And now I worry whether modern man, having opened a Pandora's Box of technological change, can learn to treat the earth as well.

The next leg in my summer's odyssey took me south of the Noatak to a geological oddity: the Great Kobuk and Nogahabara sand dunes. Just south of the Kobuk River, more than 350 square miles of dunes rise above the flat spruce-muskeg; the Nogahabara dunes lie about a hundred miles farther southeast.

Confronted by mile upon mile of golden sand almost devoid of plant life, I felt miraculously transported to the hot deserts of our arid Southwest. My sense of geographic confusion only increased when I spotted a lone moose browsing in a muskeg pond nearby. A moose in the desert?

The dunes resulted in part from centuries of glacial rock-grinding and river erosion. Composed of wind-blown sediment carried from streams draining glaciated mountains, they began their march across the land unknown centuries ago. Some are still marching. I watched the wind swirl and eddy across the dune surface, carrying sand grains from east to west. The western edge of the dunes is like some great water-less tidal wave in slow motion, swallowing the spruce and muskeg. Part way up the dunes' border, hundreds of tiny trees seem to sprout from the sand. But it's the death, not the birth, of a forest.

On a grander geological scale are the upheavals of southwest Alaska. Katmai National Monument is the center of historic volcanic activity. A series of explosions ripped the region in June 1912. The few humans present to witness the cataclysmic event reported that the top of 7,500-foot-high Mount Katmai simply blew off. Volcanologists later reported that not Katmai but another volcano, Novarupta, actually exploded. Thirty-three million tons of rock, pumice, and ash burst into the sky in an incandescent cloud, then fell back to earth, spreading an ashen blanket up to 300 feet deep. The blast directly affected 42,000 square miles and cooled the entire Northern Hemisphere — the cloud of particles spewed forth spread around the earth and reflected part of the sun's energy back into space.

In 1916, the second of five National Geographic Society expeditions led by Dr. Robert F. Griggs, a botanist, explored Katmai and discovered a great valley smoth-ered in hot volcanic ash; buried snow and water had been heated by the ash and was erupting in thousands of fissures of steam and gas. Griggs named the region the Valley of Ten Thousand Smokes. The surveys led to establishment of the monument.

Today the ash deposit has cooled and steam no longer shrouds the valley. Yet the awesome work of earth's inner fires remains to amaze those who enter this arena of volcanic power. Mount Katmai's summit, which collapsed during the eruption of No-varupta, cups a blue-green lake. Dead trees thrust gaunt and naked from the ash, and stream-cut canyons wind through the thick brown accumulation of volcanic material.

Katmai is second only to Alaska's Glacier Bay National Monument as the largest unit administered by the Park Service. Most of its 2,792,137 acres are under study for wilderness designation, from the bays and fiords along the Shelikof Strait, through the central area of volcanic mountains, to the moraine-made lakes and rivers where the arctic forest meets the tundra of Bristol Bay's coastal plain.

A backpacker into Katmai finds reassuring evidence of nature's wondrous ability to heal even the catastrophic wounds of volcanic eruption. Grasses and scrubby willow and alder have invaded parts of the denuded valley, and these plants have brought the moose into areas once barren of wildlife.

Katmai's most impressive animal, however, is the Alaska brown bear. About 500 of these huge mammals, some weighing 1,500 pounds and standing nine feet tall, find refuge in the monument. I've watched them feast on roots and grass during the spring and gorge on summer's river runs of salmon; the bears can leap with the agility of a cat to pluck dinner from swift streams.

Proposed additions north and southwest of the monument should significantly help this magnificent animal survive here by extending its range and safeguarding its salmon streams. Just north of Katmai the Interior Department also hopes to protect two other areas around Lake Iliamna and Lake Clark Pass, both with important brown bear habitat as well as other valuable wildlife. Iliamna, covering a thousand square miles, is Alaska's largest lake. These tracts contain the state's most popular sport fishing for trout and salmon, along with the spawning grounds of the richest red salm-on commercial fishery in North America.

The Lake Clark Pass region is the meeting point for the northern end of the Aleutian Range and the southern tip of the Alaska Range. Two dozing volcanoes, rugged seacoasts, dozens of high glaciers, and scores of glacier-carved lakes give rich diversity to a wilderness only 100 air miles from Anchorage.

Katmai and the neighboring lake areas aren't the only havens for brown bears in southern Alaska. National wildlife reserves protect them on Kodiak Island and the Kenai Peninsula, but in the panhandle they face not only hunters but also the drastic alteration of habitat from extensive timber cutting in Tongass National Forest.

During my summer as a salmon fisherman along this beautiful coast, I spent my off-days exploring the hundreds of islands between Juneau and Ketchikan. The big brownies made my wanderings easier, for they had worn wide trails for me to follow. I whistled and sang as I walked these paths, a technique to prevent a surprise confrontation with half a ton of disgruntled bear. The technique failed me only once. I was descending a steep trail beside a noisy, rushing stream, the way canopied with tall Sitka spruce and hemlock. Lichens, like old men's beards, hung from tree limbs.

The wind was blowing toward me as I climbed down a small cliff. I turned a bend and froze in my tracks. A mother bear and two cubs stood several dozen yards away, stiffly facing in my direction. Bears have poor vision but a superb sense of smell. This one, apparently, couldn't catch my scent, because she lifted on her hind legs and weaved slightly as though trying to detect by my odor just *what* I was. Then she dropped on all fours and charged my petrified form.

Anyone who has seen a brown bear crash through thick underbrush knows that flight was impossible. On she came, to within a dozen yards. Then she stopped, just as a breeze tossed my scent her way. A visible shock passed through her body as she recognized the smell. In an instant, mother and cubs vanished in the thickets.

Brown bears, however, do not always veer off, and for decades encounters such as these have led to the shooting of brownies. Now concern grows over the impact of timbering in the lush coastal forest. In clear-cut tracts gashed by too many logging roads, rains may gully the slopes. Salmon streams may silt up from rapid erosion. There are rules to minimize environmental damage in logging zones, and studies indicating that bear and salmon populations hold their own. Yet the fears remain. With Alaska's primitive forests vanishing at an alarming rate and undisturbed wildlife habitat dwindling, conservationists urge that most of Admiralty Island, the west coast of Chichagof Island, and the finest glacial fiords receive wilderness protection. This would add significantly to Forest Service wilderness proposals, which embrace some 2.5 million acres out of a total of nearly 21 million in Tongass and Chugach, the nation's largest national forests.

Logging threatens a land uniquely wild here. One can wander for months through thousands of waterways hemmed by wooded shores without seeing the same view twice. The waters teem with whales, seals, and fishes. Each island beckons the traveler to explore once more, to search out the secrets of life hidden deep inside portals of spruce and draped moss. A rich variety of birds grace the skies, and the bald eagle, more common here than anywhere else in the United States, wheels high over the mud flats, seeking fish marooned in shallow pools by the surging tides.

My final days in Alaska during a recent summer were spent close to North America's highest peak, Mount McKinley. The Indians called it *Denali*, the Great One. It seems to float, cloudlike on the horizon, a 20,320-foot pyramid of snow visible from both Anchorage and Fairbanks.

The wedge of streamlined feathers hurtles down on a duck flapping over the tundra. Strong feet flash out—and duck plumage explodes at the powerful blow. Thus "stoops" a peregrine falcon, perhaps the swiftest of birds, taking prey on the wing. It may reach 65 miles an hour in level flight, nearly three times that in a dive. Delighting in aerial acrobatics, it may harry a flock or a lone bird with no attempt at harm.

Man's pressures and pesticides have nearly erased from cliffside eyries in the old 48 states this prized bird of the ancient sport of falconry. But it holds its endangered own on Alaska's Yukon River, the Arctic Slope, and in the Aleutian Islands. There it returns from winter quarters to old nest sites spaced 6 to 10 miles apart.
DRAWING BY GEORGE FOUNDS

307

White men have been drawn to the mountain since 1897, when W. A. Dickey, a prospector, wrote an article about the spectacular peak he had seen the previous year. Dickey had named it for presidential candidate William McKinley. In 1902 Alfred H. Brooks of the U. S. Geological Survey became the first on record to set foot on its slopes, but it took two hardy sourdoughs, William Taylor and Pete Anderson, to conquer its north peak in 1910. Three years later a party of four led by Archdeacon Hudson Stuck reached the south, or true, summit.

Crown of the 600-mile-long Alaska Range, Denali dominates Mount McKinley National Park, 3,030 square miles of wilderness that includes Muldrow Glacier, whose stagnant snout rests within a mile of the park road. Rolling tundra spreads a low green apron to the west of the foothills, and as I walked those plains it seemed as though I were back on the North Slope of the Brooks Range.

Underfoot dry lichens, grasses, and sedges crackled with each step, releasing the pungent odors so typical of the Arctic. Ground squirrels, a favored food of bears, jerked themselves to attention at my approach, waiting until I crossed the invisible boundary of their territory to dive underground with piercing warning whistles. Prostrated willow and birch formed tangled, close-knit mats in small depressions—harsh testimony to the desiccating winds of winter.

Like the tundra, Denali's wild creatures have adapted to extremely rigorous conditions, yet to prosper they depend upon a complex environmental system that extends beyond the park boundaries, a system that can be easily thrown out of balance. Here again, substantial additions to the park—north and south—must be acquired. Much of this land serves as winter territory, particularly during unusually severe seasons. The dilemma of space affects the wolves probably more than any of the other large carnivores. The boundaries simply aren't wide enough to protect their hunting range. And when they forage outside the park, they fall prey to man.

What makes the need for these buffers especially critical now is the increase of people and the greater pressure on wildlife as a result of the completion of the Anchorage-Fairbanks Highway running along the eastern edge of the park. A single month may find more visitors than during a whole year before the road was built.

The answer to the environmental problems of McKinley and many other areas in Alaska may lie in a three-part solution: demarcation of reserve boundaries based on entire ecosystems; prevention of pollution from the outside, such as pesticides, atmospheric contamination, and sullied water; and control of human numbers intruding on wild areas.

The obstacles to such action are immense. Mining, logging, oil drilling, agricultural land clearance, highway construction, poorly planned urban and second-home settlement, facilities for mass tourism, building of dams and military installations—lumped together they spell development. The confrontation between those who wish to develop rapidly and "bring Alaska into the 20th century" and those who wish to protect major portions of the state's wilderness cuts across traditional group attitudes, even splitting native Alaskans on the issue.

Whichever way the development pendulum eventually swings, Alaska's fate is critical to people outside the state. America's northlands embrace a spiritual resource important to everyone, wherever they live. The great glacial complex of the Wrangells, the vast mountain country of the Brooks Range, the howl of a wolf in Mount McKinley National Park—all offer unique experiences of irretrievable value. As the world shrinks, the world's wilderness shrinks with it. The question now facing Alaskans, Americans, and global human society is, "How much wilderness?"

Silvered threads skein a valley in the central Brooks Range— one of some 200 rivers, many still unnamed, that drain these Arctic ramparts. Alluvial fans—triangular deposits of silt and debris washed down from the heights—hem the mountains' tundra-clad flanks. Hiking and mapping the region in the 1930's, Bob Marshall reveled in "the freedom from trails and human signs in this remote country." He found canyons aglow with flowers and marveled that "every bend in every valley held beyond it the ...mystery of unknown worlds."
JOHN P. MILTON

308

ALONE IN THE ARCTIC

Steven C. Wilson

I left Fort Yukon, its ravens, mosquitoes, swallows, and a wide and muddy rumbling as the driftwood-laden spring runoff folded under the overhanging banks of the Yukon River. I'd spent a couple of hours between planes sitting among the willows, sharing my lunch with the raven upon whose riverbank I was trespassing. Now I was heading north again. We slipped through blue-gray wisps and tails of the season's northernmost rain shower, leaving summer south of the Brooks Range, droning between its windswept peaks toward a landing on Alaska's North Slope.

I don't have destinations, either in time or place—just a project's beginning and ending. Nor do I enjoy "adventure," concurring with Stefansson that adventures in wilderness travel are almost always the result of poor preparation, knowledge, or judgment. The wilderness is a place where one must *stay* comfortable, because there is no place to go to *get* comfortable. After hundreds of miles and nights out, I have a good kit—every item light, sturdy, and multipurpose—which lets a human animal travel wild, as self-sufficient and unconcerned as the snowy owl I was stalking along the Jago River this June in the Arctic National Wildlife Range.

Three times he had flown away. Each time upwind. So I waded the river and hiked a mile or two upwind to a somewhat higher spot where I let the wind whip my clothes dry, then hunkered down to wait. The owl was gradually moving my way. He would make a long gliding flight and land at the next pingo, surveying the lemming highways for a goodly time, then a few flaps and another long glide. In a couple of hours he would be working well within range of my 180-mm lens.

Pingos, conical hills built up by freezing and thawing of subsurface water, are the highest and driest places on the tundra. Here burrowers make their homes and raptors and foxes sit and dine, leaving their casts and droppings, an informal inventory of the vicinity's prey. I picked apart some old owl casts lying beside me: five

Wind's invisible sinews tug the author's tent at a winter campsite in the Brooks Range. Photographing arctic wildlife, Wilson has spent weeks at a time beyond human company. Yet—he insists— he was not alone and enjoys this bleak, solitary land, especially the North Slope. "Its openness and simplicity, with fewer life forms, make it easier to see what needs a plant or animal has and how it satisfies them."

ENTHEOS

beautiful, perfect lower jawbones and two complete skulls of lemmings. I wrapped them in lichens and stowed them in empty film cans as mementos.

The owl gave a few strong flaps, lifted off his perch, and sailed low toward me. I followed with the camera. Fast focusing assured me he was going to move in *very* close so I held off, not using any exposures for distant "insurance" shots one often makes after a long stalk or wait. My bird was maybe 20 yards away, in a low glide, when he suddenly back-winged, false dived, twirled, and turned. Steady, pumping wingbeats sped him away downwind. Neither he nor I had noticed the rock ptarmigan that—erupting in flight—had spooked him. I hadn't made one exposure.

Frustrating but no less beautiful, the day made me keenly aware that I harvest the wilderness but don't manage it. An owl's vote or a ptarmigan's is as meaningful as mine. Using my own senses, and photographic and other tools that affix the visual and sound images of the wilderness, I furnish my family and myself food and shelter, and for me something else—quite as important, yet strangely elusive:

I sat under a cloud and watched a willow for a hundred years, twist and struggle out of the ground, unfurl a hundred seasons of green—the sky so still, the day so gentle—it was just a pulsing of the afternoon. (Journal note, Kavik River Camp)

Garden of the winds: Delicate ice flowers embellish a lake near the Canning River. Plants submerged in the shallows emit moist gases through pinholes in the covering ice: Winds crystallize and mold the vapors. In this boreal land of little rain but much water, permafrost to depths of 2,000 feet keeps water near the surface in marshes, ponds, and meandering streams. The Canning forms part of the western boundary of the vast Arctic National Wildlife Range, under study for Wilderness Act designation. One-third the size of Ohio, the ANWR was established in 1960 to preserve portions of

ENTHEOS

the unique Arctic environment big enough for nature to maintain the balanced array of life. The range contains the calving grounds of the Porcupine caribou herd; it is also home to grizzly, musk ox, wolf, and moose—among large mammals—and to fascinating worlds-in-miniature revealed by hand lens or microscope. Breakup of ice, often sudden and thunderous, signals the onset of summer. Then day and night sunshine brings a resurgence of life to the land. Accessible by air, yet lacking all but nature's facilities, the ANWR is open to camping, hiking, and quiet contemplation.

The temperature by the Kavik is above freezing for the first time this season, enough sun-warmth for photosynthesis to be well under way. And I sense a willow's hundred years along the cutbank of the river, undisturbed and undisturbing. . . .

Wilderness is perhaps something you live, rather than just visit.

One of my first times above the Arctic Circle was on a solo trek in the western Brooks Range during the migration of the Barren Ground caribou. I'd been dropped off in the Baird Mountains on the pass between the Cutler and Redstone drainages. It was a fine day, the sort of short, crisp day in late winter that one senses is given us nonmigratory animals, intending that we prepare for the celebrations of spring. Pilot Tony Bernhardt helped me unload his Super Cub. He was packing snowshoes and a tin of unleaded gas up the ridge to my base campsite when he noticed a dense fog rolling up the valley from the North Slope. He dropped the gear and ran toward the plane hollering, "Good luck, goodbye." The plane disappeared into the fogbank just before it lifted off. I heard it climbing and turning, heading back down Redstone Valley toward Tony's home base at Kobuk.

With the fog and cold rapidly pushing through the range, my camp demanded

313

ENTHEOS

Heeding a timeless tradition that heads them northward in spring to calve, caribou cows bunch before fording a willow-edged river. Caribou, the only deer having antlered females, migrate through passes in the Brooks Range to calving grounds on the tundra, perhaps 400 miles from their winter range. Bulls follow.

The margin of life is slim. Vital urgency attends a newborn's first lesson: learning to stand. In severe weather he must be on his feet quickly or freeze to the ground and die. With mother's encouragement, success—and a meal—reward the effort. Calves a few days old can outrun a man.

attention. I'd picked a spot for the tent a hundred or so yards west of as active a caribou trail as we'd spotted in several days' flying. It was right at the break of the pass with unobstructed views south down the Redstone, where the caribou were coming from, and also north. While fog blotted out the views, I stomped the stakes into the packed snow, secured the tent, stowed my gear, and organized camera equipment. In my pockets I stuck extra rolls of film, boxes of dried mincemeat, matches—just out of habit because wind and snow really aren't fire material—some nylon cord, thermometer, compass, knife, wind gauge, and binoculars. Carrying a small shovel, I headed down to the caribou trail to dig a bury blind, a hole to conceal myself for photographing when the long, single-file lines of migrating animals came into range.

By the time I got back to the tent the wind was up around 40 knots, the temperature down near zero. I crawled in and went to sleep. Hours later, in the blackness and noise of that wildly flapping tent, I was trying to keep my sleeping bag perched on a steep mound of snow the wind had packed under the floor. The floor itself was beating hard enough to lift me off the ground—then I remembered the ease with which I had pushed the stakes into the snow and the sheer drop-off to the south of my tent site, downwind only a dozen feet or so.

I unloaded my first partially exposed rolls of arctic wilderness film, screwed them tightly into cans, and put them in my inside pocket with a note asking that they be processed. I tried to take a wind reading. I couldn't; the white ball just blew up into the measuring pipe and jammed. All the great historic snows that had ever fallen between me and the North Pole were blowing into my tent through the minuscule triangular hole in the back which a manufacturing seamstress hadn't quite stitched tight. I knew I was going to get blown clear off this planet. . . .

When I woke it had grown light, that bitter green glow I had seen before only in Midwestern hailstorms and an Atlantic hurricane. The tent zipper tab came down a couple of feet before it hit packed granular snow. I reached out and around to try a stake. It felt tight. The guy rope stake, too, seemed tight. The stake on the left front corner felt as if it was embedded in concrete. With the blizzard and falling temperature the stakes had frozen into the ground and nothing short of a volcanic eruption was going to move them. I suddenly felt more like an Arctic explorer. I dug out the inside of the tent and reloaded the cameras. Then I put on my white camouflage parka and confronted the elements. Getting to the right place and staying alive was not all that was required of me; I also had to be able to photograph. I went to shovel out the blind and wait for the caribou.

Wilderness and the wild condition have long frightened men, as you can readily see from dictionary definitions which apply such words as "desolate, barbarous, unruly, destructive," such phrases as "confusing multitude or mass . . . not amenable to control, restraint, or domestication." Yet wilderness seems none of those to me, having both order and integrity and—amid stark necessity—a gentleness. Nor need it be of large size—wilderness is both a place and a state of mind. Here man need not remain a spectator; he can be part of that wildness when he limits his efforts to filling his animal needs using renewable resources.

315

Adaptations of plants and animals intrigue me: the insulation provided by hair, fur, or layers of blubber; the long nose of the caribou that helps warm the air it breathes to ease the chill to the lungs. Away from my native environment, I usually feel more secure mimicking nature's solution to a problem than relying on my own brilliant idea. My nose doesn't match the caribou's, but I can fold the ruff of my parka forward like a snout. Like the caribou, I avoid running in cold weather; rapid breathing gives the air less time to warm up. Some animals tunnel under the snow to escape subfreezing winds. Others put their backs to the storm, lie down, and let the snow build up a shelter; dead air space holds their body heat. Caught out in wind and snow, I also burrow down and wait out the storm. Unendowed with fur or blubber, I always take my sleeping bag.

In themselves, these techniques are of little use elsewhere. What is of value is knowing that in any environment we can learn directly from other forms of life.

On the Slope in winter, the very emptiness becomes a positive thing. You realize that you are the only person around. There is no external cheerfulness, no color, few sparks of aliveness — just wind and cold and snow. You sense a responsibility. If there is to be any laughter, any brightness or springiness, you have to be it. It has to come from you. You sense why Eskimos need to be a happy people. There's sheer survival value in being cheerful. In the white simplicity you reach out for something alive to

ENTHEOS

"The open life of him who lives by the hunt keeps . . . the thrill of endeavor and achievement, a thing never to be bought. . . ." Since 1921, when Stefansson published The Friendly Arctic, firearms have supplanted the Eskimo's bows and arrows; and snowmobiles largely have taken the place of his dogsleds.

For one group of Eskimos in inland Alaska, the first sign of caribou migrating through the central Brooks Range is still a summons to the hunt, as it was for their nomadic ancestors. About a hundred Nunamiuts living at Anaktuvuk Pass rely on caribou as the bulwark of their diet. Skins, stitched with sinew, become clothing, sled blankets, bed covers in their

winter "white-man" cabins, and floor covers in canvas tents used when villagers move to hunting and fishing camps in summer.

The men of one household usually make up a hunting party. As the columns of caribou near, the marksmen hold fire, letting many animals pass so their scent trail continues past the hunters; subsequent herds will then follow the same trails. Successful hunts during spring and fall migrations produce tons of food, fabric, thread, tools. Eskimo tradition honors a dead animal's spirit—or iñua—and wastes none of its substance.

Frost-rimed antlers and bones mark the spot where an old bull died, its flesh perhaps to nourish a grizzly bear, wolf, or flower.

identify with—even things that are not alive may seem friendly. There are places where Eskimos have piled up rocks. When you're scanning the empty horizon and see the upright shape, it gives you a momentary sense of relief, though you know it's not a man or a caribou. And when an Eskimo finds a shed caribou antler, he'll stick it upright. The first time I was out with Tony Bernhardt, who is full-blooded Eskimo, he did that as if it were second nature. I asked why.

"Oh, just so they'll know that someone has been here."

The Slope is big country; the wildlife range alone is 130 miles east to west and 150 miles north to south. It is both immense and delicate; an anachronism to most temperate-zone dwellers. It's quiet country. Lying still, listening but not looking, I become very aware of small, individual noises—the squeaky beep of a spider, a creature you don't think of as having a voice. Once I heard a fox walking by. Slowly, I turned to look. He was about half a mile away.

The day risen so gently, plump and pungent, broke at nine-thirty with the throbbing of a helicopter heading onto the range. A dozen choppers were scurrying about the Canning River area on busyness for the oil, gas, and pipeline companies, dropping off petroleum geologists and fledgling biologists and environmentalists, picking up a sling load of aviation fuel *(Continued on page 325)*

ENTHEOS

Layers of storm cloud and sun striate
a summer vista of tundra and north-facing
mountains. Vagaries of weather as well
as vast distances try the traveler's
ingenuity. Hikers on the trailless Slope
may set a course by distant peaks, then
have the peaks coalesce in clouds,
shimmery heat waves (right), fog (center),
or snow. An awareness of wind
direction abets the compass; sky maps
—reflected colors of terrain on the
undersides of clouds—help experts tell
what lies over the horizon. Prevailing
hues hint at the Arctic's seasonal shifts of
mood, from summer's mauve to autumn's
amber-yellow to late winter's steely white.

Large in spirit, Arctic terns blitz
a mammal intruding on their sandspit.
Besides earth's champion migrator — Arctic
terns wing from one polar zone to the
other — scores of bird species nest
on the sandbar-sheltered north coast.
A whistling swan, arctic nester named
for its high-pitched call, flexes snowy
wings. Plumage fit for queen-seeking
garbs a king eider drake rising from
a pond. Among northern phalaropes,
females wear the finery; males usually sit
on the eggs — come storm or high water.

ENTHEOS

In the fever of an Arctic summer day—
2,040 sunlit hours long—flowers in
bright profusion erupt upon the tundra.
Aglow at midnight, glacier avens adorns a
coastal meadow; wide-angle lens captures
a top-of-the-world arc. Low-growing and
frugal like most boreal plants, a starwort
twinkles among netleaf willows.
Opened seedpod of a rush rears above
the low-circling sun. Inch-high moss pinks
mat a gravelly riverbank. Mountain avens
dominates an upland meadow.
Its home in jeopardy because of coveted
riches that lie beneath, a marsh-marigold
blooms above a natural oil seep.

here or empty drums there, whomping off to get plastic bottles filled with water. Their camp was on a river but so was their garbage dump, so they flew water in.

Soon the summer "rain" of mosquitoes and the magical flight song of the male Lapland longspur replace the fading drone of the helicopter and recapture my attention. Since May 10 the sun has been circling in the sky, giving me now four hours of "sunset" each "night." Around 3 a.m. it becomes morning; the light changes from soft yellow to harsh, bright white. The wind picks up and animals increase their activity—except the nocturnal ones, which include me. I'm on a night shift schedule. At about 11:30 a.m. I head for a bedding spot to sleep the hot, burnt-out hours.

A heather garden that has stabilized a relict sand dune about a half-hour hike to the northwest appears as a possible "home." About twenty minutes out onto the soggy carpet of polygons that separates me from it, a pair of rough-legged hawks flying southeast bomb down on me in protest, wheeling and turning—so the cutbank on the far side of the river must have looked like a home to them also.

I spend an hour watching the pair, mewing and soaring above the swollen river. It is a scorcher today, still and hot, with shimmery heat waves, yet the ground is patched with snow. Bumblebees and spiders are out, a few butterflies, mostly black. Now one hawk sits on the nest, a tangle of driftwood reordered upon a jagged granite rock jutting six or eight feet over the west bank of the river. The other hawk cruises back and forth every minute or two, first sailing out across the river and circling above me, maybe fifty feet high, then soaring upriver out of sight and back, taking maybe thirty seconds for each leg of the trip. I know I'm pressuring him on this side of the river. Tracks indicated to me later that a sow grizzly with a cub was his upriver concern.

Once he sailed out over me and away to the northern horizon. In a minute or two I spied his destination through my glasses: another hawk shimmering in and out of the heat wall vision of the horizon. They circled, sparred, and dived for a minute or more, then my hawk abruptly left and, sailing over me with a high, zooming dive, landed on his perch on a snowbank a hundred yards or so from the nest. I thought of the many legends and rituals of man that honor the hawk, perhaps in homage, for he sees much farther than we. Another thought from that hawk: Time and distance are not as significant as lives up here.

Binoculars become almost a part of the body. You see a few elemental things happening again and again; with patience you begin to perceive how one happening

Rivers like shining serpents twine over the gently inclined plain, north to the sea. The Brooks Range, whose topmost peaks rise above 9,000 feet, serrates the horizon in this southerly view. The geography becomes geometry as wet, shallow soils freeze and thaw, defining polygonal ditches amid the vegetation. Tussock-forming cottongrass is the chief plant of foothill meadows. In bloom the tussocks, along with lichens, are forage for caribou, here in the pale pelage of summer. The tundra is enjoyable by man and beast for the few brief weeks of truce between winter's paralytic cold and summer's siege of bloodthirsty insects. The author found the former more endurable. "Hiking in July is a rubber boots and bugdope affair. You just can't exaggerate the Alaska mosquito."

ENTHEOS

cooperates with another. Eventually, the interrelatedness of all living things becomes apparent. Why others need wilderness or don't need it, I couldn't say. I need it to understand what I know.

The delight of summer is animals with their young. This June I watched a semi-palmated sandpiper nesting. After her four babies hatched, she took them on short walking trips. Home was then inside her feathers. One of the little birds seemed dumb. He'd get on top of something and couldn't get off. The mother would push him and he'd fall. The other three didn't mind falling. They would just bail out, get up, and go on their way. But the fourth really seemed afraid and, being slow in that one thing, became very much a retarded sandpiper. And sure enough, he was the first casualty. By the time the mother took them wading out for food, the other three could walk with the current and maintain balance. But the little dumb one couldn't. He walked out into deep water and disappeared down the stream.

Nine a.m. on the Fourth of July, the weather clear, the temperature 52° F. and virtually no wind. Lying belly down on a pingo four or five miles from the Arctic Ocean, I have been in the midst of a steady stream of caribou — and mosquitoes — since 3 a.m. A major caribou movement is one of those intense, indelible encounters we are rarely privileged to experience. At first it is just the incredible numbers of animals moving past me, the constant grunting and talking, the clicking walk as ligaments rub against bone, the animals pausing now to graze, trotting over within twenty or thirty feet to check me out, the calves gamboling, the herd speed perhaps a mile or two or three per hour; so efficient is the lawn-mower effect that the herd *must* keep moving or ruin its range.

Then I begin noticing individual animals: a cow and nursing calf, a barren cow, a pesky year-old bull, another calf apparently searching for its mother, two calves reared up on hind legs like stallions, or teddy bears! About half the cows in this post-calving concentration have calves. Now interactions become clear: calves nursing and then grazing with their mothers, then frisking all through their own local groupings of a couple of hundred animals, seldom appearing to become lost; calves bounding across a river with an obvious thrill at the challenge and excitement of swift, icy water, then with a wild exuberance racing and prancing across a wind-glazed snowbank. A bull stands on three legs delicately touching the tips of his sensitive, developing antlers to the scent gland in a rear hoof, all spread out and strange-looking like a Henry Moore sculpture. Bands of mature bulls majestically contain the herd by positioning themselves at the forefront. And countless animals display the most predictable thing about caribou: curiosity.

When I started hiking back to my tent, a two-year-old bull trotted alongside me for four or five minutes, tail and nose high. He sped up and circled me once, about fifty yards away, then again and again. It was an eight- or ten-mile hike back, counter to the herd movement, but he continued circling me most of the way. When his interest seemed to wane, I'd hunker down and "graze" for several seconds or I'd whistle like a deer; both seemed to encourage him. I didn't need any encouragement. It had been a day beyond belief, a deeply rich ending to a potent trip.

For me, wilderness has to do with awareness . . . caring . . . and not encroaching.

Midsummer night's sun illuminates a channel between land's end and bird-inhabited islands in Beaufort Lagoon. Nearing the end of a six-week sojourn in which he traveled on foot, by 'copter, plane, and truck, Wilson paddles a metal canoe that doubles as a sled on ice. "The Arctic wilderness," he muses, "is a fine place to experience how the human animal can fit into the earth's web of life — and why he must. Every place is a home."

ENTHEOS

A BACKPACKING PRIMER

Harvey Manning

In the late hours of a long day, an endless hill turning my pack into stone, sun shriveling my brain and wilting my legs, bugs besieging my eyes and ears and nose, I've often thought how grand it would be to roam across the land as a disembodied spirit. But then the path gentles into a meadow gloriously abloom, bugs blow away in a divine breeze, snowmelt cools my head and sluices my throat. And I realize wilderness wouldn't be half as much fun without a body. The hard work is what makes the water taste so good.

Though horses, burros, and canoes offer alternatives to backpacking in some areas, most people most of the time have little choice. If they want to go wild it will be not only afoot, but with a certain amount of staggering and gasping under the weight of the stone.

Overnight nibbles at the edge of wilderness start the vibrations, whet the appetite, and unlimber the muscles. But the minimum time for a satisfying jaunt is about a week—long enough for body and soul to begin swinging in wild rhythms, yet short enough to keep the pack from becoming a crushing burden.

My intent, therefore, is to describe the equipment, food, and techniques needed for an easy, safe, and happy nine-day backpack. I will make full use of the modern materials—nylon, plastic, aluminum—and food preparations that lighten the traveler's travail, extend his range, and lessen his impact on the wild lands.

This last point is crucial. Some 20 million people have tried backpacking, and the number grows every year. We can no longer afford the luxury of sleeping on a bed of fresh-cut evergreen boughs, or of building up a roaring campfire after every mealtime. Many of the cherished woodcrafter ways are passing into memory—and the sooner the better, if wilderness is to survive.

The planning is for a party of three—the smallest safe number except on the easiest, most heavily traveled trails. A solo hiker, when injured, can only shout, wait, and hope; off the beaten track in empty country he can die as a result of nothing more than a broken leg or a concussion. In a party of two, one hiker may depart to seek help—but must leave the other unattended, and an injured person may thrash about in delirium and really come to grief.

The wilderness I have in mind is not subarctic or desert, not jungle or icefield; call it an "average" summer wilderness of the old 48 states, which doesn't rule out some rugged hikes or brushes with stormy weather. And the backpackers I have in mind are beginners.

There are as many ways to run a wild land as a city household and no two veterans agree on every point. Explore the literature, or join an outdoor club, and you'll find multiple and conflicting manifestations of the ultimate wisdom. By the end of his first nine-day trip, a beginner will be far down the path toward eccentricity, eager to sneer at the pontification of experts.

Every now and again a youth sets out for the wilds carrying no food or equipment, wearing naught but shorts and sneakers, seeking a spiritual experience. The quest has always interested me, though never enough, in 35 years of hiking, to try it. I did, around the age of 13, tinker with a "no-weight" pack buoyed by helium-filled balloons, but when I discovered the cost of the balloons, I gave it up. Such examples may have little practical value, yet they are instructive for novices, whose commonest blunder is overloading.

Though seasoned backpackers often carry much more, an adult in fairly good condition can comfortably haul about one-third his weight (not counting excess fat). The formula works as well for many teen-agers; the average 16-year-old boy, or 14-year-old girl, can shoulder an adult load.

The outfit recommended here weighs 40 to 45 pounds, including boots on feet, clothing on body, and pack on back loaded with personal gear and one-third the weight of items that serve the entire party. So a 165-pounder can afford to add some "luxuries." But a 100-pounder, unless traveling with big, kind companions, must go over the outfit item by item to reduce the 40 pounds to 33.

It can be done. Not necessarily by making a cooking pot do double duty as a rain hat, in the manner of a strange chap I met once, or by cutting pockets from pants and breaking half the teeth from a comb, but by shopping for the lightest equipment, going superlight on food, perhaps even dispensing with borderline essentials.

In the listing that follows, the weight given for group items (such as tarp, first-aid kit, cooking equipment, and food) is the total weight of each item. Food stocks can be divided, but draw the line at ripping a tarp in three. Some juggling will be necessary in order to apportion the loads equitably.

EQUIPMENT

Boots (4-5 pounds in men's size 10, 3½-4½ in women's size 7). Choose carefully! Since boots tend to look pretty much alike, pay special attention to the total weight, which indicates how tough

DILL COLE

the guts of the boots are. If they're too light, the feet may get battered; if they're too heavy, legs suffer from lifting unneeded leather and metal perhaps 20,000 times a day. For mixed terrain the most versatile models are those described by mountain shops as "medium-weight hiking (or trail) boot," or "lightweight climbing boot." They should have a hard toe, rubber-lug sole, padding at least around the instep and ankle, and uppers that extend about two inches above the ankle. They should feel snug with two pairs of socks. Break them in thoroughly before the trip.

Socks (1 pound). Three pairs—two to wear, one spare; wool-nylon, or wool with nylon reinforcing. For tender feet add a light cotton, nylon, or silk sock next to the skin and spares for frequent changes. *Underwear* (½ pound). One set, whatever is usual in casual city life. Nine days in one set of underwear seems grim, but the additional weight may turn out grimmer.

Trousers (1¾ pounds). Wool is best for warmth when wet; for bone-dry country, cotton suffices. Any castoff from city wear will do, as will military-surplus or thrift-shop bargains. *Shorts* (½ pound). Light cotton swimming shorts or jeans hacked off above the knees. Generally, hike in shorts but don trousers for cold nights, storms, or extended exposure to sun or briars. Back in my Boy Scout days we put on long pajamas under our hiking shorts to avoid sunburn; trousers are a whole lot better.

Shirt (1 pound). Long-sleeved, wool, medium weight, with tails reaching below the midriff. *Sweater* (1 pound). Long-sleeved wool pullover. People prone to the shivers go into raptures with a down-filled sweater-jacket, no heavier than wool but warmer. *Parka* (½ pound). Waterproof, windproof, single-layer nylon shell, with hood and front opening—for rainy, windy spells. *Hat and bandanna* (¼ pound). A wool stocking cap is my choice in cold weather. Whatever the kind, it should be capable of covering the ears. The bandanna can be tied to serve as a sun hat. *Sunglasses* (¹/₁₀ pound). A must in sunny country, especially on snow, to prevent eyestrain, headache, even temporary blindness.

Packframe and bag (3¾ pounds). Look for a body-contoured frame of tubular

aluminum alloy with padded shoulder straps, backbands to keep the metal from pressing flesh, and a waist belt to transfer most weight from shoulders to hips, thus reducing strain on the spine. Match it with a heavy-duty, water-repellent nylon bag with three to five outside pockets. A dozen manufacturers offer sturdy, comfortable models from around $30 to $60. Beware of look-alike designs costing much less; many of them are almost certain to disintegrate during a nine-day trip. If you must buy in the under-$20 bracket, the best choice is the traditional Trapper Nelson with wood frame and canvas bag. I carried a Nelson thousands of miles over 28 years. They may be hard to find today; the trend is all to the metal frames.

Sleeping bag, with stuff bag and carrying straps (3½ pounds). My choice is a mummy bag of slant-tube construction, with a nylon shell, filled with two pounds of goose down. It will keep the average person warm down to 20° F. If the price —$60 to $100—is appalling, shop for a mummy bag with three pounds of polyester, warm merely to 32° but costing much less. Carry it in a waterproof nylon stuff bag strapped to the bottom of the packframe. *Sleeping pad* (1⅛ pounds). A 28- by 56-inch pad of ¼-inch-thick Ensolite to keep out the chill of the cold, cold ground. The pad also provides a bit of cushioning—for more, place clothes between bag and pad. For a pillow, fill the stuff bag with clothes.

Groundsheet (1 pound). A 9- by 12-foot sheet of .002-inch thick, or 2 mil, polyethylene keeps the sleeping bag dry. *Nylon tarp, poles, pegs, and rigging line* (3½ pounds). The waterproof tarp should

have at least eight grommets at corners and around the edges. Polyethylene tarps are available too; they're cheaper than nylon, but much more vulnerable to punctures, and to shredding in a high wind. Two aluminum telescoping or take-apart poles extending to seven feet, eight aluminum pegs, and a 50-foot coil of ³/₁₆-inch nylon cord will free the party to rig a shelter without a hunt for handy trees, sticks, and boulders. The sketches illustrate two ways to rig, with and without trees.

In buggy areas take mosquito netting for the shelter's open ends. Most hikers who travel in buggy or stormy country buy a tent sooner or later, but that's another and much more expensive story.

One-burner butane stove with five fuel cartridges (4 pounds). Simple to

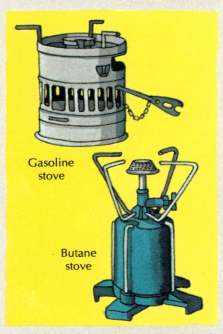

Gasoline stove

Butane stove

operate, the butane stove is favored by beginners. Veterans mostly use stoves burning white gas or kerosene, costing and weighing about the same, somewhat harder to operate but more efficient at low temperatures. A butane cartridge weighing ⅝ pound burns roughly three hours; for this trip five cartridges will do all the cooking without wood fires.

Grate (½ pound). A 5- by 15-inch grate of tubular stainless steel, large enough for two pots, allows much simpler cooking on a wood fire than fiddling around with woodcrafter rigs. *Matches and fire-starters* (¼ pound). Strike-anywhere or safety matches in a poly bag and an emergency supply of wind- and waterproof matches in a plastic box. For starting wood fires with wet fuel, take candle stubs or fuel tablets. *Cooking pots* (1¾ pounds). A nest of 1-, 2-, and 3-quart pots, with lids that also serve as skillets or plates. Or save money and weight

with coffee cans and a light frypan. Include a pot-scrubber and a bar of soap or bottle of biodegradable detergent.

I regard the following as individual equipment, though many a party carries only one flashlight or first-aid package:

Kitchen kit (½ pound). Pocket knife which includes a can-opener blade and other tools. Also a plastic or Sierra Club cup, spoon, and 1-quart screw-cap poly bottle for a canteen.

Toilet kit (½ pound). Toilet paper (about ⅔ roll), small cloth towel, toothbrush and paste, two handkerchiefs, comb and mirror. Only the first item is essential. *Repair kit* (¼ pound). A couple of feet of light steel wire in case the packframe comes apart at a joint; assorted safety pins, large needle and spool of heavy thread; several feet of Ripstop tape for tarp, parka, and sleeping bag repairs. The nylon cord for tarp-rigging doubles for repair duty, as well as for spare bootlaces.

First-aid kit (½ pound). In a serious emergency a party rarely has the right supplies. The following items are a bare minimum for healthy, cautious hikers: half a dozen Band-Aids, an Ace bandage, several 3-inch-square gauze pads, a yard of 2-inch adhesive tape, a dozen each of salt pills and aspirins, Chap Stick, needle, moleskin or molefoam, antiseptic, small first-aid manual, all carried in a plastic box. For areas of doubtful water add purification tablets. Where appropriate, add sunburn lotion, insect repellent, and a snakebite kit with instructions.

Flashlight, with two spare cells, spare bulb (¼ pound). For camp use and emergency night travel, but not reading in the sleeping bag (for that, add more spare cells). A plastic-case AA-size flashlight with two alkaline cells gives three to four hours of useful light at moderate temperatures. Tape the switch in OFF position to prevent power wastage in pack. *Map and compass* (¼ pound).

For ordinary trail hiking any compass will do that is sturdily built and has grid lines for map alignment. More on maps later; keep them in a poly bag for protection against wear and weather. *Extras.* Your back is your conscience on whether to haul camera, notebook, pen, binoculars, paperback, playing cards for stormbound days, a flask for special events.

FOOD

Food has been more written about and has triggered more quarrels than any other aspect of backpacking. I've seen a grown man sulk all week because the nut ration consisted entirely of cashews and nary a filbert.

I feel just brave enough to instruct novices in how to feed themselves on that first nine-day wilderness venture—after which they'll be as scornful of my wisdom as the veterans.

I'll assume you're more interested in seeing country than fooling around the stove and thus will settle for simple fare.

DILL COLE

On a nine-day trip we need not worry overmuch about a "balanced" diet; the main requirement is enough calories to keep the machine moving and stave off hunger pangs. The point is to pack *calories* rather than a lot of water and paper. Water is of course essential. In heavily traveled areas, spring, stream, or lake water often must be purified with tablets or by boiling. In desert wilderness frequently the entire supply for a day or two must be hauled—about a gallon (8 pounds) per man per day. Even in drenched country a full canteen should be carried on the trail; dry stretches can be excruciatingly long no matter how loud a valley is with waterfalls.

For solids, choose foods either naturally low in water content—pasta, cereals, margarine (which keeps longer than butter), sugar, and the like—or that are processed to remove most of the water.

Lighten the load by using few canned goods and by shucking excess paper and glass; put loose foods such as sugar and flour in poly bags, and peanut butter and jam in wide-mouthed poly bottles.

There are two basic sources for backpacker food supplies. By defining meals as physical necessities with no element of joy, a menu can be assembled at the average supermarket for about $1 per man-day. My own method is to lay a foundation at the supermarket, then visit a mountain shop for dehydrated vegetables, specialties unavailable elsewhere, and such freeze-dried and other goodies as I can afford.

How much food? An adult of average size and appetite can do very well on two pounds a day of dry-type foods with excess packaging removed. Lighter eaters, and those able and willing to shed some body weight, can manage on 1½ pounds. For the ravenous, 2½ pounds is scarcely enough. By stressing fats, you can pack more than twice the calories per pound you get in dry carbohydrates or proteins. Make every effort to keep the total weight at 14 to 18 pounds per person to avoid the major danger of overloading. An extra pound a day means nine more pounds on your back at the trailhead, often enough to crush both back and spirit.

To organize the commissary, draw up menus for the nine days and from this compile a list of all required items. When shopping, estimate needed quantities but don't fret about exactness. With a set of scales on hand and a supply of poly bags and poly bottles in assorted sizes, stage an assembly party an evening or two before departure. Distribute all foods except staples (margarine, salt, sugar, coffee, and the like) roughly into one-day piles of three meals. Weigh the one-day piles; the total should be somewhat less than the daily maximum to allow for staples carried separately. Pare weight to the desired figure. Assemble complete meals and package them in poly bags, with slips inside clearly denoting ''oatmeal breakfast,'' ''bean supper,'' or whatever, closing the bags with paper-wrapped wires. Be sure to include all cooking instructions.

Following is a sample low-cost nine-day menu (minus the first breakfast and last supper), based on the principle that hunger, not variety, is the spice of trail cuisine. Remember to measure out the required amounts of such staples as sugar, coffee, dry milk, several ounces of salt and about half a pound of margarine per person; include tiny shakers of pepper, garlic salt, and other desired spices.

Instant breakfast, no cooking (two days). Dry juice mix; dry cereal with sugar and dry milk; fig bar. *Quick breakfast,* prepared with hot water only (four days). Juice mix; instant oatmeal or

farina with added raisins, dates, or dried apples, plus sugar and milk; instant cocoa or coffee. *Luxury breakfast,* for rainy or lazy days (two days). Dried apples, apricots, peaches, or pears boiled up with sugar added; main course of fried bacon and pancakes (expect some disasters while learning the art) with margarine and jam; cocoa, coffee. Alternate main course: dehydrated hashed brown potatoes and a packaged omelette containing bits of freeze-dried bacon or ham.

Standard lunch (nine days). Lunch may be a single feast or a series of snacks; the rule is, when hungry or staggering, stop and eat a little. The standard lunch includes one or two items from each of three categories. *Bread:* dense, durable pumpernickel or the like; sea biscuit, pilot bread, or similar; spread with margarine and things from the protein and sweet departments. *Protein:* peanut butter, cheese, hard sausage, nuts, jerky. *Sweets:* jam, honey, candy, dried fruits, juice mix.

Quick supper, requiring only boiling water, for bad weather and late, weary arrivals in camp (three days). Pea soup mix, puff-dried carrots, freeze-dried ham, soy-bean ''ham-like'' bits, all boiled up in a single mess; cookies and

tea or coffee. Alternate: freeze-dried hash which rehydrates and cooks almost instantly with addition of boiling water.

Average supper (four days). Soup; main dish of quick-cooking macaroni and cheese; dehydrated spinach or carrots topped with margarine; gelatin or instant pudding; hot drinks. Alternates: instant potatoes which require only hot water, powdered milk, and margarine; stir in chipped beef, chunks of sausage, or canned or freeze-dried meat. Instant rice with canned chicken or tuna. *Luxury supper,* if just once you can fling money to the wind (one day). Freeze-dried tomato juice; freeze-dried cottage cheese; freeze-dried hamburgers or pork chops; dehydrated yams with margarine; freeze-dried beets; no-bake pineapple cheesecake; coffee, brandy, and cigars.

While by no means Spartan, this sample menu for the most part ignores the gourmet touches cherished by every old trail hand. Many are detailed in backpacker literature, and a beginner soon creates his own chef's specials. Some of mine may start the juices flowing.

Hot bread. A Bisquick-type flour mix makes pancakes, biscuits, and (with jam or wild berries) fruit turnovers and upside-down cakes baked in a collapsible reflector oven weighing 2½ pounds. (A lighter one can be improvised with aluminum foil and sticks.)

Beef jerky. Commercial jerky is durable and nutritious but pure boredom alongside ''semi-jerky'' made at home. Slice strips of steak, roast, or stew meat about an inch thick and an inch wide and several inches long. Place on a pan in oven at minimum heat. Watch carefully to avoid excessive cooking, since the main aim is drying. In 18 to 24 hours, depending on degree of ''jerkiness'' desired, remove from oven and wrap tightly in aluminum foil, then poly bags.

DILL COLE

The strips have shrunk to scraps, each pound reducing to about ¼ pound. But what luscious scraps!

Ice cream. I don't mean snow stirred with juice mix, but honest-to-gosh ice cream. Dig a small hole in a snowfield, line with poly. Spread snow on the bottom, mix with salt. Atop this place a pot containing ice cream mix prepared according to directions. Using a tamping stick, fill the space between poly and pot with snow and salt. Every 10 to 15 minutes add more salt and snow to the freezing ring and stir the thickening ice cream. In about an hour, rejoice! Real ice cream—or, if you can't spare enough salt (about ⅓ pound), at least a splendid milk shake.

Fish. One evening years ago I cast hungrily into a mountain lake so thick with trout that they kept colliding when they leaped into the air; yet I caught nothing, while losing half my blood to a cloud of mosquitoes. In a flash I realized the mosquitoes were using the fish as bait to catch me! I gave up the sport forever. Since then my technique has been to buddy up to fishermen on the trail, admire their catches, and wipe saliva from my lips. It works at least as often as a fishing pole. I remember a trip where our menu-planner went really light and

we were sadly facing a supper of hard-boiled eggs and crackers when a fisherman came by trying to get rid of a dozen surplus trout before the game warden caught him. A historic fish fry *that* was. Remember, if you plan to fish, allow for the weight of the tackle.

Wild fruits. Any beginner quickly learns to crop edible berries, a delight by themselves or added to cereal, pancakes, or biscuits. A word of caution, however, about "living off the land." It can be dangerous, destructive—and illegal. You must obey the fish and game laws of the jurisdiction. As for plant life, though some national forest wildernesses encourage berry-picking, the cropping of wild foods is generally frowned upon; it is forbidden in many national park areas. In an emergency, with survival at stake, the rules may be relaxed—but safety remains a factor. Many fruits and

nuts are edible, especially the kinds eaten by birds and animals. Nearly all animal life is also edible. But, unless you have expert advice, avoid mushrooms and any unfamiliar roots and greens.

GETTING READY TO GO

A certain wild land is calling urgently, books, magazines, and reveries are bringing a particular trail into sharp focus, and it's time to stop dreaming and start making plans.

When to go. A guaranteed way to play the fool would be to specify exact seasons for all the trails of America: One year may be nothing like the next; personal preferences vary widely—some like it hot and dry, some cold and snowy. However, a few generalizations may suggest to the beginner the sort of local advice he must seek before taking off.

From the Great Plains eastward trails are open at all times except in the depths of winter. The cooler and less buggy spring and fall, particularly in the South, are thought by many the loveliest of hiking seasons.

In the more southerly mountains of the West, the bulk of the high country is mainly snow-free from late May through October, and the summer skies are clear except for brief thunderstorms. In the northern Rockies, Sierra, and Pacific Northwest the high trails mostly melt out during July, and killer storms are relatively uncommon from mid-July through August. But in the Northwest some years have no real summer, only a series of spring storms between one winter and the next.

In Southwest deserts summer is altogether too hot for hiking; early and late winter are good; best of all is early spring, when the flowers are blooming. The trails of Hawaii are superb in every month. Alaska's wilderness trails—except for southeastern and south central parts of the state—are not for beginners unless accompanied by veterans.

Spying out the land. Few American wilderness areas, and fewer by the year, lack some sort of detailed hiking guide, and when competently done such a book is the best possible planning aid. For both planning and travel, a map is essential—ideally, two maps. Topographic (contour) maps show the shape of the land. Planimetric maps, as the name implies, do not show contours but usually are more up-to-date on the location of roads and trails and other works of man. (For information on where to get maps, permits, and other data about a specific area, see page 337.)

From all the information you have gathered, rough out an itinerary, selecting campsites and planning the days' journeys, taking into account both trail mileage and elevation gain. If you do not plan a loop trip that ends where you began, allow for a hike back to the car or arrange for transportation from trail's end.

The users' permit is taking hold in the wilderness system. Make sure you have current information about the requirements. If possible, obtain the papers before you leave home.

Building muscles and calluses. A person in good health, leading a reasonably active life, can hoist a nine-day pack and set safely forth without preparation. However, a city slave whose body is soft may topple to the ground before high noon on his first day out, retreat brokenly to the car, and finish the vacation beside a motel swimming pool.

The best preparation is a series of day and overnight hikes, spread over prior months, for toughening the body and learning to rig tarp, manipulate the stove, and rehydrate food. This is the time also to learn how to pack your bag for comfort and efficiency. To minimize the backward pull of the bag, generally stow the heaviest items close to the body and high up (the purple area in the sketch above), the medium-weight gear in the center, and the lightest down low and farthest from the body. Keep the canteen, first-aid kit, map, and compass in outside pockets, the trail lunch and rain gear within easy reach. Put the other meals for the day in a single poly bag and stow it fairly high, to reduce searching and repacking. Get in the habit of carrying a small emergency ration, some candy perhaps, on your person in case you and your food supply are separated and it becomes necessary to skip a meal.

Above all, get the feet in shape—by walking, as much as possible in the boots that will be worn on the nine-day wander. Some hiking experts devote extensive space to walking, often suggesting marvelous improvements on the ancient art. None, though, has come up with so revolutionary an innovation as did a friend of mine. Feeling it was wasteful of total body resources for legs to do all the work, he was inspired to tie a cord from each ankle to each wrist so his arms could help lift his feet; on the first trial he jerked one foot from under him, fell off the trail, and rolled and bounced into an alder thicket. We were half an hour cutting him loose.

The novice should do what comes naturally, observing only the basic law that the pace must be reasonably comfortable. Beginners invariably walk too fast. If legs are dragging or lungs gasping, slow down. Set a steady pace, however turtle-like, and don't worry about the endless miles ahead; take one step at a time and the miles take care of themselves. Don't fight the terrain—shift into low gear on hills rather than attempt a gallant charge as surely doomed as that of the Light Brigade.

Rest on a fairly regular routine, perhaps five minutes every half hour, or ten

every hour, but be flexible and don't march by the clock. With plenty of time the group may stop to savor every waterfall and chipmunk and overlook; after all, that's what the trip is about.

A party of ordinary strength with fairly heavy loads may average two miles an hour on an easy trail and hike six or seven hours a day without pain. Regardless of mileage, an average elevation gain of 700 feet an hour is respectable and a day's total of 4,000 feet honorable; on an unrelenting upgrade four miles can be plenty for a day.

Now disregard the above numbers; each hiker must discover his personal maximums, which can range from half to double the figures I've suggested—and can vary from day to day.

When the feet quit, the trip ends. At the first sensation of a hot spot, remove boots and socks and apply tape, perhaps topped with moleskin. Before starting a long downhill stretch (that's where the blisters bloom) lace boots tight through the instep; if feet still slop around inside, add a pair of socks. In very hot

weather periodically doff boots to cool the feet by airing or soaking. If a blister forms, drain it by puncturing at the base with a needle sterilized in a match flame; apply antiseptic, Band-Aid, and moleskin; similarly treat a blister split open.

On steep or slippery or bumpy terrain—heather or grass "cliffs," unstable rock, damp logs, or mud—a "third leg" prevents many a slip from ending in a pratfall. A stout stick serves the purpose; Northwest and other snowy-land hikers commonly carry an ice ax.

In some wild lands an important role of the third leg is for balance in crossing streams with bridge or footlog lacking. Fording is easy enough in water of moderate depth and velocity—say, boiling not much above the knee. Wade in shorts, and barefoot if the bed is sandy and the water not too frigid. Otherwise, wear boots without socks; on the far side dump water from boots and don dry socks and damp boots. If water boils as high as the hips, the beginner had better think of the folks back home and bravely chicken out.

On steep snow the secret of success is standing up straight with weight vertically over the feet, kicking solid steps into the snow, and *not* leaning into the slope. The staff or ice ax helps maintain the vertical stance.

Of course, the novice has no business here. Snow lingers on some high trails all summer and the hiker incompetent to travel safely on snow must restrict his ambitions—or perhaps ride a slope into a pile of rocks or over a cliff, returning home via rescue helicopter.

While protecting his fragile body from being damaged by rough land, the hiker

DILL COLE

must also take care to protect fragile lands from his rough boots. Stick to established routes; shortcutting switchbacks and trampling terrain—particularly in high meadows with a short growing season—kills plants, breaks the sod, initiates erosion. Enough boots, carelessly used, can be as destructive to a tender landscape as a bulldozer.

ROUTE FINDING

Out of consideration for harassed rangers if not his own safety, the beginner should confine initial travels to well-defined trail systems. Even on "turnpike" trails it's important to study signs at the trailhead in order to start on the right path, and to stay alert for junctions so that you don't end the day miles up the wrong valley.

But signs can be missing or illegible; for this reason, if not pride in craftsmanship, from the first day of his first trip a hiker should study map interpretation, an art readily learned with a bit of application. Begin by orienting the map to the landscape, most simply done by lining

up symbols on the sheet with the natural features they represent. If no prominent features can be identified, bring out the compass. Place it on the map so that the north symbol of the dial points to the top of the map (on any standard map the top is always true north). Then rotate map and compass as a unit until the north-pointing end of the needle is the proper number of degrees west or east of true north, in accordance with the local declination—that is, the difference between true north and magnetic north (the Magnetic North Pole, located in northern Canada). Declination normally is shown on topographic maps but frequently not on planimetrics. Once oriented, the map can be read to identify visible features and to find the direction of those that are out of sight.

If a novice holds his first orientation session at the trailhead, then pulls out map and compass at each rest stop and junction, he knows where he is at every moment. At least he will discover the fact that he doesn't know in a few minutes rather than after hours of plunging deeper and deeper into confusion.

MISERIES AND HAZARDS

Describing every trouble a hiker could encounter would require a volume and might frighten him back to the city. Some of the most common ones are briefly noted here. Most national parks and forests have brochures warning against local perils; such information also is found in guidebooks. Read and heed.

Getting lost. Though in backcountry I always have known exactly where *I* was, I've spent some hours wondering where the trail was—and experienced the rush of panic that comes from disorientation. Once you feel it, you travel always with a wary eye. If you should get lost, *do not* succumb to panic. Stop and think. Have a bite to eat. Recheck the map. If you're on a trail, wait for a passerby and ask directions. If somehow off the trail, take short scouting trips; should you fail to reorient yourself, always return to the point of loss. Shout—someone may answer. (Several times, while on a trail, I've heard lost backpackers bemoaning their fate a few yards away in heavy brush, and saved them with a simple "Hello.")

Do not blindly trust the old rule that says follow a stream to civilization—it may lead deeper into wilderness. Do not separate the party. If efforts to regain the route fail, remain in one place, preferably in the open where you can be seen by search planes. Perhaps build a fire and pile on greenery to make smoke. Periodically yell (three yells at a time, or three of anything, is the international

signal of distress) and listen for answers. Again, keep cool.

Hypothermia and related ills. A common killer of wild land travelers is *hypothermia,* a condition in which the body loses more heat than it generates; older and less precise terms are "exposure" and "freezing to death." Fatal cooling can occur at temperatures far above freezing. The combination of wind and water, as in a driving rainstorm, can kill a healthy but ill-clothed hiker in a few hours. The best preventive is clothing and equipment suitable for the climate to be encountered. With the outfit I've recommended hypothermia is rarely a danger in the "average" summer wilderness.

Too much sun causes *sunstroke.* Knot the bandanna at the corners, soak it, and slip it over your head; or wear a hat, pour water on your head and neck, seek shadows. Prolonged heavy sweating causes debilitating dehydration: drink, drink, drink. At the same time, a little extra salt on your food, or a salt pill, can prevent a deficiency and resulting *heat exhaustion,* with such symptoms as weakness, nausea, headache, muscle cramps.

Lightning. When big black clouds boil into obvious menaces, get off the high, exposed ridges. When bolts are striking close, avoid broad meadows, shun tall "lightning rod" trees. Seek deep woods, brush, or dense small trees in low areas. If caught in the open, keep down; if possible insulate yourself from the ground with clothing or pack.

Altitude sickness. Lowland residents climbing abruptly to high elevations, as in the Sierra Nevada and Rockies where trails reach above 10,000 feet, normally are affected by lack of oxygen. Symptoms such as weariness, lassitude, and nausea require a slower pace, deliberate "overbreathing," and frequent rests.

Poisonous snakes. Consult local experts (rangers, guidebooks) about the presence of poisonous snakes. The beginner typically worries too much about snakes, which are timorous creatures; with any warning they will usually slither out of the way. If a snake is met and doesn't move off, stir it up by tossing pebbles or prodding it with a stick longer than the snake's length. No American snake will chase a human. A snakebite

kit may allay apprehension somewhat—but some experts think more deaths are caused by kits than snakes. Study the directions beforehand! Snakebite fatalities are extremely uncommon among adults in good health.

Animals. In all my years of wilderness walking I've so far been attacked just once—by a mamma grouse distrustful of my intentions toward her chicks. The first thing a beginning hiker must do is clear his mind of the tall tales invented by droll frontiersmen and paranoid shepherds. Mountain lions, bobcats, and other wild felines shun man and are rarely seen. Wolves, almost gone from the old 48 states, are innocent of the slanders perpetrated by Little Red Riding Hood. Coyotes, common in some areas, sound scary barking and howling under the moon, but they too leave man alone. Porcupine and skunk employ their weapons purely in self-defense. In summary, the wild animals of North America are nothing to worry about. With one exception: bears.

In a completely wild condition bears flee the presence of man. Noisy walking usually is enough to notify them of your coming so they can clear out. But should you see a cub, get moving, and quickly; mamma is not far away, and will not take kindly to your chasing the little teddy to get a picture.

The "problem" bears are those less than completely wild—the campground scavengers. To discourage them, hang all food from a limb or a line stretched between trees, higher than a bear can reach. Pick a spot well away from the sleeping area to avoid nasty surprises

in the night. If a raider drops in for supper, yell, or bang pots. But if he keeps coming on, get out of the way—it's now *his* supper, not yours.

If, for any reason, a bear charges, *run.* Try to climb a tree. Throw down your pack—he may spend enough time slashing at it for you to escape. If caught, go limp, act dead; the bear's resentment may be vented before in fact you are.

The above rules apply to most black bears, and perhaps the average grizzly. But any hiker contemplating a trip to the domain of the grizzly bear (mainly Yellowstone and Glacier National Parks, adjacent wild lands, and Canada and Alaska) certainly must check with the rangers to find out which valleys are dangerous at any given time.

Rendering first aid. Many a hiker, having witnessed a serious medical emergency in the backcountry, has returned home and immediately enrolled in a first-aid course. Better to take one before the first wilderness trip. Carrying a decent first-aid kit, plus an instruction booklet that has been studied in advance of need, is better than nothing.

Summoning help. Before entering a wilderness area, learn from the local ranger the procedures for summoning assistance. Observe sign-in/sign-out regulations where they exist and sign all trail registers. When going for help, make sure you have such information as the location and time of the accident, nature

of injuries, names and next of kin of the victim and other members of the party. And remember the route so you can guide rescuers to the scene.

CAMPING

The hiker must have two concerns in building wilderness homes: second, his comfort; first, the well-being of the life systems into which he intrudes his potentially destructive presence. Everywhere he must walk lightly and respectfully, strive to take only pictures, leave only footprints. Equipment previously described makes camping so manageable that less needs to be said here about How To's than about Do Not's.

Choosing a campsite. Managers of popular wilderness areas increasingly are being forced to protect fragile ecosystems by restricting camping. Where free choice still exists, hikers should avoid making camp on living plants and instead use rocky, barren ground as much as possible. Keep the camp at least 100 feet from lake shores and stream banks, where plant communities are notably delicate and the water, of course, susceptible to pollution.

The ecological conscience and human comfort can co-exist. Unlike the crudely equipped woodcrafter of olden days, today's camper does not have to whack and chop and gouge the land for

the sake of a night's sleep; he needs only a water supply and a patch of reasonably level ground. Dry, soft ground and firewood are amenities, not necessities.

To be sure, advanced students can gain an extra measure of comfort by cleverly exploiting intricacies of *micro-climates,* such as: Gales often roar through passes and ravines while yards away only mild breezes are stirring; in settled weather a ridge slope usually is warmer at night than the adjacent basin floor, into which cold air sinks. Even the novice quickly learns to seek the lee of a knoll or a clump of trees in windy weather—and in buggy weather to seek the breezes.

Building the home. The pole-and-peg kit previously described permits a tarp to be easily rigged anywhere. All that remains to complete the bedroom is to spread the ground sheet and sleeping pads and bags. Do not automatically dig a ditch around the tarp—rather, avoid dips and swales that may become ponds in a hard rain. Should a downpour come in the night, dig the minimum emergency trenches. Afterward, meticulously reconstruct the original ground surface.

Much as we old sentimentalists mourn the loss, the time is gone when the campfire can be everywhere considered the prime symbol of the wilderness home. Wood fires already are banned in portions of some wilderness areas; even where fires are still allowed, wise hikers are giving them up for reasons of convenience. When wood is scarce (or wet), the pleasures of a flame-inspired evening seminar are more than outweighed by the nuisance of gathering fuel, nursing sick coals, and coughing and wheezing in clouds of smoke.

If you do build a fire, use an established fire ring if available. If a new one is set up, place it only on mineral soil; on leaving camp return the rocks to their original locations, broadcast the ashes, and cover the burned spot with loose dirt or leaves. Use only dead, "finger-picking" wood that requires no ax or saw—do not cut living wood and do not ravage silvered logs and snags—these are part of the scenery and much too valuable to be squandered for the pleas-

DILL COLE

ure of a few people. When breaking camp, make certain no hot spots are left, on the ground or under the surface.

Good housekeeping. To conclude with several more critically important Do's and Don't's: Do not wash dishes or bodies in lakes or streams. Carry water up in the woods or onto a moraine, using soap or biodegradable detergent. Have the manners of a cat. In the absence of privies, eliminate body wastes far from watercourses. Completely cover the evidence with rocks, dirt, bark, or whatever. Where no loose materials are available, as often in meadows, dig a shallow hole and carefully replace the sod afterward.

Littering is obnoxious. It also kills people—not often, but for every fatality hundreds of hikers are scared out of their wits. At some backcountry camps, sloppy hikers have nourished a resident population of scavenger bears who depend on humans to supply tasty meals of abandoned scraps or buried garbage. Even if no combustible materials are burned, with typical backpacker foods the total garbage weight is no more than two pounds per man for a nine-day trip. On the trail, pocket food wrappers and fruit peels. In camp, if a fire is built, burn paper and plastic and food residues from cans; do not try to burn aluminum foil. At fireless camps, wash the cans along with the dishes. Pack out every particle of metal, glass, and unburned paper, plastic, and food scrap.

Take pride that a party arriving at the site minutes after you depart can find no evidence that you ever were there. Remember, the dearth of such evidence is what makes it a wilderness. And it will remain a wilderness only as long as we keep it "untrammeled by man."

336

For Maps and Facts

By now you've come to realize that a wilderness experience is no "park-your-car-and-you're-there" kind of thing. And whether you'll be hiking, canoeing, or going with burro or horse, a key to success is advance planning.

For information you need about a wilderness, the best single source is the local headquarters of the managing agency—national forest, national park, national wildlife refuge, Bureau of Land Management region, or state park. Write for brochures. Explain the kind of trip you plan and any special interests—hunting, fishing, climbing, wildlife, photography. Ask about weather usual for dates you'll be there. About outfitters, permits, special regulations. And just before going, write again; a forest fire or other development may prompt alternate plans.

For a local headquarters address, write the appropriate national agency:

Forest Service
U. S. Department of Agriculture
Washington, D. C. 20250

National Park Service
U. S. Department of the Interior
Washington, D. C. 20240

Bureau of Sport Fisheries & Wildlife
U. S. Department of the Interior
Washington, D. C. 20240

Director (130), Bureau of Land Management
U. S. Department of the Interior
Washington, D. C. 20240

The Bureau of Land Management can also provide data about the many undesignated public lands of Alaska that offer a wilderness experience.

Addresses of state wilderness parks:

Adirondack State Park; Catskill State Park
Department of Environmental Conservation
Albany, New York 12201

Allagash Wilderness Waterway
Department of Parks & Recreation
Augusta, Maine 04330

Baxter State Park
P.O. Box 540
Millinocket, Maine 04462

Custer State Park
Hermosa, South Dakota 57744

McCurtain County Wilderness Area
Department of Wildlife Conservation
P.O. Box 53465
Oklahoma City, Oklahoma 73105

Mt. San Jacinto Wilderness State Park
P.O. Box 308
Idyllwild, California 92349

Porcupine Mountains Wilderness State Park
Route 2
Ontonagon, Michigan 49953

Most local headquarters can provide planimetric maps of their wilderness areas. At some you can obtain small-scale topographic maps. But large-scale topo maps—ones concentrating on small areas—give much more needed detail.

The U. S. Geological Survey has a helpful, free pamphlet: "Topographic Maps." It also has free indexes of topos published for the states. From the appropriate index you can order at moderate cost the quadrangle maps covering the area you are interested in. To get pamphlet and state index, write:

Distribution Section
U. S. Geological Survey
　1200 S. Eads Street
　Arlington, Virginia 22202
or Federal Center
　Denver, Colorado 80225

Commercial outfitters near wilderness areas offer guided outings by foot, boat, horse, or pack stock. So do a number of local and national groups. Trips range from easy to rugged, mountain to desert, springtime to winter, and for youths, adults, or families. Among major organizations with outing programs:

American Forestry Association
1319 18th Street N.W.
Washington, D. C. 20036

Appalachian Mountain Club
5 Joy Street
Boston, Massachusetts 02108

Appalachian Trail Conference
　(through its member groups)
P.O. Box 236
Harpers Ferry, West Virginia 25425

Sierra Club
1050 Mills Tower
San Francisco, California 94104

The Wilderness Society
1901 Pennsylvania Avenue N.W.
Washington, D. C. 20006

Our wilderness system continues to evolve through proposals, public hearings, and government action. Within the states, efforts grow to identify and preserve tracts as natural areas, if not wilderness. Citizens can play a stronger role by joining local or national movements. The Wilderness Society and Sierra Club are powerful voices for wilderness expansion. Other major groups include:

Federation of Western Outdoor Clubs
16603 53rd Avenue South
Seattle, Washington 98188

Friends of the Earth
529 Commercial Street
San Francisco, California 94111

Izaak Walton League of America
1800 N. Kent Street
Arlington, Virginia 22209

National Audubon Society
950 Third Avenue
New York, New York 10022

National Parks & Conservation Association
1701 18th Street N.W.
Washington, D. C. 20009

Nature Conservancy
1800 N. Kent Street
Arlington, Virginia 22209

Don't overlook as information sources literature that may be available at a nearby mountain shop or public library.

INDEX

Text references appear in lightface type, illustrations and illustrated text in **boldface.**

G

Galiuro Wilderness, Ariz. 103
Game management 145, 152
Gates of the Arctic, Alaska 281, 295, 300, 305
Gates of the Mountain Wilderness, Mont. 147
Gearhart Mountain Wilderness, Oreg. 35
Geese: nesting grounds 29, 296
Geological Survey, U. S. 337
Geology: alluvial fans **309**; delta 296; earthquakes 51, 57; erosion **90**, 91, 92, **94-95, 138-139, 162,** 191, sandstone formations 88, 91, **94;** "folding" **90,** 92, 115; glacial action 38, 51, **68,** 90, **162,** 190, 296, 306, lakes **66-67, 153,** 190, 216, erratics **59,** 79; grabens 113; sedimentation **90-91;** volcanic activity 39, 51, **54-55,** 90, 116, **122-125,** 306
Georgia: wilderness areas, proposed 12, 227, 228-229, 244, **246-247,** 250-251, map 228
Giant Forest, Sequoia Nat. Park **53,** 58
Gila Primitive Area, N. Mex. 103
Gila Wilderness, N. Mex. 10, 13, 15, 16, 90, 103
Glacier Bay Nat. Monument, Alaska **280,** 295, 306
Glacier Lake, Wyo. **153**
Glacier Nat. Park, Mont. 147
Glacier Peak Wilderness, Wash. **19,** 34, 37, 40, **42-43,** 49, 50, 51, 60, **82-87;** map 37
Glacier Primitive Area, Wyo. 147, 164
Glaciers 34-35, 38, 39, 40, 51, 86, 164, 216, **280,** 281, 282, 283, 284, **285,** 293
Glen Canyon Nat. Recreation Area, Utah 92, 103
Goat Rocks Wilderness, Wash. 34, 51
Goat Trail, Alaska 293
Goat Trail, Ark. **205**
Gore Range-Eagles Nest Primitive Area, Colo. 26, 147
Grand Canyon Nat. Park, Ariz. 15, 103
Grand Gulch Primitive Area, Utah 103
Grand Teton Nat. Park, Wyo. 145, 147, 148
Granite Fiords, Alaska 295
Grapevine Mountains, Calif. 105, **110-111**
Grasses: foxtail barley **4-5;** prairielands **184,** 190-191, **191,** 201, 202, 203; salt grass **109,** 113
Great Basin, desert 89, 90 see also Capitol Reef
Great Gulf Wilderness, N.H. 227, 232, 241
Great Kobuk Sand Dunes, Alaska 281, 284, **286-287,** 295, 305-306
Great Sand Dunes Nat. Monument, Colo. 147
Great Smoky Mountains Nat. Park, N.C.-Tenn. 225, 227, **266-279;** area 269; geology 267, 272, 277; map 228; wildlife 267, **268,** 269, 272, **272-273,** 275, 278
Great Swamp Wilderness, N.J. **4-5,** 11, **224,** 225, 227, 230; birds 225, 230; plant life **224,** 225
Great Western Divide, Sierra Nevada 58, 59
Great White Heron Nat. Wildlife Ref., Fla. 227
Greenstone Ridge Trail, Isle Royale Nat. Park 204

Gregory Bald, Great Smoky Mountains **266,** 267, 269, 272
Guadalupe Mountains Nat. Park, Tex. 103, **117**
Gulf Islands Nat. Seashore, Fla. 227

H

Hagemeister Island, Alaska 295
Haleakala Nat. Park, Hawaii 35, **61**
Hanaupah Canyon, Death Valley 115
Hart Mount Nat. Antelope Ref., Oreg. 35
Havasu Lake Nat. Wildlife Ref., Ariz. 103
Hawaii: wilderness areas, proposed 35, **61**
Hawaii Volcanoes Nat. Park 35
Hawaiian Islands Nat. Wildlife Ref. 35
Hayden Valley, Yellowstone Nat. Park 136, **140-141**
Hazen Bay Nat. Wildlife Ref., Alaska 295
Hazy Islands Nat. Wildlife Ref., Alaska 295
Hells Bay Trail, Everglades 251
Henry Mountains, Utah 90, **94-95,** 101
High Sierra, Calif. 28, 57-59, **59,** 60; defined 57; map 36; wilderness areas **17, 19,** 34, 57, 60, proposed **53,** 57, 60; see also Minarets Wilderness
High Sierra Primitive Area, Calif. 35, 37
High Sierra Trail 37, 58-59, 60
High Uintas Primitive Area, Utah 103
Hoh River rain forest, Wash. 38
Homestead acts 13
Hood, Mount, Oreg. 40, **46-47,** 51
Hoover Wilderness, Calif. 35
Horicon Nat. Wildlife Ref., Wisc. 186
Humbug Spires Primitive Area, Mont. 147
Hunting 10, 15, 135, 152, 337
Huron Islands Nat. Wildlife Ref., Mich. 186

I

Idaho 133; wilderness areas 12, **132,** 147, 152, proposed **132,** 136, **144,** 147, 150-151, 152, 157, map 149
Idaho Primitive Area 145, 147, 150-151, 152, 157; map 149; wildlife 136, **144,** 145, studies 152, 157
Iliamna, Lake, Alaska 295, 306
Illinois: wilderness area, proposed 186
Image Lake, Wash. 83, **86**
Imperial Nat. Wildlife Ref., Ariz. 103
Imuruk, Alaska 295
Indiana Dunes Nat. Lakeshore, Ind. 25, 191, 192, **200**
Indian Peaks, Colo. 147
Indians: cliff-dwellings 119, **126,** 129; pictographs 105, **127,** 150, **221**
Insects, control of 135-136
Interior, Department of the 25, 283, 284, 293, 300, 306
Inyo Nat. Forest, Calif. 64
Irish Wilderness, Mo. 186
Island Bay Nat. Wildlife Ref., Fla. 227
Isle Royale Nat. Park, Mich. 186, 204
Izaak Walton League 9, 25, 222, 337
Izembek Nat. Wildlife Range, Alaska 295

J

Jackson Lake, Grand Teton Nat. Park 145
Jarbidge Wilderness, Nev. 103
J. N. "Ding" Darling Nat. Wildlife Ref., Fla. 227
Jo, Mount, Adirondacks 242
John Muir Trail, Calif. 19, 37, 59, 63, 64, 79, 80

John Muir Wilderness, Calif. 12, 35
John's Lake Bayou, Tex. 203
Johnson, Lyndon B. 26, 50
Johnson, Cape, Wash. **32**
Joshua Tree Nat. Monument, Calif. 35, 103
Joyce Kilmer-Slickrock Wilderness, N.C. 227

K

Kalmiopsis Wilderness, Oreg. 34
Kansas: prairielands 201, 202
Katahdin, Mount, Maine 231
Katmai Nat. Monument, Alaska 295, 306
Kenai Fiords, Alaska 295
Kenai Nat. Moose Range, Alaska 295
Kentucky: wilderness areas, proposed 227
Kephart, Mount, Great Smoky Mountains **268-269,** 275, 278
Key West Nat. Wildlife Ref., Fla. 227
King Salmon Capes, Tongass Nat. Forest 295
Kings Canyon Nat. Park, Calif. 35, 37, 57, 58; map 36
Kipahulu Valley, Hawaii **61**
Kluane Nat. Park, Canada 284
Kobuk River, Alaska 284, **286-287,** 305
Kodiak Island, Alaska 282, 295, 307
Kodiak Nat. Wildlife Ref., Alaska 295
Kofa Game Range, Ariz. 103
Koyukuk, Alaska 295
Krusenstern, Cape, Alaska: prehistoric sites 295, 305
Kuskokwim, Alaska 295

L

Lacassine Nat. Wildlife Ref., La. 186
La Garita Wilderness, Colo. 147
Lake Chelan Nat. Recreation Area, Wash. 37, 50
Lake Clark Pass, Alaska 295, 306
Lake Mead Nat. Recreation Area, Ariz. 103
Lake Woodruff Nat. Wildlife Ref., Fla. 227
Land use 16, 25, 26, 28; control of: legislative 242, 282-283, 284, 293, 300, voluntary 231; exploitation of resources 14, **22-23,** 50, 51, 222, 243; grazing **20-21,** 26, 40
Lassen Volcanic Nat. Park, Calif. 34, 51, 52, **54-55**
Laurel Fork Wilderness, Va. 227
Lava Beds Nat. Monument, Calif. 34
Le Conte, Mount, Great Smoky Mountains **270-271,** 272, 275, 277, 278, **279**
Leopold, Aldo 10, **13,** 15-16, 90; quoted 11, 13, 16, 17
Lewis and Clark Nat. Forest, Mont. 157, 158
Linville Gorge Wilderness, N.C. 227
Litter 19, **27,** 107; disposal 169, 278, 336
Little Pend Oreille Nat. Wildlife Ref., Wash. 34
Little Missouri River, N. Dak. 189, 191, 192
Lolo Nat. Forest, Mont. **22-23**
Lost Dutchman Mine, Superstition Mountains 119, 120, 122, 125, 129
Lostwood Nat. Wildlife Ref., N. Dak. 186
Louisiana: state bird **257;** wilderness areas, proposed 186
Lumbering 14, 16, **22-23,** 28, 50, 51, 199, 204, 207, 222, 230-231, 232, 243, 250, 267, 269, 307; "selective logging" 231
Lyell Fork, Tuolumne River, Calif. 80, **81**

Composition by National Geographic's Phototypographic Division, Lawrence F. Ludwig, Manager. Color separations by Colorgraphics, Inc., Beltsville, Md.; Graphic Color Plate, Inc., Stamford, Conn., Progressive Color Corporation, Rockville, Md., The Lanman Company, Alexandria, Va. Printed by Fawcett Printing Corporation, Rockville, Md., and Judd & Detweiler, Inc., Washington, D. C. Binding by R. R. Donnelley & Sons Company, Chicago, Ill. Paper by Oxford Paper Company, New York, and Simpson Lee Paper Company, Vicksburg, Mich.

Library of Congress data
National Geographic Society, Washington, D. C., Book Service

Wilderness U.S.A.
(World in Color Library)
1. Wilderness areas—United States.
2. Camping—United States.   I. Title.
QH76.N26   917.3'04   73-10213
ISBN 0-87044-116-7

ACKNOWLEDGMENTS

The editors are grateful for the unstinting assistance of authorities across the nation from Capitol Hill to Katmai—archivist and ecologist, botanist and zoologist, historian and hiker, as well as the rangers and supervisors who reviewed material on wildlife and wild land in forest, park, and refuge.

In the U. S. Forest Service our particular thanks go to Nolan C. O'Neal, Assistant Director of the Division of Information and Education; Alan J. Lamb, Assistant Director, and Robert A. Rowen, Chief, Special Areas Branch, both of the Division of Recreation; Gerald W. Gause, Public Information Officer, California Regional Office; James W. Hughes, Public Information Officer, Pacific Northwest Regional Office; Edwin C. Rockwell, Assistant Recreation Officer, Inyo National Forest; Dr. Robert C. Lucas, Principal Geographer, and Robert W. Mutch, Research Forester, both of the Intermountain Forest and Range Experiment Station; and Dr. Miron L. Heinselman, Principal Plant Ecologist, North Central Forest and Range Experiment Station.

In the Department of the Interior we received invaluable aid and guidance from Theodor R. Swem, Assistant Director, Cooperative Activities, H. James Howe, Chief, Wilderness Branch, and James H. Husted, Staff Assistant, Alaska Planning Group, all of the National Park Service; from Larry Means, Refuge Manager, and James Gillett, Wilderness Planner, both of the Bureau of Sport Fisheries and Wildlife, and Wayne Boden, Outdoor Recreation Planner, Bureau of Land Management.

Consultants in specialized fields included Dr. Alexander Wetmore, Research Associate and former Secretary, and Dr. Ronald H. Pine, Associate Curator, Department of Vertebrate Zoology, both of the Smithsonian Institution; Dr. Theodore Dudley, Research Botanist, National Arboretum; Linda West, Naturalist, Capitol Reef National Park; Dr. Lyman Benson, Professor of Botany, Pomona College; Dr. Durward L. Allen, Professor of Wildlife Ecology, Purdue University; and Dr. W. Leslie Pengelly, Professor of Wildlife Biology, University of Montana.

From the book's inception The Wilderness Society was a constant source of encouragement and information, especially from Ernest Dickerman, Harry Crandell, Kay Younger, and Douglas Scott. Many other conservation groups generously assisted us. And for their lasting inspiration we acknowledge a great debt to Henry David Thoreau, John Muir, Aldo Leopold, and Robert Marshall.

The Eskimo song on page 300 is from Knud Rasmussen's *Intellectual Culture of the Copper Eskimos,* Copenhagen, 1932, by permission of Knud Rasmussen's heirs.